W9-BQM-112

Dryden in Revolutionary England

Dryden in Revolutionary England

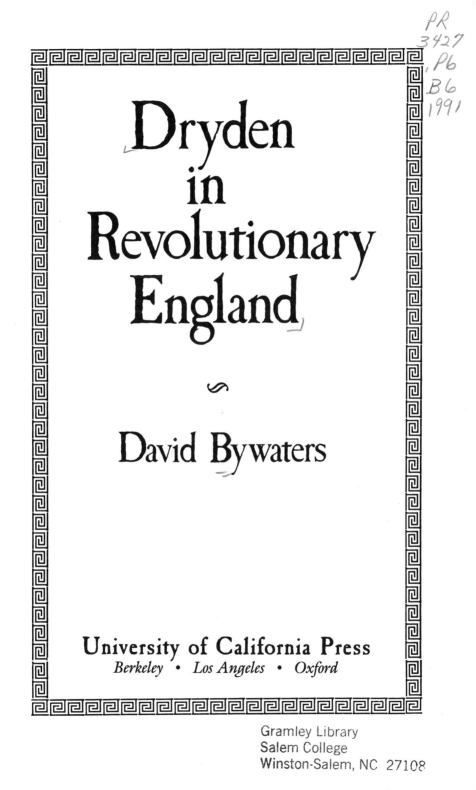

David Bywaters

University of California Press
Berkeley • Los Angeles • Oxford

University of California Press
Berkeley and Los Angeles, California

University of California Press
Oxford, England

Copyright © 1991 by The Regents of the University of California

Library of Congress Cataloging-in-Publication Data

Bywaters, David A.
  Dryden in revolutionary England / David Bywaters.
    p. cm.
  Includes bibliographical references and index.
  ISBN 0-520-07061-5 (cloth)
  1. Dryden, John, 1631–1700—Political and social views.
2. Political poetry, English—History and criticism. 3. Great
Britain—History—Revolution of 1688—Literature and the revolution.
4. Great Britain—Politics and government—1689–1702. I. Title.
PR3427.P6B9 1991
821'.4—dc20   90–38470
                                                                          CIP

Printed in the United States of America
1 2 3 4 5 6 7 8 9

To Steven N. Zwicker

Contents

Preface   ix

Acknowledgments   xiii

Introduction   1

1. "Echo's of Her Once Loyal Voice"   9
    The Hind and the Panther

2. "Adhering to a Lost Cause"   34
    Don Sebastian and *Amphitryon*

3. "The Favour of Sovereign Princes"   75
    King Arthur and *Cleomenes*

4. The Poet, Not the Man: Poetry and Prose,
    1692–1700   104
        I. Rhetorical Definition of Poet and Audience   107
        II. The Political Rhetoric of the Translations   124
        III. The Relation Between Poetry and Politics   129
            Original Verse   131
            Prose   133

    Epilogue   163

    Notes   167

    Index   191

Preface

My purpose in this book is to describe the rhetorical strategies by which John Dryden, in his published works between 1687 and 1700, sought to define contemporary politics and to stake out for himself a defensible place within them. Seeking to discover and explain their polemical and rhetorical concerns, I have tried to situate these works in political and literary contexts with which Dryden and his readers would have been demonstrably familiar. I have excluded from consideration all anachronistic political or literary information so that I may see these works as clearly as possible from their point of view. This methodology is hardly new to Dryden studies—it informs Edmond Malone's biography as well as James Winn's, Samuel Johnson's criticism as well as Steven Zwicker's. I have chosen it not because of its novelty but because of its explanatory power for this particular body of work.

However, I feel that such an approach also has some general advantages over other methods of literary study now in vogue. Traditional humanist criticism, which assumes that great works of literature embody universal truths, has been for two decades under sustained attack. Some object that the linguistic signs that make up literary works are not sufficiently stable to embody any coherent meaning, others find in canonical works not universal truths but expressions of elite ideology; I have rejected the humanist approach on practical rather than theoretical grounds. Any universal truth that a modern critic can claim to discover in a text must be either relatively plain and therefore in no need of reiteration, or dubiously embodied in the text, or dubiously universal. Humanist critics in this century have struggled mightily to avoid obviousness on the one hand and implausibility on the other; but the New Critical strategies for negotiating this terrain have come to seem increasingly worn and arbitrary. Historical criticism, on the other hand, while it may not claim to explain everything in a given text, may at least claim to have a plausible basis for explaining something that modern readers, accustomed to the circumstances of their own time, have overlooked or misconstrued.

Traditional humanism has given way in recent years to a set of approaches—deconstructive, postfreudian, neomarxist—that turn literary works to uses that their authors and original audiences could not have imagined. Whereas the humanist critic may at least claim to serve the text—to display its structure or define its meaning—these new approaches serve theories about language, psychology, or political economy, which literary texts are made to illustrate and confirm. Such critics often feel obliged to disprove or disregard the text's apparent meaning in order to arrive at something deeper that reflects what the critics think is a universal truth about the relation between signifier and signified, or ego and id, or cultural dominance and subversion. I have no quarrel here with deconstruction, postfreudianism, or neomarxism. But the exclusive application of these and similar theories to past literature has the unfortunate effect of drawing us into a kind of historical solipsism that allows us to see nothing in the past but our own reflection.

In undertaking such a project as this I am, I concede, forced to begin by making a number of assumptions the validity of which is now often contested—that language can refer to something outside itself, that the meaning a careful reader draws from a text may approximate that which a careful writer embodied in the text or which another careful reader may find in it, that we may escape the habits of thought and expression that prevail in our own age sufficiently to understand those that prevailed in another. I cannot prove the validity of these assumptions, any more than I can prove that the pen I use has an existence independent of me. I embrace them because they seem to me valid, just as my pen seems to exist; and because if they are false, the purpose of all literary and historical study seems to me obscure.

Aside from these, I have sought to avoid making any assumptions or drawing any conclusions about Dryden's work or seventeenth-century politics that cannot be verified by evidence drawn from the writings of the period. I include in my analysis only the contingent political phenomena of that period in which both author and audience were demonstrably interested. The English political nation in these years may or may not have been engaged in a centuries-long struggle to bring forth a liberal democracy, or to justify and maintain an inequitable distribution of material goods; it was verifiably divided on the immediate question of who should govern, how much power the government should have, and how it should use that power, and I have restricted myself to this relatively narrow range of issues. Dryden's work in the period may or may not embody moral truths. It certainly contains general precepts on human behavior, but whether these are noble ideals or insidious pronouncements of a classicist, patriarchal elite is a question that must be decided with reference to abstract values rather than textual and historical evidence, and therefore I have let it alone. Whatever Dryden's commitment to Christian humanism or patriarchal elitism, he was quite demonstrably committed to his own survival as a poet at a time when the conflict between his known principles and those of the majority of his audience left him publicly discredited. I have therefore confined my study to the means by which he sought to achieve this end.

I am not blind to the disadvantages inherent in this method. It would be pleasant, for example, if Dryden's political ideals were such as we might ourselves unequivocally endorse—if Dryden could be shown to have made a brave stand against the political dragons that we ourselves detest. Unfortunately, this is not the case. While Dryden's loathing of war seems admirable, his regret at the interruption of the lineal succession, and at James's failure to maintain and increase the power of the monarch, is difficult to share. There is something attractive in Dryden's contempt for the equivocations by which the old Tories justified their desertion of James; but there is little to recommend their motives or Dryden's for having adhered to him in the first place. The most apparently persuasive argument Dryden advanced before 1688 for preserving the lineal succession—that its interruption would bring violence and anarchy—turned out to be quite simply wrong. If, however, Dryden's example does not invite direct imitation, it requires us at least to imagine a society that operated under ideological pressures very different from our own, and so reminds us that our own are not perhaps any more natural or inevitable than those of the seventeenth century. The nature of the Revolution and Dryden's response to it shows us with striking clarity that entire nations may strive to preserve the most obviously pernicious institutions even against their own interest simply because those institutions are embedded in conventional ways of imagining the distribution of power and authority. The English political nation had every reason in 1688 to discard the monarchy as well as the monarch, or at least to make the throne elective rather than hereditary. However, the Convention Parliament not only failed even to discuss this possibility (except insofar as the more conservative members attempted to blacken their opponents by complaining that their policies advanced it), but in order to avoid it they were forced upon obvious fictions of abdication that supplied the Jacobites with a talking point for years after. Dryden was no political hero—his principles were not necessarily admirable, and he was capable of bending them for polemical and perhaps personal advantage—but his story can tell us a good deal about political institutions and about the relation between politics, polemic, and art. The method I have employed in the following study must, however, find its ultimate justification in its ability to explain not the general nature of history, psychology, or language, but the specific nature of Dryden's works from 1687 to 1700.

Acknowledgments

The Newberry Library, the William Andrews Clark Memorial Library, and the graduate schools of Washington University and Northern Illinois University provided fellowships that helped me complete this book. An earlier version of the first part of chapter 2 appeared in *The Journal of English and Germanic Philology* under the title "Dryden and the Revolution of 1688: Political Parallel in *Don Sebastian*" (85 [1986], 346–365).

Several friends and colleagues have read parts of the book and offered useful comments, among them Anna Battigelli, Andrea Carlson, Bill Covey, Tom and Julie McCourt, Jody Ollenquist, Mary Sanders, Sean Shesgreen, and my wife, Lisa Chase Bywaters.

My greatest debt is to three of my teachers. John M. Wallace introduced me to the study of the relation between literature and history in seventeenth-century England, and has given me advice, encouragement, and assistance at several crucial moments. Carol Kay read the manuscript at various stages, always offering acute observations and helpful suggestions. Roughly a quarter of this book is drawn from a dissertation written under the direction of Steven N. Zwicker; all of it, however, has had the benefit of his detailed attention, his sharp and subtle intelligence, his sure understanding of Dryden, and his apparently limitless knowledge of seventeenth-century politics and culture. As a teacher, a scholar, and a critic he has provided me with an invaluable model for a career that would probably have foundered early without his generous aid. This book is gratefully dedicated to him.

Introduction

Certainly, if a Man can ever have reason to set a
value on himself, 'tis when his ungenerous Enemies
are taking the advantage of the Times upon him, to
ruin him in his reputation. And therefore for once, I
will make bold to take the Counsel of my Old Master *Virgil, Tu, ne cede malis; sed, contrà, audentior
ito.*

(Preface to *Don Sebastian*)

I suffer no more, than I can easily undergo; and so
long as I enjoy my Liberty, which is the Birth-right
of an *English* Man, the rest shall never go near my
Heart. The Merry Philosopher, is more to my Hu-
mour than the Melancholick; and I find no disposition in my self to Cry, while the mad World is daily
supplying me with such Occasions of Laughter.

(Dedication of *Amphitryon*)

Let this suffice; Nor thou, great Saint, refuse
This humble Tribute of no vulgar Muse:
Who, not by Cares, or Wants, or Age deprest,
Stems a wild Deluge with a dauntless brest.

(*Eleanora*)

What I now offer to your Lordship, is the wretched
remainder of a sickly Age, worn out with Study, and
oppress'd by Fortune: without other support than the
Constancy and Patience of a Christian.

(Dedication of Virgil's *Pastorals*)

> I think my self as vigorous as ever in the Faculties of
> my Soul. . . . What Judgment I had, increases rather
> than diminishes; and Thoughts, such as they are,
> come crowding in so fast upon me, that my only
> Difficulty is to chuse or to reject; to run them into
> Verse, or to give them the other Harmony of Prose. I
> have so long studied and practis'd both, that they are
> grown into a Habit, and become familiar to me.
>   (Preface to *Fables*)

As these quotations would suggest, Dryden's attitude towards himself and his work after the Revolution is not easy to define: he
veers between indignant defiance, amused detachment, and patient
resignation; he complains of poverty, illness, and exhaustion; he
exults in increasing powers. The long study that has worn him out
in 1697 has made verse and prose habitual to him in 1700. He
sometimes sinks beneath his misfortunes, sometimes benignly dis-
regards them; and sometimes overcomes them with heroic effort.
This variousness has given rise to a number of conflicting critical
views of the late Dryden. Some critics find "an old man's benignity
and practiced ease" or a "vital and buoyant happiness";[1] others
emphasize his "sense of personal decline," or his "bitterness and
resentments, the disappointments of disillusionment, the sense of
his own talents unused or scorned."[2] No one, however, seriously
doubts that these and similar passages embody more or less directly Dryden's personal feelings, that they are expressive rather
than rhetorical. Indeed, one critic has argued that private doubts
and disappointments become the mainspring of Dryden's art after
1685.[3]

If we read these passages in isolation, we may find nothing to
prevent us from taking them as the spontaneous outpourings of a
troubled soul. To explain their inconsistency, we need only suppose that like any sufferer Dryden was given to frequent shifts in
mood, sometimes complaining of his woes, sometimes defying
them, and sometimes bearing them with patient resignation. But
these passages appear in works aimed at a public that well knew
his circumstances and was curious about his response to them.
After his conversion, he was violently abused as a hireling eager to

adapt his politics and his religion to the government that paid him; after the Revolution he could defy his critics by pointing to his continuing loyalty to James and Catholicism. In doing so, however, he needed to use circumspection. Had he apostatized, had he even maintained silence concerning his political and religious beliefs, his critics would have seized on these new signs of inconstancy to abuse him the more: indeed, before he was able to reaffirm his principles in *Don Sebastian*, he figured in an anonymous lampoon purporting to be his loyal address to William. Yet any open defense of James or Catholicism was liable to be construed as a dangerous attack on the government or a traitorous declaration of sympathy with the ambitions of France. In these and other autobiographical passages Dryden deploys a subtle rhetorical strategy intended to disarm his attackers of both sets of weapons. He mentions his loyalty to his church and king only in order to describe its cost in fame and money, and his success in bearing that cost. His age and his poverty render him harmless to his opponents, while his experience has placed him beyond the reach of petty topical disputes. The new government's forbearance toward him, his recurring illnesses, his patriotic hatred of the French, and especially his immersion in a transcendent literary world, all are made to explain or to imply a renunciation of politics.

Dryden did not in fact renounce politics after the Revolution: his works from 1689 through 1700, from *Don Sebastian* through *Fables*, are filled with partisan references to William's usurpation, or the undeserved sufferings of James and his supporters, to the evils of unnecessary war, to the hypocrisy of governments that extend their power under the pretense of reform and liberation. But if these works are addressed to the potentially hostile audience Dryden seems to anticipate in his prefaces and dedications, we may well ask what such references are doing in them. This is the question I try to answer in the following study. What emerges from it is neither the embittered outcast nor the mellowed sage of tradition, but a poet still fully engaged with his experience and still able to combine the power of a close critique of politics with the authority of literary art.

I have chosen to discuss at greatest length those of Dryden's works that most fully and clearly exemplify the nature of his engagement with politics. Thus though I am concerned with a number of works commonly considered among Dryden's most important—*The Hind and the Panther, Don Sebastian, Amphitryon, The Discourse of Satire*—I have given other such works, particularly *Fables*, relatively short shrift and have lavished attention on still others—*King Arthur, Cleomenes*—commonly thought unworthy of it. My aim has been not to establish Dryden's "greatness" but to understand his political rhetoric and trace its evolution under changing political circumstances. I begin with *The Hind and the Panther* since it presents many of the same problems in interpretation as the postrevolutionary works. By early 1687 Dryden had already lost the audience to which he had habitually addressed his political rhetoric: the "more moderate sort" could hardly be expected to join the court in promoting a religion almost universally feared and despised. He had earned the obloquy of his former allies by his part in the controversy over the papers on the duchess of York's conversion, and in *The Hind and the Panther* he makes no attempt to conciliate either the Anglicans or the Dissenters. Indeed he attacks both groups and so leaves himself no one to persuade. The Hind's prophetic fable ends not with a "series of new time" but with an all-devouring tyrant. Yet despite his despair of attracting adherents or effecting change, Dryden clearly has much to say about contemporary politics and wants to be understood. In part he wants to defend himself against the charge of having changed his principles for personal gain; and so he argues that he has gained nothing, and more importantly, that though in his personal religious beliefs he has been moved from error to truth, in his political principles he has remained a model of constancy in comparison with his attackers. Throughout the poem he opposes the principles and rhetoric of the exclusion crisis Tories, which he claims as his own, to the dangerous practices of the newly rebellious Anglicans.

Dryden's tone in *The Hind and the Panther* is not persuasive but admonitory. He accuses the Anglicans of deserting a position of political rectitude and warns them that in so doing they have exposed themselves to fatal attack from their actual enemies. He suggests that when the revolution is over, they will acknowledge the justice of his predictions. He wishes to be seen as assured of the admiration, if not of his erring contemporaries, at least of an enlightened posterity. And in one way, both he and his opponents

knew that his claim upon posterity was assured. As the foremost
poet of his day, he could claim by virtue of his place in a transcendent literary tradition an authority surpassing that of any tran-
sient political faction. Dryden was to be sure an old hand at in-
forming political issues with literary authority: in *Annus Mirabilis*,
for example, he had lent Virgillian dignity to England's commercial rivalry with Holland, and in his verse tragedies he had meant
to invest his society with the values of epic poetry. But in *Don
Sebastian* (1689) and *Amphitryon* (1690), as well as in *The Hind
and the Panther*, only the poet is given this kind of authority;
Dryden claims that his literary qualifications allow him to see
clearly and completely the debasement and disorder of contemporary English politics. Thus in *The Hind and the Panther* he lays
claim to a native poetic tradition that had enabled Chaucer and
Spenser to penetrate the deceits of their times, and to Aesopian
fable, a genre in which the fabulist is endowed with calm wisdom
while the characters he describes wander in endless delusion. In
Don Sebastian he mixes farce with high tragedy in order to ridicule
the rebels and to elevate the values of such characters as Sebastian,
Almeyda, and Dorax, who either represent Dryden's political allies
or function as exemplary contrasts to his enemies. *Amphitryon* is
a farce of mistaken identity, and Dryden uses the genre to expose
the differences between the two claimants to the identity of the
king of England. But it is also a version of Molière's version of
Plautus, again part of a long and authoritative literary tradition.

Unlike *The Hind and the Panther*, these two postrevolutionary
plays contain no direct political attack; having lost his pension
with his laureateship, Dryden wrote these plays avowedly for
money and could not afford to stake their success on his audience's
willingness to tolerate his view of the Revolution. But the com-
prehension of his immediate audience was not necessary to his
rhetorical purposes in these plays. He neither hopes nor wishes to
sway public opinion; he wishes to be seen, by careful readers if not
casual theatergoers, as rebuking the revolutionaries before the tri-
bunal of posterity and predicting the consequences of their acts
with a confidence that future events will vindicate. The moral Dryden announces but leaves unexplained in the preface to *Don Sebastian* is that usurpers destroy all authority, including their own,
and so can engender only political chaos. But if he expected such

chaos before and immediately after the Revolution, he seems by 1690 to have begun to change his mind. Like *The Hind and the Panther* and *Don Sebastian*, *Amphitryon* ends with a prophecy; in this play, however, Dryden seems to expect not anarchy, but a stability upheld by the tyranny of William and the self-interested hypocrisy of his agents.

Political conditions had changed markedly since the Revolution by 1690. England was now engaged in a full-scale war with France, and among the Williamites the old Whig and Tory parties began to reemerge in a new form in order to debate the conduct and financing of the war or the merits of a strong fleet as opposed to a standing army. Within the growing parliamentary opposition were many of Dryden's former allies, most notably the marquis of Halifax, whom he had celebrated in *Absalom and Achitophel* as Jotham, and to whom he dedicated his next work for the stage, the semi-opera *King Arthur*. In this work Dryden's political rhetoric operates on two levels. On the one hand, he seeks to engage the Williamite opposition: compliments to Mary in the *Dedication* and to William in the concluding series of songs, and an insistent British nationalism that permeates the play, assure a Williamite audience of the author's essential loyalty to the large causes of freedom and justice, despite his refusal to abandon his belief in the legitimacy of James's title and the truth of his religion; while references to the blessings of peace and the commercial and military benefits of the sea support the opposition's political agenda. On the other hand, beneath this celebratory rhetoric runs a current of irony that undermines not only the martial values by which William was distinguished but also his title, as a foreign prince, to the British throne. Dryden borrows heavily from a wide assortment of literary models, and he uses these to elevate the society he describes as well as to establish his own literary stature; but the reality of English politics is so grossly out of line with the literary ideal that Jacobite readers are invited to contrast rather than compare Dryden's Arthurian Britain with its contemporary counterpart.

Perhaps led by the success of these tentative gestures towards conciliation, Dryden turned in his next play, *Cleomenes*, to a parallel in which he might reconcile his admiration for James with his support of England over France, and by which he might suggest to the government the political value of supporting a patriotic Jacobite. Again he turns to a literary model that might elevate both the poet and his subjects, both James and William. Cleomenes, an obvious parallel to James, suffers in the play at the hands not of those who supplanted him but of those to whom he fled for aid. In losing his throne, he falls victim rather to the fortunes of war than to a self-seeking political faction. Antigonus, the foreign conqueror, makes no appearance in the play, but his benevolent forbearance is described at length by an emissary from Sparta and pointedly contrasted with the rape and pillage Cleomenes expects. Dryden thus finds a way of admiring James without condemning William and his supporters.

Cleomenes, however, was very nearly banned from the stage—its performance was twice prohibited because of its supposed Jacobitism—and perhaps in response to this episode Dryden abandoned his effort to conciliate the court. He did not, however, return unchanged to his attack on the Revolution. He grew even more emphatic in reminding us of his place in literary tradition and in elevating the literary above the political. Whereas in his earlier work he looked to literary tradition for standards by which he might measure the degraded condition of contemporary politics, in his last works he looks upon this condition as normal. Politics is always and inevitably a source of cruelty and injustice, hypocrisy and corruption; the arts alone are capable of real improvement, and governments can achieve lasting fame only by fostering such improvement. Through such claims as these, Dryden is able to present himself exclusively as a poet and to make his criticism of contemporary politics dependent on his literary stature, a source of rhetorical authority which almost all his countrymen, whatever their political views, were willing to grant him. Most of Dryden's allusions to contemporary politics appear as generalizations about politics in all ages; often they are ascribed to the classic poets with whom almost everything Dryden wrote in his last years was concerned. General political allusions in criticism and translations allowed him to imply a unity of poets in all ages and to rate the governments of all ages (including his own) by their sponsorship of the arts. He refers directly to the rule of William only to complain about its failure to encourage the writing of an English prosodia, or its unjust use of the laureateship.

Although I am interested in close political analysis of Dryden's late works, I intend neither to reduce those works to a few crude topical particulars nor to trace in them the signs of large historical trends of which the author and his audience were not aware. My purpose is rather to study the artistry by which Dryden creates a rhetoric subtle enough to suit his very delicate political circumstances and very complex polemic purposes, and powerful enough to serve these purposes well. The fall of James II both strongly provoked this poet to political satire and deprived him of the central social and political position from which his best satire had previously been launched. By translating his political experience into the authoritative terms of classic and native poetic tradition, he creates in his late work a political rhetoric that rivals in power and surpasses in subtlety that of his laureate years.

I. "Echo's of Her Once Loyal Voice": *The Hind and the Panther*

In the year preceding the publication of *The Hind and the Panther*, James II alienated irrecoverably his natural allies, the Anglican Tories who had supported his claim to the throne during the exclusion crisis. He had spent the fall of 1686 attempting to persuade, with bribes and threats, individual members of parliament to repeal the Test Act, which prevented Roman Catholics from holding public office. After this "closetting" failed, James turned in the spring of 1687 to a different strategy: he published a Declaration of Indulgence according religious liberty to Protestant dissenters as well as to Catholics. This move infuriated the Anglicans, who joined the Whigs in insisting that James's promises could not be relied upon, that he would take the first opportunity to revoke the Declaration as Louis XIV had revoked the Edict of Nantes, and that he would turn himself eventually to converting the nation by force.

If the task of defending governmental policies was, therefore, difficult in itself, for Dryden it was further complicated by his own beliefs and circumstances. His recent conversion to Catholicism, which seemed to his enemies and many of his former allies an act of shameless self-interest and servility, lessened his authority as a public spokesman. The year before he had had a part in defending the authenticity of certain papers purporting to prove the conversion to Catholicism of James's first wife, and this first appearance before the public as a Catholic had not met with a reassuring response. Moreover, he harbored strong doubts (documented in his letter to Etherege of February 1687) about the practical ad-

visability, if not the aim, of James's policies, which must have
made them nearly impossible for him to defend.

The result is an extraordinarily complex poem that has baffled
and annoyed generations of readers. As most readers of the poem
from the time of its first publication to the present have recognized, the concerns of *The Hind and the Panther* are mainly
political.[1] The great controversy over Roman doctrine to which it
reacts arose not from a sudden and universal resurgence of interest
in questions of faith, but from widespread fear of James's radical
policies, especially of his unprecedented extension of his dispensing
power that culminated in April 1687 with the Declaration of Indulgence. Yet however apparent the poem's general intention, the
details of its political program are far from clear. We would expect
the champion of the royal party to adopt the position of the court,
yet in *The Hind and the Panther* the very dissenters whose tender
consciences James was in May 1687 busily attempting to assuage
appear as bears, boars, and wolves cursed with an "innate antip-
athy to kings." To explain this discrepancy, a tradition has arisen
that claims Dryden changed his poem, as he was once supposed to
have changed his religion, to suit the policy of the court. As
Macaulay puts it, "At first the Church of England is mentioned
with tenderness and respect, and is exhorted to ally herself with
the Roman Catholics against the Protestant Dissenters; but at the
close of the poem [written after James's Declaration] the Protestant Dissenters are invited to make common cause with the Roman
Catholics against the Church of England."[2] This error has been
ably refuted by the most recent editor of the poem,[3] but the problem it was developed to solve remains. Not only does Dryden fail
to "invite" the dissenters at the end of the poem, he fails throughout to accord any "tenderness and respect" or even tolerance to
the Anglicans. *The Hind and the Panther* attacks every significant
political party of its time, and if Dryden had been attempting in
this poem to form public opinion as he had done with such success
in *Absalom and Achitophel*, so general an attack would have been
far worse than useless. In 1687 Dryden could not and did not
write with any such purpose. He turns from persuasion to reproof
and admonition, from arguments based on precedent to precepts
and predictions embodied in fables. The rhetorical authority that
Dryden had habitually drawn from his claim to represent a unified
or unifiable nation is replaced by a different kind of authority

drawn from the poet's professed mastery of and participation in a venerable and transcendent literary tradition.

As advocates of Macaulay's revision theory have observed, the satiric portraits of the dissenters that dominate the beginning of the poem make little sense in light of James's Declaration and Dryden's endorsement of it in the *Preface*. Dryden's claim there to have aimed his satire only at those who have refused to support James's policies is belied not only by the opening portraits but even by those sections of the poem that praise the Declaration. Those of the sects, for example, who admire the Hind as she drinks her "sober draught" under the Lyon's protection do not wholly escape blame:

> Some, who before her fellowship disdain'd,
> Scarce, and but scarce, from in-born rage restrain'd,
> Now frisk'd about her, and old kindred feign'd.
> Whether for love or int'rest, ev'ry sect
> Of all the salvage nation shew'd respect.
>
> (I.544–548)[4]

And those birds which in the Hind's fable avail themselves of the Landlord's edict are hardly flattered:

> His Gracious Edict the same Franchise yields
> To all the wild Encrease of Woods and Fields,
> And who in Rocks aloof, and who in Steeples builds:
> To *Crows* the like Impartial Grace affords,
> And *Choughs* and *Daws*, and such Republick Birds.
>
> (III.1247–1251)

Further, even in the *Preface* Dryden's invitation to the sects just misses being a satire upon them. Rather than celebrate their loyalty, he merely asks why he "may not suppose" that, as "some Diseases have abated of their Virulence," so the sects may abandon their republican principles; and in the three following paragraphs, all on the Declaration, he comes nearer threatening than praising them. The first of these flatters James: Dryden replaces the "stretched" figure of the dissenting addresses—that James had *"restor'd God to his Empire over Conscience"*—with a "safer" one that emphasizes the link between James's radical extension of his prerogative and the dissenters' safety: "Conscience," Dryden tells us, "is the Royalty and Prerogative of every Private man." The

next paragraph scourges the "Pride and Obstinacy" of those who
refuse to be grateful for the Declaration; and Dryden's angry insistence here that such gratitude "ought in reason to be expected"
is somewhat qualified by his earlier remark that more dissenters
have come over to James "than I could reasonably have hop'd."
He concludes his discussion of the Declaration with a scarcely
veiled threat:

> Of the receiving this Toleration thankfully, I shall say no more, than
> that they ought, and I doubt not they will consider from what hands
> they receiv'd it. 'Tis not from a *Cyrus*, a Heathen Prince, and a For-
> eigner, but from a Christian King, their Native Sovereign: who expects
> a Return in *Specie* from them: that the Kindness which He has Gra-
> ciously shown them, may be retaliated on those of his own perswasion.
> (Pp. 120–121)

Dryden's loathing of the dissenters appears to have been so strong
that he could not, even to advance the ends of his king and patron,
entirely give it up.

Yet he might nonetheless have restrained himself from venting
it with such force and thoroughness in the poem if he had not in
fact been after bigger game than the Fox and Wolf. The real objects of Dryden's satire in part I and throughout *The Hind and the
Panther* are not the dissenters, but the Anglicans, the party he had
left only a year or two before and in support of which he had
written all his political poetry since the Restoration. His description of the dissenting sects initiates a rhetorical strategy that structures the entire poem and is subtly calculated to suit the uncomfortable position in which his sudden and sharp reversal of
allegiance had left him. Since in accusing the sects of rebellious
pride, Dryden does exactly what the Anglicans had done during
the exclusion crisis (and what he himself had done in *Absalom and
Achitophel*, *The Medall*, and *Religio Laici*), he may, when he turns
the same accusations against the Anglicans, suggest that they are
guilty of the crimes they affect to abhor, that they have altered
their old principles of loyalty and obedience, and that he alone has
preserved—despite his apostacy—any real claim to integrity and
consistency. This strategy of confronting new Anglican practice
with old Tory principle is varied and developed throughout *The
Hind and the Panther*; it never lies far beneath the surface,
whether of religious history, doctrinal debate, or Aesopian fable.

Dryden's parade of sectarian beasts, then, merely sets the stage for his introduction of the Anglican Panther: the order in which he introduces these beasts, and the digressions with which he interrupts his description of them, are designed to implicate the Anglicans in the crimes of which they accused the sectaries. Dryden begins with a group of sects that the nation almost unanimously hated and feared. Presbyterians, Anglicans, and Catholics could join in condemning the religions of the men who had levelled Munster in the sixteenth century and England in the seventeenth, and even these loathed Anabaptists and Independents could join their Christian brethren against the atheists and Socinians. Yet Dryden makes the last insignificant sect the occasion of nearly a hundred lines of personal confession and doctrinal argument, no doubt recognizing that his affecting confession of faith is the more likely to carry the sympathy of the Protestant reader as it is proposed in opposition to the blasphemy of the deists. In the doctrinal digression that follows he leads us carefully from arguments for the divinity of Christ, the main subject of dispute between Socinians and orthodox Christians, to arguments for transubstantiation, a main subject of dispute between Protestants and Catholics;[5] and the parallel thus suggested between Socinians and Protestants continues through the ensuing description of the Wolf. The Presbyterians, unlike the Independents and deists, made up a numerous and respectable party; Dryden therefore undermines their authority by contaminating them with the taint of their more radical enemies. Thus the Boar and Bear may lay waste the woods of Britain, but the Wolf is more destructive even than these (I.154–160); he shares with the Fox a common ancestry, and a common predisposition to violence and rebellion (I.190 ff.).

Thus far the great majority of Anglicans would have agreed with Dryden's assessment of the sects; a few years earlier they would even have applauded his spirited description of the rebellious depredations of the Fox and Wolf. This is followed, however, by a digression no less carefully placed and constructed than that which follows the description of the Fox. The lines against Louis's persecution of the Huguenots would have won Anglican assent as readily as those against the Socinian heresy; the revocation of the Edict of Nantes was a potent weapon for Anglican controversialists, who used it to assess the value of a popish king's promises to heretics. But Dryden is no more interested in Louis than in the

Socinians: again, he introduces Anglican accusations against their proper objects only that he may later turn them against the Anglicans themselves. Dryden's account of the creation, with its suggestions of the benignity not only of prelapsarian man but of James II (I.262, 266, 271, 275), begins this transfer of blame; his account of the fall of man advances it further:

> Then, first rebelling, his own stamp he coins;
> The murth'rer *Cain* was latent in his loins,
> And bloud began its first and loudest cry
> For diff'ring worship of the Deity.
> Thus persecution rose, and farther space
> Produc'd the mighty hunter of his race.
>   (I.278–283)

Rebellion and persecution, closely linked in Anglican polemic since the tyranny of the rebels during the interregnum, are here brought together to justify the anti-Anglican policies of James, who both "provides protection" for unruly Protestant beasts (I.289–290) and prevents them from persecuting in their turn (I.299–304). The connection between these sins, thus early established through myth and metaphor, recurs throughout the poem to define and condemn the recent behavior of those Anglicans who had so often used the same polemic strategy against the dissenters.

At the end of this chain of allegory stand the Anglicans themselves. Just as the blasphemy of the Fox is transferred to the Wolf, so the rebelliousness and cruelty of the Fox and Wolf are transferred in turn to the Panther.[6] The faint praise with which Dryden introduces the beast, and which has misled many readers into supposing that the abuse of the Panther in part III results from sudden changes in court policy, is part of a simple rhetorical strategy well described by Aristotle: "Another way, available for the accuser, is to praise at great length some trifling merit of the accused, and then to put a great slur upon him concisely, or to list a number of his merits, and then condemn him for one bad quality that bears heavily on the case."[7] Having alluded to the fairness and nobility of the Panther, Dryden suggests her adulterous connection with the Wolf, traces her lineage from Heresy and Sacrilege, and accuses her of Mohammedanism in her contempt for fasting and of Calvinism in her abuse of the Eucharist. Another brief passage of

praise ends, like the first, in a reference to her adultery with the
Wolf; and we can hardly admire her for being "the fairest member
of the fallen crew" when we have just heard Dryden's recitation of
the religious and political crimes by which that crew is distinguished. The whole case against the Panther concludes with a
charge that returns at intervals throughout the poem and is central
to its political meaning:

> For how can she constrain them to obey
> Who has herself cast off the lawfull sway?
> Rebellion equals all, and those who toil
> In common theft, will share the common spoil.
> . . . .
> If she reform by Text, ev'n that's as plain
> For her own Rebels to reform again.
>   (I.454–457, 460–461)

> So hardly can Usurpers manage well
> Those, whom they first instructed to rebell:
> More liberty begets desire of more,
> The hunger still encreases with the store.
>   (I.517–520)

The Anglicans not only share the rebelliousness of the sects but are
themselves the great source and example of that rebelliousness. No
argument could have better suited Dryden's purpose: to charge
with betrayal that party which, only a few years before, had
boasted of its position as the great prop of monarchy and scourge
of rebellion. As the Panther "stands herself accused" by the sects
from "that scripture which she once abus'd / To Reformation," so
throughout the poem the Anglicans stand themselves accused by
the strategies and arguments which, during the exclusion crisis,
they had used so forcefully against the Whigs.

The charge of inconsistency that underlies Dryden's use against
the Anglicans of old Tory polemic in part I is made explicit at the
beginning of part II. The Panther has accused the Hind of cow-
ardice during the Popish Plot, when, though her "priestly calves
lay strugling" in the snare of the Whigs, the Hind herself escaped
(II.1–17). The allegorical incoherence of this statement is obvious;
but the Hind chooses to counter it on more telling grounds. Although she now changes the object of her attack from political to

doctrinal inconsistency, the political implications of doctrine are never far from Dryden's mind. The Panther was silent in "the main question" of the Eucharist until the Test Act:

> The *Test* it seems at last has loos'd your tongue.
> And, to explain what your forefathers meant,
> By real presence in the sacrament,
> (After long fencing push'd, against a wall,)
> Your *salvo* comes, that he's not there at all:
> There chang'd your faith, and what may change may fall.
>   (II.30–35)

Though the Hind may have fled the persecution of the Whigs, the Panther altered her very nature to escape the same danger:

> Long time you fought, redoubl'd batt'ry bore,
> But, after all, against your self you swore;
> Your former self, for ev'ry hour your form
> Is chop'd and chang'd, like winds before a storm.
>   (II.54–57)[8]

Thus the Test, since 1685 the main source of controversy between James and the Anglicans, is made a sign of Anglican inconsistency. Dryden claims that it had been forced upon the Anglicans by the Whigs, and that its revocation would therefore be entirely consistent with old Tory principles. Transubstantiation had been an object of derision to English Protestants of all kinds long before the Test Act, but this hardly matters to Dryden. He is primarily interested not in the doctrine itself, but in its political consequences, and this is no less true of all the points of dogma under discussion in part II.

As in part I, the case against the Panther in part II is constructed with old Tory polemic.[9] The Hind's next speech—an invocation of the infallibility of Pope and councils—brilliantly demonstrates this technique. Not only does the government of the Catholic church bear a striking resemblance to the ideal of constitutional government to which all good Englishmen subscribed[10] but refusal to submit to it is attended with precisely the same consequences that the Tories once feared from the exclusion bill:

> But mark how sandy is your own pretence,
> Who setting Councils, Pope, and Church aside,

> Are ev'ry man his own presuming guide
> . . . .
> All who can read, Interpreters may be:
> Thus though your sev'ral churches disagree,
> Yet ev'ry Saint has to himself alone
> The secret of this Philosophick stone.
> These principles your jarring sects unite,
> When diff'ring Doctours and disciples fight;
> Though *Luther, Zuinglius, Calvin,* holy chiefs
> Have made a battel Royal of beliefs;
> Or like wild horses sev'ral ways have whirl'd
> The tortur'd Text about the Christian World;
> Each *Jehu* lashing on with furious force.
>   (II.105–107, 110–120)

No one had been a greater master of Tory polemic than the poet laureate himself, and the anger and sharpness of Dryden's satire against the Whigs in *The Medall* shine throughout this passage. Just as here the Protestant sects are held together only by their rebellion against authority—"These principles your jarring sects unite"—so in *The Medall* "All hands unite of every jarring Sect" to overthrow the government. The anarchy—the "battel Royal of beliefs"—to which this rebellion leads in *The Hind and the Panther* is in *The Medall* the consequence of the exclusion bill:

> The Cut-throat Sword and clamorous Gown shall jar,
> In shareing their ill-gotten Spoiles of War:
> Chiefs shall be grudg'd the part which they pretend;
> Lords envy Lords, and Friends with every Friend
> About their impious merit shall contend.
>   (II.306–310)[11]

The Panther rejoins that "The Word in needfull points is only plain"; and in the discussion that follows, the Hind uses this principle of scriptural interpretation to strengthen the connection between the Anglicans and the levelling dissenters. If all heretics have "the same pretence / To plead the Scriptures in their own defence" (II.154–155), then all are equally rebels to authority. As Dryden had in *The Medall* claimed of the sects that "The Text inspires not them; but they the Text inspire," so in *The Hind and the Panther* the same charge, its political meaning more explicitly developed, is turned against the Anglicans:

> The word is then deposed, and in this view,
> You rule the Scripture, not the Scripture you.
>   (II.186–187)

The Tories had long argued that the deposition of political authority led to tyranny and anarchy; by applying the charge to the Panther, the Hind arraigns the Anglicans in their own court.

Such references to Tory polemic abound in part II. Like the structural parallels in part I, they are designed to taint the Anglicans with the political principles of their old enemies. Two such references hint at the specific political implications of this new Anglican whiggery. The Hind, concluding her arguments against the Panther's confused attitude towards tradition, refers again to the Anglicans' inability to curb rebellion:

> Shall she command, who has herself rebell'd?
> Is *Antichrist* by *Antichrist* expell'd?
> Did we a lawfull tyranny displace,
> To set aloft a bastard of the race?
>   (II.279–282)

The comparison of the Anglicans to Monmouth is here inevitable; and this reference to the old Protestant successor is complemented by another, less obvious, to the new. Having condemned English exportation of criminals rather than religion, the Hind digresses on the even more sacrilegious trade of the Dutch:

> Yet some improve their traffick more than we,
> For they on gain, their onely God, rely:
> And set a publick price on piety.
> Industrious of the needle and the chart
> They run full sail to their *Japponian* Mart:
> Prevention fear, and prodigal of fame
> Sell all of Christian to the very name;
> Nor leave enough of that, to hide their naked shame.
>   (II.568–575)

The Dutch had long been an object of Tory disgust and derision.[12] Dryden both taunts the Anglicans with their new republican ally and predicts an ill fate for their religion under the prince of Orange.

As the beginning of part II reminds the Anglicans of their protection of James during the exclusion crisis, so the conclusion reminds them of James's protection of them during Monmouth's rebellion. The "streaming blaze" and "chearfull azure light" that show divine approval of the Hind's peroration are compared to the "pleasing triumphs of the sky," which, according to Dryden, were visible in London after the battle of Sedgemoor and antici- pated the "news" that "three lab'ring nations did restore" (II.649– 662). In the lines that follow, Monmouth's rebellion enters the action of the poem metaphorically as a threat to the Panther:

> By this, the *Hind* had reach'd her lonely cell;
> And vapours rose, and dews unwholsome fell.
> When she, by frequent observation wise,
> As one who long on heav'n had fix'd her eyes,
> Discern'd a change of weather in the skyes.
> The Western borders were with crimson spread,
> The moon descending look'd all flaming red,
> She thought good manners bound her to invite
> The stranger Dame to be her guest that night.
> (II.663–671)

The Hind invites her to share "A grace-cup to their common Pa- tron's health,"

> For fear she might be wilder'd in her way,
> Because she wanted an unerring guide
> . . . .
> But most she fear'd that travelling so late
> Some evil minded beasts might lye in wait;
> And without witness wreak their hidden hate.
> (II.682–683, 688–690)

The Panther, "wisely weighing, since she had to deal / With many foes, their numbers might prevail" (II.693–694), accepts, and the Hind offers her permanent residence. The crimson western borders are clearly those of England on which Monmouth landed and fought: the figuration of anti-Anglican violence as weather looks forward to the Panther's fable, where the Panther delights in the storms that figure her own persecution of the Catholics. The "evil minded beasts" and "many foes" represent the threat Monmouth and his followers posed to the party which was responsible for his misfortunes. Thus the Hind's invitation shows that James, though Catholic, had protected the Anglicans from their enemies, and the Panther's acceptance reminds us of the debt of gratitude they had thus incurred. This version of James as a great Tory protector is in itself preposterous: he had at least as much to fear from Monmouth's victory as did the Church of England. But we have been carefully prepared for it by the system of allusions that, throughout parts I–II, identify the Tories of the exclusion crisis with the Catholics of the present, and the Whigs of that period with the Anglicans of the present. In part III Dryden describes this strategy and the confusion and resentment he no doubt intends to arouse in the Anglicans by employing it:

> The *Hind* thus briefly, and disdain'd t' inlarge
> On Pow'r of Kings, and their Superior charge,
> As Heav'ns Trustees before the Peoples choice:
> Tho' sure the *Panther* did not much rejoyce
> To hear those Echo's giv'n of her once Loyal voice.
>   (III.887–891)

The Hind and the Panther is, then, a consistent and thorough attack on the Anglicans; but this alone does not explain Dryden's political motivation in the poem. When a few years earlier he had launched his attack on the Whigs, he had been assured of a large body of Tories eager to applaud his work, and no doubt of a great many readers who were as yet uncommitted and might have been influenced by his arguments. When in 1687 he launched a similar attack against the Anglicans, he could rely on the support only of a small and despised group of his coreligionists; and the only uncommitted party over which he could hope to have some influence was that of the dissenters, which he begins his poem by abusing. When the poem was published, James was, like his poet laureate, attacking the Anglicans, but only as a means of wooing the party they had so long persecuted. For Dryden, an attack on the Anglicans seems to be an end in itself and so attractive an end that he is willing to sacrifice to it even those to whom James was applying for help. Some critics, remarking only Dryden's preoccupation with the Anglicans, have argued that he is attempting—at least in the first two parts of the poem—to persuade them to an alliance with the court.[13] One can, however, imagine more likely ways of going about this than mockery and derision. Two months before the poem was published even James was convinced that Anglican support for his policies was not to be had; and it would seem reasonable to credit the most astute political poet of the age with more penetration than the monarch whose stupidity was proverbial in his own time. In fact Dryden attacks, in one way or another, every recognized political faction except his own, the moderate Catholics, a party that he well knew to be powerless. If we are to understand his purpose in so doing, we must abandon the notion that his attitude towards the consequences of his work was in 1687 substantially what it had been in 1681.

This attitude, though implicit throughout the poem, emerges most clearly at the beginning of part III. There Dryden turns again to the exclusion crisis and develops more fully his account of the Panther's repudiation of her loyalty. The Hind ascribes this change to the Panther's greed and ambition and so introduces a debate over whether the Anglicans or the Catholics stand to gain temporal profit from their religion. Dryden's description of the condition of the Catholics suggests that he had little faith in their political power, and refers, no doubt, to his own uncomfortable position:[14]

> Mean-time my sons accus'd, by fames report
> Pay small attendance at the *Lyon's* court,
> Nor rise with early crowds, nor flatter late,
> (For silently they beg who daily wait.)
> Preferment is bestow'd that comes unsought,
> Attendance is a bribe, and then 'tis bought.
> How they shou'd speed, their fortune is untry'd,
> For not to ask, is not to be deny'd.
> For what they have, their *God* and *King* they bless,
> And hope they shou'd not murmur, had they less.
>
> (III.235–244)

The autobiographical reference is even clearer in Dryden's famous and moving description of the Hind's manner of disciplining her wayward sons:

> If joyes hereafter must be purchas'd here
> With loss of all that mortals hold so dear,
> Then welcome infamy and publick shame,
> And, last, a long farwell to worldly fame.
> 'Tis said with ease, but oh, how hardly try'd
> By haughty souls to humane honour ty'd!
> O sharp convulsive pangs of agonizing pride!

Down then thou rebell, never more to rise,
And what thou didst, and do'st so dearly prize,
That fame, that darling fame, make that thy sacrifice.
                                                    (III.281–290)

Such confessional passages, though they are to become frequent in
his prose after the Revolution, are new in Dryden's poetry and
indicate an important change in his view of his work. His conversion had deprived him of the authority he had enjoyed during
the last years of Charles's reign as a spokesman for the Tories and
Anglicans: as a Catholic, Dryden would no longer be able to persuade a Protestant nation. Rather than ignore this rhetorical hand-
icap, Dryden attempts to make it work in his favor: we are to
believe him because, he claims, he has chosen personal principle
over political effectiveness, while the Anglicans have abandoned
their loyal principles in order to advance their political agenda.
Dryden attacks every prominent party of his time not so that he
may persuade anyone to do anything, but so that he may record
in verse the relation of his principles to the faithlessness and hypocrisy with which he felt himself surrounded and of which he
knew himself accused.[15] He is primarily concerned with the Anglicans because, if he is to display the truth of his new party, he
must demonstrate the falsity of his old one and the moral rectitude
of his change. Further, to repair the loss of the rhetorical authority
he had once derived from his allegiance to this party, he creates for
himself another and rather different rhetorical position, grounded
in classic and native poetic traditions, from which he may encounter the claims of his opponents.

The beast fable was popular during the Restoration—new editions of Aesop were published regularly throughout the period—
and enjoyed a privileged generic status.[16] On the one hand, such
fables were held sufficiently simple and obvious to form the characters of children; on the other, they were considered an ancient
vehicle of wisdom, especially such wisdom as penetrated and opposed political deceit and hypocrisy. The preface of *Aesop Improved* (1673) assures us that a "due compliance" with the lessons
of its fables "had preserved divers individual persons, and not only
persons but families, and not only families but kingdoms, from
those causes which have proved their ruin." The preface of *Aesop
Explained* (1682)—though this work, which includes "the plain

meaning of the *Grammar* Rules unfolded to the Youth's capacity
by way of Question and Answer," seems primarily directed towards children—nonetheless presents its fables as an antidote to
Whig machination:

> considering that it might prove of great Advantage, especially in these
> tumultuous Times, wherein men use Fraud and Equivocation, to carry
> on their devilish Designs, I have prepared this Book, as a Looking-
> Glass, wherein are lively represented the Insinuations, Frauds, Deceits,
> and Equivocations that are now on foot. . . . As touching the *Fables* in
> general, I need say but little: *Solomon* himself sends us to the *Ant* for
> wisdom . . . and a better than *Solomon* bids us to be as Wise as *Ser-
> pents*, and as innocent as *Doves*. You may by well choosing, the Pre-
> cepts and Instructions which are here laid down in these Morals, es-
> cape many Devices, Dangers, and Troubles, which others less wary
> have run themselves into.

Roger L'Estrange, Dryden's ally who like him suffered for his support of James, prefaces his 1692 translation of Aesop with large
claims for the authority of the genre: "What can be said more to
the Honour of this *Symbolical* Way of Moralizing upon *Tales* and
Fables, than that the Wisdom of the Ancients has been still wrapt
up in *Veils* and *Figures*." The dedication of another translation,
written in the same year as *The Hind and the Panther*, emphasizes
the genre's ability to express moral truths in difficult political circumstances:

> This Book ascrib'd to *Aesop*, in a Plain and Simple Form, contains the
> Substance of Moral Philosophy, and perhaps as much Truth in order
> to the Conduct of life, as History itself commonly affords us, since 'tis
> the Misfortune of Mankind, that the Present Times as little dare to
> relate Truths, as the Future can know them.[17]

Aesopian fable has, then, a number of uses for Dryden. Its generic
character suggests simplicity, moral wisdom, and innocence, qualities well suited to set forth the virtues of a policy that the majority
of his audience thought tortuous, dubious, unprecedented, and im-
moderate, and its ability to discover and censure the frauds and
deceits of contemporary politics is no less appropriate to Dryden's
beleaguered political position. Most important, it allows Dryden
to write not as the hireling scribbler of a tyrannous court but as a
classic poet in a great tradition, looking down on public affairs

from the privileged point of view supplied him by a venerable genre.

The fable allows Dryden to claim allegiance also to a more specific and no less honorable tradition. Throughout the Restoration, English literature was generally believed to have had only two canonical nondramatic poets. Whenever Englishmen had occasion to celebrate the literary accomplishments of their nation, they inevitably thought of the Elizabethan dramatists and of Chaucer and Spenser.[18] The presence of these two poets throughout *The Hind and the Panther* is, then, no accident. Dryden's occasional use of archaic diction and syntax, his modelling the Hind's fable after Chaucer's *Nun's Priest's Tale*, his reference to Spenser's *Mother Hubbard's Tale* (the Protestant associations of which Dryden neutralizes by emphasizing its attack on the Whig heroine Elizabeth), all serve to place his poem in the great English tradition. The last of these occurs in a passage of self-defense, emphatically placed at the beginning of part III, which summarizes all the generic claims of the poem:

> Much malice mingl'd with a little wit
> Perhaps may censure this mysterious writ,
> Because the Muse has people'd *Caledon*
> With *Panthers*, *Bears*, and *Wolves*, and Beasts unknown,
> As if we were not stock'd with monsters of our own.
> Let *AEsop* answer, who has set to view,
> Such kinds as *Greece* and *Phrygia* never knew;
> And mother *Hubbard* in her homely dress
> Has sharply blam'd a *British Lioness*,
> That *Queen*, whose feast the factious rabble keep,
> Expos'd obscenely naked and a-sleep.
> Led by those great examples, may not I
> The wanted organs of their words supply?
>
> (III.1–13)[19]

Dryden is led by these examples throughout his poem: his conversion, though it deprived him of the support of the great majority of his contemporaries, did not deprive him of his claim to a place in English poetic tradition. By asserting that claim, he is able to attack contemporary politics from the only tenable position that James's policies and his own new principles had left him.

The Hind and the Panther, then, confronts political affairs on its own peculiar terms. It attempts not to change their course but

to translate them into the authoritative language of Aesopian fable
and English verse. Parts I and II expose what Dryden would have
us see as the true nature of the Anglicans by entangling their new
policies with their old principles; and the language of fable, with
its powers of penetrating deceit and hypocrisy, supports this strategy. In part III this language comes to dominate the poem. The
lines that precede the Panther's fable argue the innocence and patience of the English Catholics, and the base motives of the Anglican attack upon them: disdain, envy, spite, malice, interest,
pride, jealousy, and revenge (III.70–74). In so doing they serve as
an excellent introduction to the Panther's fable, which, as a rhetorical expression of the Panther's malice, corroborates these
claims,[20] while as a fabular translation of Anglican polemic it exposes the weakness and inconsistency of the Panther's ideas and
behavior.

The attack on popery in the Panther's fable bears almost no
similarity to the Anglican antipapist polemic of its time. In Gilbert
Burnet's *Reasons Against Repealing . . . the Test*, an Anglican tract
that appeared several weeks before the poem and to which the
poem alludes,[21] we are reminded of *"the Councils of the Lateran,*
that decreed the *extirpation of all Hereticks*, with severe sanctions
on those *Princes* that failed in their Duty, of being the *Hangmen
of the Inquisitors*," of "the *Council of Constance*, that decreed,
that *Princes were not bound to keep their faith to Hereticks*," of
"the *Gunpowder Plot*," of "the *Massacre of Ireland*," and especially of what, since the revocation of the Edict of Nantes, the
Catholics

> have done, and are still doing in *France*; and what feeble things *Edicts*,
> *Coronation Oaths*, *Laws and Promises*, repeated over and over again,
> prove to be, where that *Religion* prevails; and *Leuis le Grand* makes
> not so contemptible a Figure in that *Church*, or in *our Court*, as to
> make us think, that *his example* may not be proposed as a *Pattern*, as
> well as his *aid* may be offered for an encouragement, to act the same
> things in *England*, that he is now doing with so much applause in
> *France*.
>
> (P. 4)

In a later tract, which may allude in turn to *The Hind and the
Panther*, Burnet thus cautions us against James's campaign for
tolerance:

If papists were not fools, they must give good words and fair promises,
till by these they have so far deluded the poor credulous hereticks, that
they may put themselves in a posture to execute the decrees of their
church against them; and though we accuse that religion as guilty both
of cruelty and treachery, yet we do not think them fools.[22]

But it is as comic fools, rather than violent knaves, that Dryden
has the Panther portray the Catholics:

> The *Swallow*, privileg'd above the rest
> Of all the birds, as man's familiar Guest,
> Pursues the Sun in summer brisk and bold,
> But wisely shuns the persecuting cold:
> Is well to chancels and to chimneys known,
> Though 'tis not thought she feeds on smoak alone.
> From hence she has been held of heav'nly line,
> Endu'd with particles of soul divine.
> This merry Chorister had long possess'd
> Her summer seat, and feather'd well her nest.
>   (III.427–436)

In fact Dryden gives the Panther not the Anglican anti-Catholic
language of James's reign, but the Tory anti-Catholic polemic of
the exclusion crisis,[23] a language in which he had himself been
very proficient. In *Absalom and Achitophel*, the Jebusites are both
silly and harmless; and the Whig version of the Catholics as in-
cendiaries watching their opportunity to assassinate the king and
burn the kingdom is dismissed with derision. Similarly, Father Petre, to whom Burnet ascribes "much more *Force* and *Passion*"
than the French scourge of Huguenots Pére La Chaise,[24] is in the
Panther's fable little more than a harmless buffoon, another version of Dominic in *The Spanish Fryar*: "He says he's but a friar,
but he's big enough to be a pope; his gills are as rosy as a turkey
cock; his great belly walks in state before him, like an harbinger;
and his gouty legs come limping after it: Never was such a tun of
devotion seen."[25]

> A church-begot, and church-believing bird;
> Of little body, but of lofty mind,
> Round belly'd, for a dignity design'd,
> And much a dunce, as *Martyns* are by kind.
>   (III.462–465)

This depiction of the Catholics had the same purpose in 1687 as in 1681—to defuse fear of popery by revealing the harmlessness of its object. By giving it to the Panther, Dryden again opposes old Tory with new Anglican attitudes.

This consistency is realized, however, not by our unassisted comparison of these attitudes—Dryden could not here depend on his audience's willingness to recall such small matters—but by the juxtaposition in the fable of this old Tory polemic with new Anglican policy. The harmlessness of the victims of Anglican persecution emphasizes the cruelty of that persecution:

> The latter brood, who just began to fly
> Sick-feather'd, and unpractis'd in the sky,
> For succour to their helpless mother call,
> She spread her wings; some few beneath 'em craul,
> She spread 'em wider yet, but cou'd not cover all.
> . . . .
> The joyless morning late arose, and found
> A dreadful desolation reign a-round,
> Some buried in the Snow, some frozen to the ground:
> The rest were strugling still with death, and lay
> The *Crows* and *Ravens* rights, an undefended prey.
> (III.613–617, 622–626)

The Panther's own fable thus arraigns Anglican policy no less effectually than the Hind's; yet Dryden, if accused of manufacturing the evidence, could have found sources for all the elements of the fable either in Anglican polemic of the exclusion crisis or in present Anglican behavior.

The Panther's fable becomes even more damning when read in conjunction with the Hind's. The fable of the pigeons presents a rival version of affairs and a rival prophecy. The Panther's absurd Swallows become the Hind's mild and maligned poultry; and whereas the Panther predicts a massacre of Catholics, the Hind predicts a massacre of Anglicans. But the parallels between the two fables run far deeper than this. Both fables are based on the same plot: in each, a nation of birds, too eager to advance its interests, follows a false leader, and by misusing a period of grace, provokes an unexpected doom. Thus the two fables correspond to one another both in plot-structure (Swallows equal Pigeons) and in historical reference (Swallows equal poultry); and from the counterpoint between these two systems Dryden forms a complex political lesson. Thus combined, the two fables bring together, in one final and authoritative statement, the oppositions between Catholic/Tory principles and Dissenting/Anglican practices that structure the political meaning of the entire poem.

The most obvious of the plot-correspondences between the two fables is that between the Swallows and the Pigeons: both follow false leaders to their doom. The acts and motives, however, that lead them to do so are strikingly contrasted. Though the Swallows respond to forces the real reference of which is political, these forces—the penal laws—are represented in their fable as weather. They are wild fowl, and, like the Hind's sons who "pay small attendance at the Lyon's court," cannot themselves act to much purpose. They are vulnerable to forces they can neither control nor clearly anticipate, and their only choice is whether or not to flee these forces.[26] Further, they are misled into the act that sets their plot in motion by nothing more wicked than their desire that their young should escape inevitable misfortune:

> The sickly young sat shivring on the shoar,
> Abhorr'd salt-water never seen before,
> And pray'd their tender mothers to delay
> The passage, and expect a fairer day.
> (III.457–460)

The Pigeons, by contrast, are domestic fowl. They have far more control over their destiny than the Swallows; and they must answer to a just and indulgent landlord. The motive that ultimately brings on their ruin, unlike that of the Swallows, is indefensible—envy rather than parental care:

> Our pamper'd *Pigeons* with malignant Eyes,
> Beheld these Inmates, and their Nurseries:
> Tho' hard their fare, at Ev'ning, and at Morn
> A Cruise of Water and an Ear of Corn;
> Yet still they grudg'd that Modicum, and thought
> A sheaf in ev'ry single Grain was brought.
> (III.997–1002)

Thus the Catholics can be accused of profiting by James's (to the Panther) dubious policies only because they mistakenly believe that they and their families will escape destruction, whereas the Anglicans wrongfully oppose those policies because they begrudge the

Catholics the smallest shred of protection or patronage—a political luxury that Dryden carefully figures as a biological necessity.
The Martyn appears earlier in the Panther's fable than does his
counterpart the Buzzard in the Hind's, no doubt because the evil
which must hurry each group to its ruin, though it might easily be
ascribed to the malicious Pigeons, could not conveniently be laid
to the charge of the Swallows. But the superstition by which the
Martyn advances himself does have a corresponding term in the
Hind's fable. Though he may have some selfish interest in mis-
leading his followers, the Martyn is himself "In Superstition silly
to excess" (III.471), and seems to believe in his false prophecies:

> his advice
> Was present safety, bought at any price:
> (A seeming pious care, that cover'd cowardise)
> . . . .
> For he concluded, once upon a time,
> He found a leaf inscrib'd with sacred rime,
> Whose antique characters did well denote
> The *Sibyl's* hand of the *Cumaean* Grott:
> The mad Divineress had plainly writ,
> A time shou'd come (but many ages yet,)
> In which, sinister destinies ordain,
> A *Dame* shou'd drown with all her feather'd train,
> And seas from thence be call'd the *Chelidonian* main.
> At this, some shook for fear, the more devout
> Arose, and bless'd themselves from head to foot.
> (III.477–479, 486–496)

Catholic superstition is, then, harmless and rather absurd. The
Martyn's use of it will injure only his followers and, indeed, himself. Protestant superstition, by contrast, is based rather on hatred
than on fear; the Pigeons consciously exploit it to incite mob violence against the devout poultry. Fearing that the "Holy Deeds"
of the poultry may "o're all their Arts prevail,"

> An hideous Figure of their Foes they drew,
> Nor Line, nor Looks, nor Shades, nor Colours true;
> And this Grotesque design, expos'd to Publick view.
> One would have thought it some Ægyptian Piece,
> With Garden-Gods, and barking Deities,
> More thick than *Ptolomey* has stuck the Skies.
> All so perverse a Draught, so far unlike,

It was no Libell where it meant to strike:
Yet still the daubing pleas'd, and Great and Small
To view the Monster crowded *Pigeon*-hall.
                                    (III.1042–1051)

Thus even if the Catholics are, as the Anglicans charge, superstitious, they are at least free of that "ribbald Art" that has, Dryden
suggests, stigmatized the Protestants since Luther, and of which
the Panther's fable is itself a notable example.

The Swallows hold an election on, and foolishly vote to follow,
the Martyn's counsel:

The question crudely put, to shun delay,
'Twas carry'd by the *major* part to stay
                                    (III.524–525).

The Pigeons hold a corresponding election which, though no less
foolish, is far more pernicious: they choose the means rather of
inflicting than of avoiding harm. Further, in contrasting the issues
on which the Swallows and Pigeons vote, Dryden again arraigns
the Anglicans with their own polemic. Whereas the Swallows, in
voting on questions of policy, adhere to the principles of the English constitution, the Pigeons, like exclusionist Whigs, extend the
electoral process to questions of succession: on the advice of "One
more mature in Folly than the rest" (III.1107), "all agreed/Old
Enmity's forgot, the *Buzzard* should succeed" (III.1134–1135).
Both groups, however, are equally guilty of fatally confusing religious with political leaders:

His point thus gain'd, Sir *Martyn* dated thence
His pow'r, and from a Priest became a Prince.
He order'd all things with a busie care,
And cells, and refectories did prepare,
And large provisions lay'd of winter fare.
                                    (III.527–531)

Their welcom Suit was granted soon as heard,
His Lodgings furnish'd, and a Train prepar'd,
With *B*'s upon their Breast, appointed for his Guard.
He came, and Crown'd with great Solemnity,
God save King *Buzzard*, was the gen'rall cry.
                                    (III.1136–1140)

Even here, however, the Pigeons lose by the contrast: only the Pigeons' vote is unanimous; the "stagers of the wiser sort" who argue against the Martyn's proposal have no counterparts in the Hind's fable. Further, the Swallows' leader is rather a fool than a knave, whereas the Pigeons' is a tyrant indeed. During the exclusion crisis, the Whigs had accused the Catholics of concealing a thirst for arbitrary power beneath religious zeal, and the Anglicans had accused the sectaries of the same imposture: thus in suggesting that the Anglicans promote tyranny under cover of religion, Dryden is turning against them the charge that they had so frequently brought against the Whigs, while in showing that the Catholic leader is merely a fool vainly seeking a means of escape, he refutes the Whig charges against the Catholics.

A period of grace follows the rise to power of both the Martyn and the Buzzard; and here, as in the events that set both plots in motion, are figured again the opposing reactions of Catholics and Anglicans to James's attempts to revoke the Test and penal laws. The Swallows mistake a temporary for a permanent respite as the more extreme Catholics misjudged the efficacy of James's edicts. The Pigeons, on the other hand, foolishly abuse the "Grace the Landlord had allowed" to "form their Friends, and to seduce the crowd" (III.1199–1201) as the Anglicans availed themselves of James's parliamentary attempts to revoke the Test to consolidate their opposition. And again, the Swallows are guilty only of a desire to escape injury and an absurdly hopeful weather forecast, the Pigeons of ingratitude, cruelty, and rebellion. The occupations of the two groups in their prosperity are strikingly opposed. Both flourish and increase, but in very different ways:

> Who but the *Swallow* now triumphs alone?
> The Canopy of heaven is all her own,
> Her youthful offspring to their haunts repair;
> And glide along in glades, and skim in air,
> And dip for insects in the purling springs,
> And stoop on rivers to refresh their wings.
> (III.566–571)

> The House of Pray'r is stock'd with large encrease;
> Nor Doors, nor Windows can contain the Press:
> For Birds of ev'ry feather fill th' abode;
> Ev'n Atheists out of envy own a God:

And reeking from the Stews, Adult'rers come,
Like *Goths* and *Vandals* to demolish *Rome*.
                                        (III.1209–1214)

Though the Swallows use their false security for domestic pur-
suits, the Pigeons theirs for the practice of vice and cruelty, both
groups are equally mistaken, and both pay for their folly with their
lives. The parallel between the forces to which the two groups
succumb is carefully constructed from two distinct sets of correspondences. First, the Swallows fall victim to storms representing
Anglican persecution, while the Pigeons fall victim to a "Gracious
Edict"—the Declaration of Indulgence—which is the result of
Catholic tolerance. The Swallows are killed with cruelty, the Pigeons with kindness:

But when th' Imperial owner did espy
That thus they turn'd his Grace to villany,
Not suff'ring wrath to discompose his mind,
He strove a temper for th' extreams to find,
So to be just, as he might still be kind.
Then, all Maturely weigh'd, pronounc'd a Doom
Of Sacred Strength for ev'ry Age to come.
By this the *Doves* their Wealth and State possess
No Rights infring'd, but licence to oppress.
                                        (III.1228–1236)

Nor did their Owner hasten their ill hour:
But, sunk in Credit, they decreas'd in Pow'r:
Like Snows in warmth that mildly pass away,
Dissolving in the Silence of Decay.
                                        (III.1269–1272)

Second, the Swallows fall victim to the inevitable coming of winter, which represents the death of James and cessation of his protection, while the Pigeons fall victim to the depredations of the
Buzzard following the death of the Landlord, which last refers also
to the death of James:

Nor can th' Usurper long abstain from Food,
Already he has tasted *Pigeons* Blood:
And may be tempted to his former fare,
When this Indulgent Lord shall late to Heav'n repair.
Bare benting times, and moulting Months may come,
When lagging late, they cannot reach their home:

Or Rent in Schism, (for so their Fate decrees,)
Like the Tumultuous Colledge of the Bees;
They fight their Quarrel, by themselves opprest,
The Tyrant smiles below, and waits the falling feast.
(III.1279–1288)

Dryden is careful to make those who have in his view so patently turned against themselves in principle fall by turning against themselves in fact.

In *The Hind and the Panther*, several features of Dryden's late rhetoric emerge fully formed. He had lost by his conversion the political centrality that derived from his alliance with a strong political party and that allowed him to represent his political views as the ideals of a whole people. So he speaks not for the political nation, but against it. He authorizes such speech by claiming on the one hand consistent adherence to political principles that had carried the now ungrateful Tories through the exclusion crisis, and on the other hand participation in a timeless literary tradition that carries with it privileged insight into political affairs and an assurance of posterity's favor and attention. Long after the Anglicans have brought on their own destruction, Dryden implies, posterity will see them through his eyes, as they now see Elizabeth through Spenser's. *The Hind and the Panther* is the last of Dryden's direct analyses of English politics; in *Britannia Rediviva* he is merely a powerless observer of providential forces, hoping for the best but fearing the worst.[27] In *Don Sebastian*, his first major work after the Revolution, he is concerned with much the same set of political issues as in *The Hind and the Panther*, and he engages them by many of the same rhetorical strategies; but his loss of government protection forces him to replace statement with implication, allegorical fable with a complex form of political parallel.

2. "Adhering to a Lost Cause": *Don Sebastian* and *Amphitryon*

Though it did not improve his lot, the Revolution did much to clarify Dryden's position. He needed no longer worry about defending James's impracticable policies; and he might readily defend himself by pointing to his constancy in the face of financial loss and some personal danger. In *Don Sebastian* and *Amphitryon* he avails himself fully of this newly fortified rhetorical situation—though his political rhetoric in these plays is not so overt as in *The Hind and the Panther*, it is both more assured and more coherent. The Revolution had brought a new series of triumphant attacks upon the fallen laureate.[1] Three Whig poems of 1689 speculate whether Dryden will again change his principles with the change in government.[2] *Don Sebastian*, staged in December of this year, was the first of Dryden's works to come before the public after the Revolution; its original audience must have eagerly awaited his reaction to the events that had deprived him of office, pension, and political and religious legitimacy; and in the *Dedication, Preface,* and *Prologue* of the play Dryden carefully defines that reaction. He presents himself as harmless, impoverished, an object rather of pity than of fear, yet nonetheless constant to his religion and his principles. He finds himself in "bad circumstances" and sees "very little probability of coming out" (*Preface*, p. 65); "the bus'ness of the Field is o'er" and he concedes himself "a vanquished foe" (*Prologue*, ll. 8, 12); he desires only that "the Town may be somewhat oblig'd to my misfortunes, for a part of their diversion" (*Preface*, p. 65), and offers to "sheath his cutting Satyr" if the audience will agree not to persecute him for his Catholicism (*Prologue*, ll. 33–40).[3] Both *Dedication* and *Preface*, however, conclude with an expression of defiance, the *Dedication* with a quotation from Cicero, who like Dryden had come out on the losing side of a revolution: "Inimici mei mea mihi non meipsum ademerunt" (p. 64) [Loeb trans.: "my enemies have robbed me of all I had; but they have not robbed me of myself"]; the *Preface* with a quotation from the *Aeneid*: "Tu, ne cede malis; sed, contrà, audentior ito" (p. 72), which Dryden was to render,

> But thou, secure of Soul, unbent with Woes,
> The more thy Fortune frowns, the more oppose.
> (Aeneis, VI. 143–144)

As in *The Hind and the Panther*, Dryden seeks not to persuade his audience but to display before it the wisdom and integrity, in the midst of political upheaval, of his beliefs and career; to reprove the political nation for its misdeeds and to suggest their probable consequences. He makes his case by inviting comparison between the attitudes and events of his tragedy and those of recent English history: the values of heroic poetry—constancy, fortitude, self-sacrifice, and piety—are brought forth as timeless standards by which to measure the behavior of the revolutionaries.[4]

Dryden makes explicit most of these claims for himself and his party in his *Dedication* of the play to Philip Sidney, third earl of Leicester. Leicester is "secure in your own merit; and all Parties, as they rise uppermost, are sure to court you in their turns." On this sentence of praise Dryden hangs a lengthy digression on the instability of contemporary politics and the greed and ambition that propel them: the "leading men"

> rise and fall in the variety of Revolutions; and are sometimes great, and therefore wise in mens opinions, who must court them for their interest: But the reputation of their parts most commonly follows their success; few of 'em are wise, but as they are in power; Because indeed, they have no sphere of their own, but like the Moon in the *Copernican* Systeme of the World, are whirl'd about by the motion of a greater Planet. This it is to be ever busie; neither to give rest to their Fellow creatures, nor, which is more wretchedly ridiculous, to themselves.
>
> (P. 60)

Among these busy men must be classed the successful revolutionaries, and Dryden seems to have them in mind in his exultant description of their probable fall:

Ambitious Meteors! how willing they are to set themselves upon the Wing; and taking every occasion of drawing upward to the Sun: Not considering that they have no more time allow'd them for their mounting, than the short revolution of a day; and that when the light goes from them, they are of necessity to fall.

(P. 60)

Dryden here implicitly contrasts the honor and wisdom of his own constancy with the deplorable folly of those who in his view had abandoned their principles and deserted their sovereign; and this polemic agenda determines, as we shall see, the play's moral and much of its action. Dryden is able to introduce his views so openly here because of the public character of his dedicatee. Leicester had been an active servant of the Parliament and Cromwell during the interregnum; he had retired from public life after the fall of Richard Cromwell. Dryden thus describes the motive for this retirement:

But who wou'd trust the quiet of their lives, with the extravagancies of their Countrymen, when they were just in the giddiness of their turning; when the ground was tottering under them at every moment; and none cou'd guess whether the next heave of the Earthquake, wou'd settle them on the first Foundation, or swallow it?

(P. 61)

As the quotation of Cicero at the end of the *Dedication* suggests, Leicester's fall at the Restoration has a parallel in Dryden's at the Revolution. Both men have responded nobly to misfortune, and Dryden hints that this moral similarity far outweighs their political differences.

Yet despite this rhetorical conflation of Republican and Royalist, Dryden takes care to hint even within the *Dedication* at the probable resurgence of his own party. To Atticus and Leicester

the Friend was always more consider'd ... than the cause: And an *Octavius*, or an *Anthony* in distress, were reliev'd by them, as well as a *Brutus* or *Cassius*; For the lowermost party, to a noble mind, is ever the fittest object of good will.

(P. 62)

If Leicester is Atticus, and Dryden's "lowermost party" that of Octavius and Anthony, William's must be that of Brutus and Cassius, and, we may infer, no more likely to endure than its original. The political implications of this are, however, carefully enfolded in authoritative literary claims. Leicester is not only Atticus, the great Roman patron, but a Sidney whose sponsorship of poetry rivals that of his Elizabethan great-uncle: "There is another *Sidney* still remaining, tho there can never be another *Spencer* to deserve the Favor. But one *Sidney* gave his Patronage to the applications of a Poet; the other offer'd it unask'd." However we may take Dryden's disclaimer, his placement of himself and his patron in the context of a long literary tradition dignifies both. Though at present Dryden suffers with the "lowermost party," he remains, with Cicero and Spenser, part of a transcendent literary tradition to which politics is ultimately irrelevant.

Dryden shows a similar desire to remove himself from his age in his prefatory account of his play:

> Having been longer acquainted with the Stage, than any Poet now living, and having observ'd how difficult it was to please, that the humours of Comedy were almost spent, that Love and Honour (the mistaken Topics of Tragedy) were quite worn out, that the Theaters cou'd not support their Charges, that the Audience forsook them, that young men without Learning set up for Judges, and that they talk'd loudest, who understood the least: all these discouragements had not only wean'd me from the Stage, but had also given me a loathing of it. But enough of this: the difficulties continue; they increase, and I am still condemn'd to dig in those exhausted Mines.
> (Pp. 65–66)

We may trace the political causes of this weariness if we remember that Dryden's most recent work for the stage, *Albion and Albanius*, had concluded with "Love and Honour" claiming "an equal place" in Albion's "glorious race." Dryden feels that England is no longer capable of sustaining the heroic values that in his earlier plays he had sought to impart to it. He responds by emphasizing literary technique over societal values:

> And I dare boldly promise for this Play, that in the roughness of the numbers and cadences, (which I assure was not casual, but so design'd) you will see somewhat more masterly arising to your view, than in most, if not any of my former Tragedies. There is a more noble daring in the Figures and more suitable to the loftiness of the Subject; and besides this some newnesses of *English*, translated from the Beauties of

Modern Tongues, as well as from the elegancies of the *Latin*; and here
and there some old words are sprinkled, which for their significance
and sound, deserv'd not to be antiquated; such as we often find in
Salust amongst the *Roman* Authors, and in *Milton's Paradise* amongst
ours.
(Pp. 66–67)

The discussion of literary techniques and the invocation of classi-
cal precedents to justify them had been a prominent feature of
Dryden's presentation of his plays throughout his career; but here
he implicitly presents this appeal to literary tradition as a defensive
reaction against the exhaustion of contemporary English culture
and society.

This defensive detachment shapes much of Dryden's political
commentary in the play itself. The values by which his opponents
are condemned arise naturally from the action; and the action is
based on literary and historical sources that Dryden takes care to
enumerate and describe in his *Preface*: Don Sebastian, for example, is drawn from Portuguese history:

We are assur'd by all Writers of those times . . . that some years after
[the battle of Alcazar], when the *Spaniards* with a pretended title, by
force of Arms had Usurp'd the Crown of *Portugal*, from the House of
Braganza, a certain Person who call'd himself Don *Sebastian* . . . appear'd. . . . 'Tis most certain, that the *Portugueses* expected his return
for almost an Age together after that Battel; which is at least proof of
their extream love to his Memory; and the usage which they had from
their new Conquerors, might possibly make them so extravagant in
their hopes and wishes for their old Master.
(Pp. 67–68)

Sebastian clearly resembles James, also the victim of a foreign
usurper: the alteration of a few proper names would make this a
Jacobite history of the Revolution and prophecy of its consequences. Throughout the play the virtues for which the Jacobites
praised James—justice, martial courage, piety—are attributed to
Sebastian. Dorax lists them early in Act I, and long before his
reconciliation to his king:

Brave, pious, generous, great, and liberal:
Just as the Scales of Heaven that weigh the Seasons.
(I.i.103–104)[5]

To the English Catholics, the most important of these virtues was
piety; only piety could not have been derived from any of Dryden's
sources;[6] and Dryden's concern for the virtue in the *Preface* shows
the importance he places on the reader's recognition of it: "In the
drawing of his character I forgot not piety, which any one may
observe to be one principal ingredient of it; even so far as to be a
habit in him" (p. 68). However, Dryden does nothing here to force
us to identify Sebastian with James, and later indeed he raises some
important obstacles to an easy identification of the two. If we see
any resemblance, we are to understand it as arising accidentally
from our own application of Dryden's heroic standards to contemporary England.[7]

In the play itself this application is supported only by a few
brief allusions, which however are sufficient to allow us to impute
to the Jacobites all the lofty virtues of Sebastian and his followers.
Sebastian and Muley-Moloch, for example, contend for the sovereignty of Almeyda's hand in pointed metaphors:

> *Emp.* Thou art not marry'd to *Almeyda*?
> *Seb.* Yes.
> *Emp.* And owns't the usurpation of my Love?
> *Seb.* I own it in the face of Heav'n and thee
>   No Usurpation, but a lawful claim,
>   Of which I stand possest.
> *Emp.*   Sh' has chosen well,
>   Betwixt a Captive and a Conqueror.
>   (III.i.168–173)

Sebastian's subjects present in their unfailing loyalty to their unfortunate king an instructive contrast to their English counterparts.
Sebastian himself lays emphasis on their dissimilarity to the general run of subjects:

> For Subjects such as they are seldom seen,
> Who not forsook me at my greatest need;
> Nor for base lucre sold their Loyalty,
> But shar'd my dangers to the last event,
> And fenc'd 'em with their own.
>   (I.i.396–400)

The loyalty of the Portuguese arises apparently from their religious
beliefs; it is pointedly contrasted with the love of mutiny endemic

among the Moors. The only admirable Moor, Almeyda, is a Christian convert; and Dorax claims to have given up his religion in order to abandon his loyalty to Sebastian: "I left," he says, "my foolish Faith / Because it wou'd oblige me to forgiveness" (II.i.237–238). His renewal of loyalty to his king involves also a renewal of faith: he is "in one moment . . . reconcil'd / To Heaven, and to my King, and to my Love" (IV.iii.648–649). The Portuguese thus resemble the Catholic supporters of James; their religion in the play is Catholicism in fact as well as in application. Dryden takes care to point this out in a parody of the Protestant view of popery. Benducar describes Sebastian's wedding ceremony, as conducted by

> A puffing Fryar;
> Close wrap'd he bore some secret Instrument
> Of Christian Superstition in his hand:
> My servant follow'd fast, and through a chink,
> Perceiv'd the Royal Captives hand in hand:
> And heard the hooded Father mumbling charms,
> That make those Misbelievers Man and Wife.
>   (III.i.35–41)

The immediate literary precedent of this "puffing Fryar" is the Martin in the Panther's fable, and he functions in much the same manner.

The serious plot ends at a great distance from English politics, in the discovery of Sebastian's incest. Yet Dryden takes some care in the *Preface* to prevent the incest from presenting too great an obstacle to our admiration of Sebastian or our application of his character to James's:

> It being . . . only necessary according to the Laws of the *Drama*, that Sebastian shou'd no more be seen upon the Throne, I leave it for the World to judge, whether or no I have disposed of him according to art, or have bungled up the conclusion of his adventure. . . . This being presuppos'd, that he was Religious, the horror of his incest, tho innocently committed, was the best reason which the Stage cou'd give for hind'ring his return. 'Tis true I have no right to blast his Memory, with such a crime; but declaring it to be fiction, I desire my Audience to think it no longer true, than while they are seeing it represented: For

that once ended, he may be a Saint for ought I know; and we have
reason to presume he is.

(P. 68)

We are to attribute the incest to dramatic necessity (quite plausibly, since incest had been an important vehicle for tragedy since
Sophocles) and forget it as the one fictional part of Sebastian's
career when the play is over; and Dryden, faced with the laws of
England as well as of drama, may have found it a convenient way
of disposing of his exiled Catholic monarch. But though the incest
itself has no reference to English politics, the moral Dryden derives
from it applies clearly enough to the circumstances of James's
"abdication."[8] As John Wallace has shown, the differences between seventeenth-century literary parallels and the political events
to which they refer serve to guarantee the poet's impartiality;[9] here
they serve also to lend generality and authority to Dryden's views.
The "general moral" of the play is indeed so general that it may
be applied with equal plausibility to Sophocles's *Oedipus* and to
the human race after the Fall:

And let *Sebastian* and *Almeyda*'s Fate,
This dreadfull Sentence to the World relate,
That unrepented Crimes of Parents dead,
Are justly punish'd on their Childrens head.
(V.i.724–727)

Yet despite its grand generality, this moral applies no less neatly to
revolutionary England. It had been so applied again and again in
contemporary Jacobite polemic. One writer, for example, professes to be

confounded . . . with Horrour, to look onely back upon the Miseries
we have hitherto felt; but when I consider that *Pandora*'s Box is just
open'd, and view a long Train of War, Famine, Want, Bloud, and
Confusion, entailed upon us and our Posterity, as long as this Man, or
any descended from him, shall possess the Throne, and see what a Gap
is opened for every ambitious Person who can cajole the People to
usurp it: These Considerations, I say, chill my Bloud in my Veins, and
I cannot but lament my poor Countries Misfortune with deepest Sighs
and Groans. . . . [The Revolution] has brought along with it all the
Plagues we dreaded under others, and gives us nothing but a dismal

Prospect of all the Misfortunes which can befall a Nation, which hath greatly provoked God Almighty's Anger.

Such polemic suggests that Dryden's audience, or at least its Jacobite element, would have noticed the contemporary implications of Dryden's moral—that by overthrowing the settled power that ensures the stability of the state and their own safety, the Protestants had in the Revolution entailed on their own posterity the war and anarchy passed on to them by the rebels of the 1640s.[10]

Dryden does not, however, maintain a uniform distance from contemporary politics throughout the play. While the story of Sebastian consistently provides a kind of instructive counterexample for Dryden's opponents, the comic plot often directly ridicules the behavior of those opponents. In the first act of the play, Mustapha, the leader of the Moorish rabble, and the Mufti, the leader of the Moorish clergy, dispute the ownership of Antonio, who, studious only of preserving his life, cowers before them. Mustapha, threatening Antonio with his whip, advises him to "Buckle to thy Geers: Behold my Ensign of Royalty display'd over thee" (I.i.514–515); and Antonio (lying down) submits: "Hold, my dear Thrum-cap: I obey thee chearfully, I see the Doctrine of Non-Resistance is never practis'd thoroughly but when a Man can't help himself" (I.i.520–523). The Tories who made frequent professions of belief in this doctrine at the beginning of James's reign abandoned it during the Revolution. The Jacobites, and Dryden among them, retained their belief and bitterly resented the Tories' desertion.[11] Antonio, then, for the moment at least, represents a Williamite Tory; Dryden ironically suggests that such a man will recognize the doctrine only in submitting to superior force. While Mustapha is exaggerating Antonio's value to a prospective buyer, the Mufti appears, berates Mustapha for attempting to "Take Mony twice for the same Commodity" (I.i.569–570), and asks what has become of Alvarez, whom Mustapha has already sold. Mustapha answers that "while I was managing this young robustous Fellow, that old Spark who was nothing but Skin and Bone, and by consequence, very nimble, slipt through my fingers like an Eel, for there was no hold fast of him, and ran away to buy himself a new Master" (I.i.586–590). Dryden here implicitly portrays the Anglican clergy and the London mob as the dual leaders of a nation that will buy a new master as the one or the other should direct it. Whereas the high-minded behavior of James and his allies is elevated in the serious plot, the self-interested baseness of the revolutionaries is in the comic plot given the farcical treatment that in Dryden's view it richly deserved.

Dryden's most pointed political commentary, however, comes neither in the tragic story of Sebastian's incest, nor in the farcical story of Antonio's theft of the Mufti's daughter, but in a third plot—the story of the rebellion against Muley-Moloch. This plot partakes of both tragedy and farce; it dominates the first four acts of the play; and it embodies the concealed "moral" that in his *Preface* Dryden invites judicious critics to discover. This plot may at first suggest rather Williamite history than Jacobite prophecy, for though the causes of the Moorish rebellion clearly represent the Jacobite view of the causes of the 1688 Revolution, Muley-Moloch, the victim of the Moorish rebellion, is a tyrant, as James was only to the Williamites. Muley-Moloch's tyranny has, however, nothing to do with his overthrow, which is owing rather to the rebellious nature of his subjects. The Mufti is provoked to rebellion not by Muley-Moloch's cruelty, but by his mercy: the Emperor protects the Christians from the Mufti's legally and religiously based attempt to enslave them much as James had protected the Catholics from the Anglicans' attempt to persecute them and exclude them from power. Like Dryden's Whigs in other poems, Benducar rebels not so that he may free the Moors from tyranny, but so that he himself may tyrannize in his king's stead. The Mufti incites the mob against Muley-Moloch by frightening it with the prospect of a Christian succession; and the mob, though it affects concern for religion, rebels only that it may plunder. In *Don Sebastian*, as in *Absalom and Achitophel, The Medall, The Duke of Guise*, and *The Hind and the Panther*, a group of self-interested rebels plot to overthrow their king under color of serving their religion, what in the *Dedication* of the *Aeneis* Dryden contemptuously calls the "modern Motive to Rebellion."[12] It need not surprise us that this combination of Whigs, mob, and clergy should succeed in *Don Sebastian* where in the pre-Revolutionary work it had so often failed.

The Moors, then, represent the English Protestants,[13] and particularly the Anglicans who, Dryden felt, were provoked to rebellion by James's refusal to allow them the part in government that they claimed as their right:

> They love Religion sweetn'd to the sense;
> A good, luxurious, palatable faith.
> Thus Vice and Godliness, prepost'rous pair,
> Ride cheek by joul; but Churchmen hold the Reins.
> And, when ere Kings wou'd lower Clergy greatness,
> They learn too late what pow'r the Preachers have,
> And whose the Subjects are.
>
> (III.i.411–417)

In his note on this passage, Miner cites the following lines in *The Hind and the Panther*, concerning which he remarks that there were "parallels drawn between Mohammed and Luther by numerous Catholic controversialists in the debates over the celibacy of the clergy and the saintliness of life":

> Though our lean faith these rigid laws has giv'n,
> The full fed *Musulman* goes fat to heav'n;
> For his *Arabian* Prophet with delights
> Of sense, allur'd his eastern Proselytes.
> The jolly *Luther*, reading him, began
> T' interpret Scriptures by his *Alcoran*;
> To grub the thorns beneath our tender feet,
> And make the paths of *Paradise* more sweet.
>
> (I.376–383)[14]

The Revolution, far from obliging Dryden to avoid political commentary, did not oblige him even to alter the terms in which he wrote it.

Dryden's account in the *Preface* of his alteration of Muley-Moloch's life and character differs substantially from his account of his alteration of Sebastian's:

> I must likewise own, that I have somewhat deviated from the known History, in the death of *Muley-Moloch*, who, by all relations dyed of a feaver in the Battel, before his Army had wholly won the Field; but if I have allow'd him another day of life, it was because I stood in need of so shining a Character of brutality, as I have given him; which is indeed the same, with that of the present Emperor *Muley-Ishmael*, as

some of our *English* Officers, who have been in his Court, have
credibly inform'd me.
(P. 70)

No laws of drama dictate this alteration—the reader is not asked
to believe it only during the play; and it is suggestive that Dryden
should have stood in need of a "shining character of brutality,"
which resembled that of a "present emperor." Muley-Moloch is,
as various critics have observed, but another version of Dryden's
stage tyrant and resembles in many ways his predecessors in
Tyrannick Love, The Conquest of Granada, Aureng-Zebe, and
other plays. Yet the William of contemporary Jacobite pamphlets
and poems was hardly the glorious deliverer of Whig history;
he was far more like Maximin, Boabdelin, and Muley-Moloch
than Macauley's Protestant hero. The writer of one such pamphlet
publishes a supposed letter of William's which, he says, "plainly
discovers a Temper *solely* bent to pursue his own private *Gran-
deur* . . . and with that transport as to disregard the ruining himself, and sacrificing all his other Engagements, and predetermined
general *Goods,* rather than to suffer the Diminution of the least
Tittle of it." A contemporary poem corroborates this view of William: "this kingly lion would blood all the crown / If fate gives him
life till his claws be but grown."[15]
Muley-Moloch is no less interested in consolidating his power;
like the Jacobites' William, he is looking forward to the tyranny he
can exercise after his claim to the throne is secure:

> What's Royalty but pow'r to please my self?
> And if I dare not, then am I the Slave,
> And my own Slaves the Sovereigns,_____'tis resolv'd,
> Weak Princes flatter when they want the pow'r
> To curb their People; tender Plants must bend,
> But when a Government is grown to strength,
> Like some old Oak, rough with its armed Bark,
> It yields not to the tug, but only nods,
> And turns to sullen State.
>   (II.i.46–54)

Moreover, Benducar promises Muley-Zeydan—whose character
as an "easie Fool" and relationship to Muley-Moloch suggests
Prince George of Denmark—to depose the Emperor in language

that recalls the doubtfulness of William's title and of the succession:

> His growth is but a wild and fruitless Plant,
> I'll cut his barren branches to the stock,
> And graft you on to bear.
>
> (I.i.53–55)

The most important topic of Jacobite polemic against William was his usurpation of the throne of his uncle, and in this he is identical to Muley-Moloch. Dryden tells us in the *Preface* that his sources mention one "*Muley-Mahumet,* who had been driven out of his Dominions, by *Abdelmelech,* or as others call him, *Muley-Moloch,* his nigh Kinsman" (p. 67). This Muley-Mahumet, whose death is mentioned at the beginning of the play, is Muley-Moloch's first cousin; in the play, however, Muley-Moloch has only prevented his cousin, Almeyda's brother, from regaining the throne and has rather dethroned his uncle, Almeyda's father, whom Dryden seems to have invented.[16] This parricidic usurpation—which is identical to William's of his uncle James II and first cousin the old Pretender—is alluded to repeatedly in the play. In one of her first speeches, Almeyda charges Muley-Moloch, whose underhand manner here resembles that attributed by the Jacobites to William, with having "Surpriz'd [her 'peaceful Father'] and his Kingdom / No provocation given, no War declar'd" (I.i.458–459). A contemporary Jacobite satirist begins his poem on the 1688 Revolution with this reference to William's usurpation:

> In times when Princes cancelled nature's law
> And declarations (which themselves did draw),
> When children used their parents to dethrone
> And gnawed their way like vipers to a crown.[17]

Almeyda describes Muley-Moloch's usurpation in exactly the same language:

> but thou, Viper,
> Hast cancell'd kindred, made a rent in Nature,
> And through her holy bowels gnaw'd thy way,
> Through thy own Bloud to Empire.
>
> (II.i.378–381)

Almeyda's genealogical relation to Muley-Moloch corresponds exactly to Mary's relation to William: she is his first cousin and the daughter of the king he has overthrown. In the *Preface* Dryden assures us that the part of Almeyda is "wholly fictitious" (p. 69); and so indeed it is, for although Almeyda corresponds to Mary in circumstance, she directly opposes her in behavior. Mary was frequently and violently abused in the year following the Revolution for usurping the throne of her own father and brother.[18] Almeyda, given the opportunity to do the same, indignantly refuses. At her first meeting with Muley-Moloch, while in danger of immediate execution, she contrasts her "purer" blood to his, which "though deriv'd from the same Source . . . is puddl'd, and defil'd with Tyranny" (I.i.430–432), and charges him with the destruction of her family:

> My murther'd Father, and my Brother's Ghost
> Still haunt this Brest, and prompt it to revenge.
> (I.i.446–447)

When later he offers her marriage and joint sovereignty—exactly Mary's position—she immediately and firmly refuses (II.i.458–468). The moral and its application to both William and Mary is even clearer in Almeyda's response to Benducar's offer of marriage:

> to me he stood
> Confest before, and own'd his Insolence
> T'espouse my person, and assume the Crown,
> Claym'd in my Right: for this he slew your Tyrant;
> Oh no, he only chang'd him for a worse,
> Imbas'd your Slavery by his own vileness,
> And loaded you with more ignoble bonds.
> (IV.iii.251–257)

Here the meaning of the parallel is derived equally from likeness and dissimilarity: the one establishes the correspondence so that the other may point the moral.

Sebastian's subjects not only represent the English Catholics; they also oppose the English Protestants, and so function as does Almeyda to show by contrast the injustice of the Revolution. They did not forsake Sebastian at his greatest need, as James's did his at the Revolution; they did not for base lucre sell their loyalty, as James's did theirs in taking the oath of allegiance to William that they might retain their offices and salaries. James's subjects are to see the contrast and judge themselves accordingly. Dryden does, however, admit one exception to his general view of the perfidy of the deserters. Many of Dryden's most important patrons—Dorset, Halifax, Rochester, Ormond—had deserted James, and perhaps to reflect their case Dryden has invented Dorax, who, though unquestionably wrong in doing so, at least rebels from "avarice ofhonor" rather than of base lucre. Dorax's contempt for "the groveling sin of Crowds," for clergy who "swell to counsel Kings and govern Kingdoms," and for court favorites who "fawn and yet betray" shows that, even before his reconciliation with Sebastian, he has sound political principles; and Dryden gives him frequent opportunities of expressing these principles to advantage. Dorax's justifications of his rebellion are, by contrast, infrequent and comparatively weak and are finally refuted by Sebastian himself. The following argument, for example, by which Dorax attempts to explain himself to Benducar, carries its own refutation:

> My Master? By what title,
> Because I happen'd to be born where he
> Happen'd to be King?
>   (I.i.86–88)

This is obviously a far better title than Muley-Moloch's to Dorax's allegiance. From what Dorax says of his rebellion early in the play, one might assume that Sebastian had merely deprived him of his lord-lieutenancy:

> Indignities, which Man cou'd not support,
> Provok'd my vengeance to this noble Crime.
> But he had strip'd me first of my Command,
> Dismiss'd my Service, and absolv'd my Faith.
>   (II.i.316–319)

Dorax has, as we discover in Act IV, a stronger motive; yet even so he comes to regret his desertion, and may therefore serve as a model for his historical counterparts: "I should," he says, "have fallen by Sebastian's side / My Corps had been the Bulwark of my King" (IV.iii.592–593).[19]

The contemporary reference of the Mufti is far more specific: in his self-interest, officiousness, lechery, demagoguery, theological juggling, and addiction to slander and defamation, he recalls Gilbert Burnet, who is so described in contemporary satire, most of which owes something to Dryden's character of the Buzzard in *The Hind and the Panther*:

> Broad-back'd, and Brawny built for Loves delight,
> A Prophet form'd, to make a female Proselyte.
> A Theologue more by need, than genial bent,
> By Breeding sharp, by Nature confident.
> Int'rest in all his Actions was discern'd;
> More learn'd than Honest, more a Wit than learn'd
> . . . .
> Oft has he flatter'd, and blasphem'd the same,
> For in his Rage, he spares no Sov'rains name:
> The Hero, and the Tyrant change their style
> By the same measure that they frown or smile.
>   (III.1145–1150, 1163–1166)

The Mufti's lechery is early established—he has paid Mustapha "a thousand golden Sultanins" for the "dainty virgin" Almeyda (I.i.232–238)—and remarked upon throughout the play (e.g., II.ii.77–80; III.ii.33; IV.ii.56). His service to Muley-Moloch represents the Jacobite view of Burnet's to William. A contemporary satire says of Burnet, "To serve all times he could distinctions join";[20] so when Muley-Moloch, having just won his war, is in the mood for a feast, the Mufti complies with a theological distinction:

> Fasting is but the Letter of the Law;
> Yet it shows well to Preach it to the Vulgar.
> Wine is against our Law, that's literal too,
> But not deny'd to Kings and to their Guides,
> Wine is a Holy Liquor, for the Great.
>   (I.i.179–183)

Dorax then puts at least the general reference beyond all doubt: "This *Mufti* in my conscience is some *English* Renegade, he talks so savourly of toping" (I.i.184–185). Another contemporary satire accuses Burnet of "pimping and plotting for Will and his mate";[21]

so in *Don Sebastian* the Mufti, commanded by Muley-Moloch to
"wrest and rend the Law to please thy Prince," justifies rape as a
glorious form of religious devotion:

> You have a Conqueror's right upon your Slave;
> And then, the more despight you do a Christian,
> You serve the Prophet more who loaths that Sect.
>   (III.i.96–98)

When the Mufti goes on to justify the murder of Sebastian, Muley-
Moloch is moved to exclaim,

> How happy is the Prince who has a Churchman
> So learn'd and pliant to expound his Laws!
>   (III.i.105–106)

The Mufti later supplies his prince with a general doctrine that
seems a Jacobite parody of the Williamite justification for the Revolution: "People side with violence and injustice, / When done for
publick good," and Muley-Moloch approvingly replies, "Preach
thou that doctrine" (III.i.377–378).

The Mufti is not, however, actually as compliant to Muley-
Moloch as he seems; throughout the play he slanders the Emperor
and plots against him, ostensibly to serve his religion, but actually
to serve himself. The Mufti's championship of the Moorish cause
is in many ways similar to Burnet's of the Anglican cause in *The
Hind and the Panther*:

> The spleenful *Pigeons* never could create
> A Prince more proper to revenge their hate:
> Indeed, more proper to revenge, than save;
> A King, whom in his wrath, th' Almighty gave;
> For all the Grace the Landlord had allow'd
> But made the *Buzzard* and the *Pigeons* proud:
> Gave time to fix their Friends, and to seduce the crowd.
> They long their Fellow-Subjects to inthrall,
> Their Patrons promise into question call,
> And vainly think he meant to make 'em Lords of all.
>   (III.1195–1204)[22]

The Mufti first rebels because Muley-Moloch does not take that
revenge upon the Christians that the Moorish religion requires,
and especially because the Emperor frees those Christians whom

the Mufti longs literally to "inthrall" (I.i.409–414). Frustrated in his greed, his lust, and his revenge, the Mufti slanders Muley-Moloch to Dorax,[23] who replies with all the arguments levelled against the political interference of the Anglicans, and the vengefulness and self-interest of Burnet, in *The Hind and the Panther*:

> *Dorax.* But when he made his loss the Theme, he flourish'd,
> Reliev'd his fainting Rhetorick with new Figures,
> And thunder'd at oppressing Tyranny.
> *Mufti.* Why not, when Sacrilegious Pow'r wou'd seize
> My Property? 'tis an affront to Heav'n
> Whose person, though unworthy, I sustain.
> (II.i.154–159)

> *Dorax.* Your Heav'n you promise, but our Earth you covet;
> The *Phaethons* of mankind, who fire that World,
> Which you were sent by Preaching but to warm.
> (II.i.165–167)

> Why then those forein thoughts of State-Employments,
> Abhorrent to your function and your Breeding?
> (II.i.183–184)

> Of all your College Vertues, nothing now
> But your Original Ignorance remains:
> Bloated with Pride, Ambition, Avarice,
> You swell, to counsel Kings, and govern Kingdoms.
> (II.i.195–198)

> Content you with monopolizing Heav'n,
> And let this little hanging Ball alone;
> For give you but a foot of Conscience there,
> And you, like *Archimedes*, toss the Globe.
> (II.i.205–208)

This theme recurs throughout the play. In Act III Dorax warns Muley-Moloch that

> To trust the Preaching pow'r on State Affairs,
> To him or any Heavenly Demagogue
> 'Tis a limb lopt from your Prerogative.
> (III.i.385–387)

This gives rise to a learned debate between Dorax and the Mufti on the clergy's role in politics. There is nothing inconsistent in Dryden's setting Burnet against William. Dryden may have suspected, or wanted us to suspect, that Burnet would accord no longer with his latest patron than with Lauderdale, Charles, and James. The complexity of the parallel allows Dryden at once to present his view of the causes of the Revolution against James and suggest that William will prove no more able to control his mutinous subjects.

Benducar and the Mobile function as does the Mufti: they recall the perfidy of their counterparts under James and suggest that William will suffer from it as well. Like the Whig leaders in Dryden's pre-Revolutionary poems, Benducar rebels so that he may rule. His method as Moore remarks resembles that of Sunderland, whom the Jacobites thought to have betrayed James while pretending to serve him.[24] Mustapha, the captain of the rabble, does not even bother to disguise the motive of his rebellion: "O, for some incomparable Tumult! Then shou'd I naturally wish, that the beaten Party might prevail, because we have plundered t' other side already, and there's nothing more to get of 'em."

> Both rich and poor for their own interest pray,
> 'Tis ours to make our Fortunes while we may;
> For Kingdoms are not conquer'd every day.
> (I.i.602–608)

In the mob scene, all the rebels come together, and the political parallel becomes quite obvious. The Mufti delivers a speech to the mob that is, as critics have remarked, a parody of the Convention Parliament and, indeed, of the whole Glorious Revolution:

> You are met, as becomes good Musulmen; to settle the Nation; for I must tell you, that though your Tyrant is a lawful Emperor, yet your lawful Emperor is but a Tyrant. . . . That your Emperor is a Tyrant is most manifest; for you were born to be *Turks*, but he has play'd the *Turk* with you; and is taking your Religion away. . . . He is now upon the point of Marrying himself, without your Sovereign consent; and what are the effects of Marriage? . . . Children: Now on whom wou'd he beget these Children? Even upon a Christian! Oh horrible . . . he is going to beget a Race of Misbelievers. . . . Therefore to conclude all, Believers, pluck up you Hearts, and pluck down the Tyrant. . . . your selves, your Wives and Children . . . our holy *Mahomet*; all these require your timous assistance . . . they claim it of you by all the nearest and dearest Tyes of these three P's, Self-Preservation, our Property, and

our Prophet. Now answer me with an unanimous chearful Cry, and follow me, who am your Leader, to a glorious Deliverance.
(IV.iii.69–113)

So far, this may be taken as referring only to the revolution against James; what follows indicates that Dryden refers also to another against James's successor. Mustapha, seeking to persuade his followers to revolt in his name rather than the Mufti's, reminds them of his past services:

Do you remember the glorious Rapines and Robberies you have committed? Your breaking open and gutting of Houses, your rummaging of Cellars, your demolishing of Christian Temples, and bearing off in triumph the superstitious Plate and Pictures, the Ornaments of their wicked Altars, when all rich Moveables were sentenc'd for idolatrous, and all that was idolatrous was seiz'd?
(IV.iii.124–127)

This is a reference to the London riots that followed the flight of James on December 11, 1688, at which Catholic churches and the houses of Catholics were plundered and destroyed.[25] The present mob is engaged in rebellion against the successor of the king—presumably Almeyda's father—against whom they were rioting when they plundered these temples. To the mob, however, it matters little against whom they rebel, so long as they may plunder:

Second Rabble. We are not bound to know who is to Live and Reign; our business is only to rise upon command, and plunder.

Third Rabble. Ay, the Richest of both Parties; for they are our Enemies.
(IV.iii.33–37)

The same is, again, true of the Mufti and Benducar: however they may talk of freedom from tyranny and preservation of religion, they will rebel only to preserve and extend their power, no matter against whom.

In *Don Sebastian* as in *The Hind and the Panther* Dryden is aware that his opponents have a view of England's future different from his own, and in the play, as in the poem, he includes their view so as to suggest its inaccuracy. In the *Preface* Dryden explains his method of building plays upon history:

> This ground-work the History afforded me, and I desire no better to build a Play upon it; For where the event of a great action is left doubtful, there the Poet is left Master: He may raise what he pleases on that foundation, provided he makes it of a piece, and according to the rule of probability.
>
> (P. 68)

On the morning before his death, Muley-Moloch has an ambiguous prophetic dream:

> methought *Almeyda*, smiling, came
> Attended with a Train of all her Race,
> Whom in the rage of Empire I had murther'd.
> But now, no longer Foes, they gave me Joy
> Of my new Conquest, and with helping hands
> Heav'd me into our Holy Prophet's arms,
> Who bore me in a purple Cloud to Heav'n.
>
> (IV.i.136–142)

The interpretation of this dream that Benducar foists upon Muley-Moloch is not at all "according to the rule of probability." Neither, Dryden would have us infer, is the fond hope that the Revolution of 1688 will prove to have brought England concord and stability under William.

Muley-Moloch, then, is William III in James II's plight but all the more vulnerable for being a usurper. By surrounding William with James's betrayers, Dryden predicts his probable fate: as James was slandered by the clergy, betrayed by the courtiers, and reviled by the mob, so shall be William. Dryden does not, however, leave the moral to work itself out only through disparities in the parallel; it is indeed "couched under every one of the principal Parts and Characters" (*Preface*, p. 71), and we may infer it by applying these parts and characters to contemporary political affairs. Moreover, it is stated in various forms by various characters throughout the play:

> *Dorax.* And wou'd his Creature, nay his Friend betray him?
> Why then no Bond is left on human kind:
> Distrust, debates, immortal strifes ensue;

Children may murder Parents, Wives their Husbands;
All must be Rapine, Wars, and Desolation.

(II.i.306–310)

Benducar. A secret Party still remains that lurks
Like Embers rak'd in ashes_____wanting but
A breath to blow aside th' involving dust,
And then they blaze abroad.

(II.i.76–79)

Almeyda. Thy Father was not more than mine, the Heir
Of this large Empire; but with arms united
They fought their way, and seiz'd the Crown by force;
And equal as their danger was their share:
For where was Eldership, where none had right,
But that which Conquest gave?

(I.i.451–456)

Antonio. ... when Kings and Queens are to be discarded, what
shou'd Knaves do any longer in the pack?

(IV.iii.169–170)

Mustapha. Nay, if he and his Clergy will needs be preaching up Rebellion, and giving us their Blessing, 'tis but justice they shou'd have
the first fruits of it.

(IV.iii.172–174)

If we add to this moral the idea of ancestral sin included in the last
four lines of the play, we may arrive at a full justification of Dryden's vision of unending and pointless revolution in the *Dedication*
and his longing there for retirement. The following four lines from
The Hind and the Panther embody both morals and might serve as
an epigraph to *Don Sebastian*:

So hardly can Usurpers manage well
Those, whom they first instructed to rebell:
More liberty begets desire of more,
The hunger still encreases with the store.

(I.517–520)

Dryden presents, then, a parallel not to the 1688 Revolution,
but to one of the endless counterrevolutions that he predicts in the
Dedication: as he tells us in the *Preface*, his plot is "purely fiction;

for I take it up where History has laid it down" (p. 67). This parallel is constructed from a series of identities and oppositions, and its complexity must have been intended to protect the Jacobite poet from the hostility of a Williamite audience. What confuses the viewer, however, need not trouble the reader:

> 'Tis obvious to every understanding Reader, that the most poetical parts, which are Descriptions, Images, Similitudes, and Moral Sentences; are those, which of necessity were to be par'd away, when the body was swoln into too large a bulk for the representation of the Stage. But there is a vast difference betwixt a publick entertainment on the Theatre, and a private reading in the Closet: In the first we are confin'd to time . . . in the last, every Reader . . . can . . . find out those beauties of propriety, in thought and writing, which escap'd him in the tumult and hurry of representing.
>
> (P. 66)

The political meaning of the printed text, though complex and oblique, is hardly impenetrable. The first act conveniently suggests a contemporary parallel for each character within a few lines of its first appearance; the *Dedication* and *Preface* strengthen some of the parallels and clarify the political morals we are to draw from them; and throughout the play Dryden is careful to provide a series of clear signs—descriptions, images, similitudes, and moral sentences—that direct us from fictional and historical characters to their contemporary counterparts.

Amphitryon seems to have been ready for the stage within five months of the first performance of *Don Sebastian*,[26] and it shares many of the earlier play's political concerns. Dryden directly refers in the *Dedication* of *Amphitryon* to one source of continuity between the two plays:

> as since this wonderful Revolution, I have begun with the best Pattern of Humanity, the Earl of *Leicester*; I shall continue to follow the same Method, in all, to whom I shall Address; and endeavour to pitch on such only, as have been pleas'd to own me in this Ruin of my small Fortune; who, though they are of a contrary Opinion themselves, yet blame me not for adhering to a lost Cause; and judging for my self, what I cannot chuse but judge; so long as I am a patient Sufferer, and no disturber of the Government.[27]

Here we have the same complex self-presentation as in *Don Sebastian* and *The Hind and the Panther*: we are to recognize Dryden's harmlessness even as we admire his consistent adherence to the "lost cause" that has ruined him. Leveson Gower stands with Leicester as a model of indulgence for Williamite readers, who, if they reject this model, show themselves the ignoble tools of faction:

> There is one kind of Vertue, which is inborn in the Nobility . . . of this Nation; they are not apt to insult on the Misfortunes of their Countrymen. But you, Sir . . . have . . . rais'd it to a Nobler Vertue: As you have been pleas'd to honour me, for a long time, with some part of your Esteem and your good Will; so in particular, since the last Revolution, you have increas'd the Proofs of your kindness to me; and not suffer'd the difference of Opinions, which produce such Hatred and Enmity in the brutal Part of Human kind, to remove you from the settled Basis of your good Nature and good Sence.
>
> (P. 223)

Moreover, in thus rising above the brutal slaves of faction, Leveson Gower can make some claim on the peculiarly Jacobite virtue of adherence to a cause, a quality that was, as we have seen, of great importance to one who had been so frequently attacked as a time-server. Such "constancy to your former Choice" is a virtue "not overcommon amongst *English* Men." He has continued "in the same Tract of Goodness, Favour, and Protection"; and retained "a kind of unmoveable good Nature" through all political changes (p. 223). As he shares Dryden's constancy, Dryden shares his noble indifference to party prejudice: "As you, Sir, have been pleas'd to follow the Example of [the play's audience] in favouring me: So give me leave to say, that I follow yours in the Dedication, to a Person of a different Perswasion" (p. 224). Dryden and Leveson Gower, then, though divided by mere political opinions, are united in this *Dedication* by far more important principles of virtue and integrity. As in *The Hind and the Panther* and *Don Sebastian*, Dryden defines an area outside and above politics inhabited by noblemen and poets, from which he may survey his enemies with detachment and perspicuity.

Again as in the earlier works, this combination of consistent adherence to principle with disengagement from petty faction is paralleled by a similar combination of patriotism unshaken by revolution with transcendence of age and country through literature. He has adapted Plautus and Molière, "the two greatest Names of Ancient and Modern Comedy" to the requirements of "our Stage," assisted by the music of Purcell, "in whose Person we have at length found an *English-man*, equal with the best abroad" (pp. 224–225). And he makes much of the Englishness of Leveson Gower's noble kindness, thereby implying, perhaps, that brutality is, like King William, a foreign import. But there is another, more extended assertion of patriotism and literary transendence here, which is as closely connected with the meaning of the play as is the prefatory vision of endless revolutions to *Don Sebastian*. Probably referring to a recent pamphlet gloating over his loss of place and pension,[28] Dryden claims that this loss "if it be a severe Penance, as a great Wit has told the World, 'tis at least enjoyn'd me by my self: And *Sancho Panca*, as much a Fool as I, was observ'd to discipline his Body, no farther than he found he could endure the smart" (p. 224). Unwilling to allow his enemies the comfort of supposing him unhappy, Dryden not only claims to have risen above his misfortunes but implies that he is prepared to deal with their source. In *Don Quixote*, Sancho gives himself "Seven or Eight" lashes and expends the rest of the six hundred required of him on the trees.[29] In the following paragraph, Dryden gives some indication of where he will bestow the rest of his:

> I suffer no more, than I can easily undergo; and so long as I enjoy my Liberty, which is the Birth-right of an *English* Man, the rest shall never go near my Heart. The Merry Philosopher, is more to my Humour than the Melancholick; and I find no disposition in my self to Cry, while the mad World is daily supplying me with such Occasions of Laughter.
>
> (P. 224)

By asserting the value of English liberty, Dryden at once denies the supposed connection between Jacobite Catholicism and French absolutism and suggests that the Williamites are obliged by their own principles to tolerate his. Having dressed his contempt of the present age in both homegrown tradition and ancient philosophy, he is free to project throughout the play his mockery of "the mad World"—of the Revolution, its causes, its justifications, and its consequences.

The *Prologue* that follows is no less like its counterpart in *Don Sebastian* than the *Dedication*: it provides the same references to the poet's renunciation of satire and the same flirtation with Jacobite polemic. In both, the audience's disfavor is briefly compared to political rebellion—to the Civil Wars in the first (l. 13), to "levelling" in the second. And both end with assurances of harmlessness. In the first Dryden reduces himself from a dangerous satirist to a poor Catholic struggling to pay his double taxes; in the second he shifts the subject from an apology for political satire, which he again claims to have renounced, to an attack on lampoons against ladies. Both prologues thus briefly and playfully embody the themes of the prose dedications: They remind us of Dryden's principles, hint at the nobility of those principles, and finally assure us that we have nothing to fear from them.

Again as in *Don Sebastian*, this disclaimer is immediately contradicted by the play it introduces. Dryden devotes the first scene of *Amphitryon* to a sustained exposition of the major political identifications and themes that he will develop throughout the play. Though it draws on the burlesque of the gods in both Plautus and Molière, the scene has no counterpart in Dryden's sources. Its action and its immediate function in the plot are both quite simple. Phoebus and Mercury speculate on why Jupiter has called them to Thebes; Jupiter joins them, explains that he wishes to impersonate Amphitryon in order to enjoy Alcmena, and sends Phoebus to delay the morning, Mercury to prolong the night and to impersonate Sosia, Amphitryon's servant. Though the bare plot provides nothing to provoke topical application, even a superficial reading of the scene itself compels such application: it is pervaded by references to councils, courts, prerogative, politics, subjects, kings, monarchs, princes, laws, arbitrary power, tyrants, governments, patriots, preferment, commissions, and deposition.[30] As usual in his postrevolutionary work, Dryden does not provide such terms without providing also some indication of how and where we are to apply them.

The scene begins with the two courtiers Phoebus and Mercury speculating on Olympian state affairs, and we can infer a great deal about that state from their language and demeanor. Jupiter's rule seems both absolute and secretive. In asking Mercury the purpose of their "consult," Phoebus places himself among a "Herd of Gods," of which the wisest are no better informed than the fools;

and Mercury counsels blind obedience: " 'Tis our Part to obey our
Father: for, to confess the Truth, we two are little better than Sons
of Harlots; and if *Jupiter* had not been pleas'd to take a little pains
with our Mothers, instead of being Gods, we might have been a
couple of Linck-Boys" (I.i.15–19). There is no deviation here from
mythological fact, but an illegitimate court upheld solely by the
absolute power of a secretive ruler is strongly suggestive of the
revolutionary government as it appears in contemporary Jacobite
satire.[31] There follows a discussion of a quarrel between Jupiter
and Juno which, though it does not confirm any specific parallel,
does at least increase our sense of the disjunction between the
power of the Olympian court and the low standards of conduct
that prevail there.[32] This sense is deepened by the arrival of Jupiter
himself, whose first speech confirms the general identification of
the consult of the gods with an ill-regulated court: "What, you are
descanting upon my Actions? / Much good may do you with your
Politicks: / All Subjects will be censuring their Kings" (I.i.57–60).
Mercury suspects Jupiter of intending to debase his "Almighty-
ship" by fornicating "in the Shape of a Bull, or a Ram, or an Eagle,
or a Swan" and so "transgressing your own Laws"; and Phoebus
welcomes "Any disguise to hide the King of Gods" (I.i.73–80).
Jupiter's identity as a tyrant is thus confirmed: he equates politics
with "subjects censuring their kings," and Mercury justly accuses
him of "transgressing his own laws." Jupiter responds to Phoebus
with the first of three related justifications for royal crime:

> I know your Malice, *Phoebus*, you wou'd say
> That when a Monarch sins it shou'd be secret,
> To keep exterior show of Sanctity,
> Maintain Respect, and cover bad Example:
> For Kings and Priests are in a manner bound,
> For Reverence sake, to be close Hypocrites.
>   (I.i.81–86)

Though William's usurpation was not secret, his intention in first
coming to England was indeed hidden, and many Tories who ral-
lied to his cause expecting only concessions from James, a regency
for his son, or the accession of Mary as sole sovereign, had reason
to complain of William as a "close hypocrite" in pretending only
to assure a free Parliament.[33]

The connection is, however, somewhat remote, and these lines may merely provide further comment on the secrecy of William's court. What follows is far more clearly appropriate to the Jacobite view of William and the Revolution and provides the basis for Dryden's political satire throughout the play. Phoebus objects that "to be secret makes not sin the less"; and Jupiter replies, "I Love, because 'twas in the Fates I shou'd" (I.i.89–93). Phoebus is not satisfied: "With reverence be it spoke, a bad excuse: / Thus every wicked Act in Heav'n or Earth, / May make the same defence" (I.i.94–96). Jupiter responds with a circular argument to which no effective answer is possible:

> Fate is, what I
> By vertue of Omnipotence have made it:
> And pow'r Omnipotent can do no wrong:
> Not to my self, because I will'd it so:
> Nor yet to Men, for what they are is mine.
>   (I.i.102–106)

We have seen that in *The Hind and the Panther* and *Don Sebastian* Dryden's most forceful satire is reserved for the Anglican Tories who reversed their political principles in order to preserve under William the power James sought to deny them. In *Amphitryon* he attacks them again. One chief Anglican justification for rendering allegiance to William consisted in a theological interpretation of his undeniable success: William's accession to the throne was the work of Providence.[34] Late in 1690, when the prominent non-juror William Sherlock took the oaths to William and published a pamphlet justifying the act, both sides of the issue were thoroughly and passionately discussed in a series of pamphlets and poems;[35] but the argument from providence had been current among Williamite clergymen from the first days of the Revolution: Burnet, for example, preached a sermon on the subject before William on 23 December 1688.[36] Dryden himself repeats the argument, together with its refutation, in his "Character of a Good Parson":

> The senseless Plea of Right by Providence
> Was, by a flatt'ring Priest, invented since:
> And lasts no longer than the present sway;
> But justifies the next who comes in play.[37]

Jupiter advances a similar justification for his crime, and Phoebus
a similar refutation. Jupiter, however, is not the favorite of god,
but god himself, and this quality, though it may have helped conceal the parallel from Dryden's enemies, is vital to his satire. Dryden's Jupiter is a god appropriate to those who chose William as
king, a god given to secrecy and crime, which he justifies by invoking the fate that he himself controls. William and the Anglicans
sought to avoid responsibility for the Revolution by ascribing it to
God's will and casting themselves as the passive and innocent
agents of that will. By making Jupiter advance the same claim—by
obligingly transforming God's chosen instrument into God
himself—Dryden exposes the fallacy of this argument. Jupiter, like
William and his followers, claims to be the passive agent of fate:
"I love, because 'twas in the Fates I shou'd." But, being omnipotent, he himself controls this fate: "Fate is, what I / By vertue of
Omnipotence have made it"; and this control clearly invalidates
his denial of responsibility. Dryden suggests that William was no
less the author of his fate, that the forces which brought him to the
throne were no less subject to his control; and that therefore he,
like Jupiter, can ultimately justify his authority only by a bare
assertion of power: "And pow'r Omnipotent can do no wrong."
Dryden's Jupiter neatly combines the Williamite view of providence with its Jacobite refutation; and in an omnipotent god the
incongruity of unlimited power with hypocrisy and injustice becomes all the more striking.

Mercury's response pours ridicule on Jupiter's argument while
it confirms the parallel between Jupiter and earthly monarchs:

> Here's Omnipotence with a Vengeance, to make a Man a Cuckold, and
> yet not to do him wrong. Then I find, Father *Jupiter*, that when you
> made Fate, you had the wit to contrive a Holy-day for your self now
> and then. For you kings never Enact a Law, but you have a kind of an
> Eye to your own Prerogative.
>
> (I.i.113–118)

Phoebus, however, attempts a more serious answer:

> *Phoeb.* If there be no such thing as right and wrong,
> Of an Eternal Being, I have done_____
> But if there be_____

*Jup.*_____Peace, thou disputing Fool:
Learn this; if thou coud'st comprehend my ways,
Then thou wert *Jove*, not I.

(I.i.119–123)

At last Phoebus is forced to capitulate: "Since Arbitrary Pow'r will hear no Reason, 'tis Wisdom to be silent" (I.i.131–132). Phoebus has earlier identified himself as a poet: Dryden here seems to have complemented his playful and mocking elevation of William with a similar elevation of himself. Like Phoebus, he had been interrupted in his discussion of right and wrong in politics by an assertion of what he considered arbitrary power, and, if we may trust his prologues and dedications, had found it wisdom to be silent. Mercury's ironic commentary confirms the identities of both king and poet:

> Why, that's the Point; this same Arbitrary Power is a knock-down Argument; 'tis but a Word and a Blow; now methinks our Father speaks out like an honest bare-fac'd God, as he is: he lays the stress in the right Place, upon Absolute Dominion: I confess if he had been a Man, he might have been a Tyrant, if his Subjects durst have call'd him to account.
>
> (I.i.133–138)

To Dryden, William was such a man, and Mercury's phrasing here suggests the extent to which power has overcome truth in revolutionary England: since his subjects dare not call him to account, he escapes not only the consequences of tyranny, but also the thing itself. As Jupiter's omnipotence can overcome logic, William's arbitrary power can alter truth. Mercury proceeds:

> But you Brother *Phoebus*, are but a meer Country Gentleman, that never comes to Court; that are abroad all day on Horse-back, making Visits about the World; are drinking all Night, and in your Cups are still rayling at the Government: O these Patriots, these bumpkin Patriots, are a very silly sort of Animal.
>
> (I.i.138–143)

Dryden was fond of casting himself as a country patriot in these years;[38] Mercury's view of such an animal—which recalls Dryden's self-denigrating identification with Sancho Panza in the

Dedication—playfully conveys his sense of political alienation and moral self-sufficiency in such circumstances.

Jupiter offers one further justification for his crime:

> That, for the good of Human-kind, this Night
> I shall beget a future *Hercules*;
> Who shall redress the wrongs of injur'd Mortals,
> Shall conquer Monsters, and reform the World.
>
> (I.i.124–127)

One critic has been misled by Jupiter's repetition of this promise at the end of the play into thinking Hercules a potential reformer of the contemporary social and political ills Dryden attacks in the play;[39] however, if the clumsy hyperbole of this speech is not enough to invite our suspicion, Dryden exposes the speciousness of Jupiter's claim in Mercury's reply: "Ay, Brother *Phoebus*; and our Father made all those Monsters for *Hercules* to Conquer, and contriv'd all those Vices on purpose for him to reform too, there's the Jeast on't" (I.i.128–130). In fact this is a parody of another of the justifications for the Revolution: William had purportedly come to England to redress the wrongs of the people and reform James's popish tyranny. Dryden had already mocked this claim in the Mufti's statement of doctrine in *Don Sebastian*: "People side with violence and injustice, / When done for public good"; and other Jacobite satirists were equally given to such mockery:

> Let no free quarter grieve you or disturb you,
> Nor think that Dutch and Dane came here to curb you.
> What though they spoil your goods and pox your wives
> So long as all our throats 'scape Popish knives?
> Deliverance! Deliverance! is all.[40]

Like the auditors of this satirist, Amphitryon requires deliverance only from his deliverer. He is threatened not by "monsters," but by the god who would invade his marriage and usurp his bed on the specious pretext of reform. Dryden suggests in Mercury's speech that the monsters and vices requiring reform were merely specters of Stuart tyranny raised by William's supporters to excuse his invasion.

Having established his parallel between Jupiter and William, Dryden devotes the remainder of this scene to a few illustrations of the absolute quality of this monarch's rule and the inability of his subjects to oppose his illegitimate and injurious exercise of power. Jupiter orders his reluctant deputies to their tasks: Phoebus to delay the morning while Jupiter enjoys Alcmena, Mercury to assume Sosia's "villanous shape." Phoebus and Jupiter depart, and Mercury is left to inform Night of Jupiter's plans. Here Dryden, while following Molière's *Prologue*, continues to provide hints of his parallel. Night greets Mercury with speculations about his activities that further establish the venality of Jupiter and his court: "what Bankers Shop is to be broken open to Night? or what Clippers, and Coiners, and Conspirators, have been invoking your Deity for their assistance?" (I.i.213–215). Mercury refers to Jupiter's deposition of Saturn;[41] Night at first threatens to "lay down my Commission" rather than serve Jupiter's wicked aims, but at length submits, giving a reason appropriate to those politicians whose allegiance to William the Jacobites ascribed to fear of the danger and trouble of resistance: "Well, I am edified by your discourse; and my comfort is, that whatever work is made, I see nothing" (I.i.248, 270–271). Throughout the first scene, then, Dryden sets up a parallel intended to expose both the specious bases for William's authority and the irresistible power that actually enforces that authority. The opposition introduced here between power and truth recurs throughout the play and provides Dryden and the reader with an unfailing source of irony and amusement.

Indeed, we may find traces of that opposition even in those episodes of the play that have least bearing on the Jupiter/William parallel and that are adapted with relatively little change from Plautus and Molière. In II.i, for example, Sosia, having come to inform Alcmena of Amphitryon's arrival, is kept at the door by Mercury, who beats him out of his identity. Mercury takes a perverse pleasure in forcing Sosia to deny what both know to be true; and in Sosia's desperate attempts to maintain some hold on that truth, we may see a distant reflection of the plight of the Jacobites under William: "I dare say nothing, but Thought is free; but whatever I am call'd, I am *Amphitryon's* Man, and the first Letter of my Name is *S.*, too. . . . Lord, Lord, Friend, one of us two is horribly giv'n to lying—but I do not say which of us, to avoid Contention" (II.i.169–175). We may draw similar reflection from

Mercury's reviling Amphitryon when he has locked him out of his own house (IV.i.137–193). Throughout the play, the power of the gods opposes the legitimate interests of the mortals.

The opposition is most pointed in the contest between the two claimants to Alcmena's bed, one false and powerful, the other true but weak. The situation resembles that in *Don Sebastian*, where the wicked king Muley-Moloch contends for Almeyda's love with the virtuous captive Sebastian: in both Dryden figures the political rivalry between William and James as an amorous rivalry the values of which may readily be transferred to a Jacobite view of the Revolution.[42] As James Garrison has remarked, Jupiter describes his love in appropriate political terms:

> In me (my charming Mistris) you behold
> A Lover that disdains a Lawful Title;
> Such as of Monarchs to successive Thrones:
> The Generous Lover holds by force of Arms;
> And claims his Crown by Conquest.
>   (II.ii.83–87)

These terms recur throughout the play. Amphitryon berates Alcmena for "all the prodigality of Kindness, / Giv'n to another, and usurp'd from me" (III.i.293–294); and later he arraigns Jupiter as "Thou base Usurper of my Name, and Bed" (V.i.144). The parallel is thus complete: the crimes that Jupiter justifies in the first scene on the Williamite pretexts of providence and public good are shown to be William's crimes of usurpation and conquest.

Dryden does not, however, restrict himself to attacking only the usurpation and its flimsier justifications: as in his earlier works on the Revolution, he claims to find its true source in the self-interest of the English public. The Pigeons in *The Hind and the Panther* and the Moors in *Don Sebastian* have their counterparts in the people of Thebes. Despite his omnipotence, Jupiter apparently cannot maintain his claim on Alcmena without the collusion of Phaedra, Gripus, and their kind, who respond not to threats and sophistry, but to money. Phaedra and Gripus have no counterparts in Dryden's sources; he establishes their political meaning in a series of direct topical allusions.[43] Phaedra's politics depend entirely on her interest: "what matter is it to me if my Lord has routed the Enemies, if I get nothing of their spoils" (I.ii.24–25). Her trust in Jupiter confirms the political identity of that god and suggests the

Jacobite view of the success of his English counterpart, who could absolve the clergy of their oath to James: "I hate to deal with one of your little baffling Gods that can do nothing, but by permission: but *Jupiter* can swinge you off; if you swear by him, and are forsworn" (I.ii.48–51). Gripus's political principles are similarly based on dishonesty and greed. Phaedra arraigns him as "Thou Seller of other People: thou Weather-cock of Government: that when the Wind blows for the Subject, point'st to Priviledge; and when it changes for the Soveraign, veers to Prerogative" (V.i.13–16). The political terms of the accusation, though they have little bearing on the play, are obviously and directly relevant to contemporary England. The same is true of an earlier description of Gripus: "He sells Justice as he uses, fleeces the Rich Rebells, and hangs up the Poor" (II.ii.123–124). This is the only reference to the action from which Amphitryon is returning as a civil war; the reference is again more appropriate to Jacobite polemic than to the play: among the supporters of James who lost wealth and position for their "rebellion" was Dryden himself, who was fleeced of his pension and taxed double as a Catholic. Like William's henchmen, Gripus upholds tyranny in order to reap its spoils; the Jacobites saw the same motive in William's supporters.

Nor are Phaedra and Gripus alone in their subordination of public rectitude to self-interest. Sosia complains of "great Lords" who

> will say *Upon my Honour*, at every word: yet ask 'em for our Wages, and they plead the Priviledge of their Honour, and will not pay us; nor let us take our Priviledge of the Law upon them. These are a very hopeful sort of Patriots, to stand up as they do for Liberty and Property of the Subject: there's Conscience for you!
>
> (II.i.19–24)

We may conclude that the English gentry are no less self-interested in their protection of liberty and property. Mercury provides a similar, though less overtly political, indictment of "the Great":

> All seek their Ends; and each wou'd other cheat.
> They onely seem to hate, and seem to love;
> But Int'rest is the point on which they move.
> Their Friends are Foes; and Foes are Friends agen;
> And, in their turns, are Knaves, and Honest men.

Our Iron Age is grown an Age of Gold:
'Tis who bids most: for all Men wou'd be sold.

       (IV.i.551–557)

Gripus and Phaedra are only part of a general trend common to
ancient Thebes and contemporary England. Gripus is typical of all
lawyers, whose "long Preambles, and tedious Repetitions . . . sig-
nifie nothing, but to squeeze the Subject" (V.i.63–64); and Phaedra is typical of the population of Thebes, France, and England:

> She's Interested, and a Jilt into the Bargain. Three thousand years
> hence, there will be a whole Nation of such women, in a certain Coun-
> try that will be call'd *France*; and there's a Neighbour Island too,
> where the Men of that Country will be all Interest. Oh what a precious
> Generation will that be, which the Men of the Island shall Propagate
> out of the Women of the Continent!

(II.ii.105–111)

Jupiter, like the Jacobite caricature of William, is forced to
maintain his false claim by pandering to this universal self-interest.
He finds quite early in the play that to gain access to Alcmena, he
must first buy off Phaedra:

> *Phaed.* Ay, my Lord, I see you are on fire: but the Devil a
> Bucket shall be brought to quench it, without my leave. . . .
> *Jup. aside.* Now I cou'd call my Thunder to revenge me,
> But that were to confess my self a God,
> And then I lost my Love! . . .
> *Phaed.* You have got some part of the Enemies Spoil I war-
> rant you. . . .
> *Jupiter, taking a Ring off his Finger and giving it.* Here, take
> it, this is a very Woman:
> Her Sex is Avarice, and she, in One,
> Is all her Sex.
> *Phaed.* Ay, ay, 'tis no matter what you say of us. What,
> wou'd you have your Mony out of the Treasury, without
> paying the Officers their Fees?

       (I.ii.154–187)

Jupiter is later forced to bribe Phaedra again so that he may see
Alcmena after her quarrel with Amphitryon. He throws her a
purse and laments that money can do more even than divine
power—and more, Dryden implies, than divine Providence as well:

"This is my Bribe to *Phaedra*; when I made / This Gold, I made a greater God than *Jove*, / And gave my own Omnipotence away" (III.i.580–582). Phaedra bargains with Jupiter as the English nation, which she explicitly represents, bargains with William: he may raid the treasury only after he has bribed its officers.

Conversely, Amphitryon relies upon the justice of his cause: he is unwilling to bribe, and so, like James, fails to attract support. In attempting to prove to Amphitryon that he had been with her the preceding night, Alcmena appeals to Phaedra, who unhesitatingly puts her allegiance up for sale: "I am to forget all that was done over-night in Love-Matters,—unless my master please to rub up my Memory with another Diamond" (III.i.202–204). When Amphitryon is forced to seek legal authority to break open his own house, Gripus will "command nothing without any Warrant; and my Clerk is not here to take his Fees for drawing it" (IV.i.314–315). Sosia himself declares for "the inviting, and eating, and treating *Amphitryon*: I am sure 'tis he that is my lawfully begotten Lord" (IV.i.343–345).[44] And Phaedra chooses the Amphitryon who has bribed her:

> *Amph* . . . Answer me precisely: do'st thou not know me for *Amphitryon*?
> *Phaed.* Answer me first: did you give me a Diamond, and a Purse of Gold?
> *Amph.* Thou know'st I did not.
> *Phaed.* Then, by the same token, I know you are not the true *Amphitryon*.
> (V.i.97–102)

Amphitryon, knowing himself to be right, naturally expects to be believed without pay; Jupiter, knowing his imposture, is happy to purchase belief for whatever it costs. In so base a nation as Thebes/England, Dryden suggests, circumstances favor the usurper.

This national bias, and its responsibility for William's success, is even clearer in the climactic trial scene. When William was advancing upon London with his 15,000 Dutch troops and assorted English followers, he claimed to intend "no other design, but to have a free and lawful Parliament assembled as soon as is possible." James replied that William's "Designs in the bottom did tend to nothing less than an absolute usurping of his majesty's crown and royal authority."[45] The postures of both contenders—William

peaceful and ready to stand a free trial; James confused and ag-
grieved at having to stand trial at all—are reflected in the postures
of Jupiter and Amphitryon. When Amphitryon attempts to attack
him, Jupiter calmly remarks on the intemperance of such behavior:

> But still take notice, that it looks not like
> The true *Amphitryon*, to fly out, at first
> To brutal force: it shows he doubts his Cause,
> Who dares not trust his reason to defend it.
>   (V.i.140–143)

Amphitryon's friends justify their inaction by their inability to de-
cide which claimant deserves their loyalty; this provides the occasion of another exchange which bears upon the Revolution:

> *Amph.* I know it; and have satisfy'd my self:
> I am the true *Amphitryon*.
>   *Jupit.* See again.
> He shuns the certain proofs, and dares not stand
> Impartial Judgment, and award of right.
>   (V.i.156–160)

The true claimant naturally resents having to trust his claim to the
judgment of third parties; the false stands only to gain by such a
process and therefore freely undergoes it. Amphitryon does not
think his own identity the proper subject of an "impartial judgment, and award of right"; Dryden implies, I think, that the kingship of England is no more than a man's personal identity the
proper subject of an election.

This is, to be sure, a parallel, not an allegory, and though many
of the obvious differences between the characters of the play and
the actual characters they reflect help advance Dryden's satire,
some do not. Thus Amphitryon is eager for battle; James avoided
it. Alcmena is guiltless of intentional wrongdoing; in Dryden's
view, England was not. Yet many of the more apparently refrac-
tory elements of the play do yield polemic meaning. The following
exchange, for example, which has no counterpart in Dryden's
sources, may seem to run directly counter to the parallel:

> *Alcm* ... my Heart will guide my Eyes
> To point, and tremble to its proper choice.
>   [*Seeing* Amphitryon, *goes to him.*
> There neither was, nor is, but one *Amphitryon*;

And I am onely his   [*Goes to take him by the Hand.*
   Amph. pushing her away from him. Away, Adulteress!
   Jupit. My gentle Love; my Treasure and my Joy;
Follow no more, that false and foolish Fire,
That wou'd mislead thy Fame to sure destruction!
Look on thy better Husband, and thy friend,
Who will not leave thee lyable to scorn,
But vindicate thy honour from that Wretch
Who wou'd by base aspersions blot thy vertue.
   Alcm. going to him, who embraces her. I was indeed mis-
   taken; thou art he! . . .
Thy kindness is a Guide that cannot err.
                       (V.i.257–272)

If we read this scene according to the parallel, we might conclude that England rightly chose William over James as the claimant most likely to favor and protect the country. Jupiter's kindness here, however, is merely apparent: he can well afford to excuse the adultery of which he is the sole beneficiary; and his own deceitful assault on Alcmena's virtue and Amphitryon's honor has provided the occasion for this specious show of kindness. He is, as Mercury points out in the first scene, the creator of the ills he pretends to remedy; and as Alcmena can protect her honor only by adhering to the ravisher who cónceals his crime, England can protect its collective political integrity only by adhering to the usurper who justifies its desertion of the true king.

Most of the play's political comment, however, is far simpler and far more direct than this. Dryden is not, as in *Don Sebastian*, teaching serious lessons on the nature of political institutions; he is rather laughing at the "mad world," exposing contemporary politics to ridicule by weaving it carefully into the farcical comedy that Plautus and Molière had made of the Amphitryon story. Dryden consistently uses the double identity that is the mainspring of this comedy to mock Revolutionary pretenses. Sosia's inability either to establish or abandon his identity reflects the Jacobites' position, and mocks the Williamites' denial of obvious fact. In conceding that Mercury has proven his claim to be Sosia, Sosia involves himself in absurdity: "Well, you are *Sosia*; there's no denying it; but what am I then? for my Mind misgives me, I am somebody still, if I knew but who I were" (III.i.278–280); and his best efforts to maintain this falsehood are eventually frustrated:

"where ever I come, the malicious world will call me *Sosia*, in spight of me" (IV.i.377–378). If William is king of England, Dryden implies, James must be somebody still. In Amphitryon's quarrel with Sosia, Dryden continues to play upon the idea of duplicate monarchs:

> *Amph.* That one shou'd be two is very probable!
> *Sos.* Have you not seen a Six-pence split into two halves, by some ingenious School-Boy; which bore on either side the Impression of the Monarchs Face? now as those moieties were two Three-pences, and yet in effect but one Six-pence_____
> *Amph.* No more of your villanous Tropes and Figures.
> (III.i.95–100)

Sosia goes on to describe his two selves in such a way as again to reflect upon the two kings of England:

> That there was two I's, is as certain, as that I have two Eyes in this Head of mine. This I, that am here, was weary: the t'other I was fresh: this I was peaceable, and t'other I was a hectoring Bully I.
> (III.i.106–109)

Dryden later suggests the advantages of such duplication for the English public:

> *Sosia.* You, my Lord *Amphitryon*, may have brought forth another You my Lord *Amphitryon*, as well as *I Sosia* have brought forth another *Me Sosia*; and our Diamonds may have procreated these Diamonds; and so we are all three double.
> *Phaedra.* If this be true, I hope my Goblet has gigg'd another Golden Goblet: and then they may carry double upon all four.
> (III.i.250–256)

Thus as in so much of his political poetry, Dryden employs the literary qualities of the genres in which he works to advance his rhetorical purposes. The play's covert political meaning is in perfect accord with its surface wit.

It is possible that in the months since *Don Sebastian*, Dryden had begun to lose the already rather problematic faith in the possibility of counterrevolution which that play implies. The only allusion to such a possibility in *Amphitryon* comes at several removes from the action, in a rondeau at the end of a pastoral dialogue conjured up by Mercury; and even this places more emphasis on present poverty than future restoration:

> Thus at the height we love and live,
>   And fear not to be poor:
> We give, and give, and give, and give,
>   Till we can give no more:
> But what today will take away,
>   Tomorrow will restore.
>   (IV.i.538–543)

Indeed, *Amphitryon* ends with a specious prophecy of reform that in fact predicts the continuation, and even extension, of tyrannic rule. Mercury and Jupiter reveal themselves to Sosia and Amphitryon and invite them to take comfort in the dubious benefits of their impersonation. Sosia recognizes this proffered consolation for what it is:

> *Merc.* You ought to take it for an honour to be drubb'd by the hand of a Divinity.
> *Sosia.* I am your most humble Servant, good Mr. God; but by the faith of a Mortal, I cou'd well have spar'd the honour that you did me.
> (V.i.316–320)

Amphitryon is given no opportunity to respond, but the solace Jupiter offers him is perhaps no less questionable:

> From this auspicious Night, shall rise an Heir,
> Great, like his Sire, and like his Mother, fair:
> Wrongs to redress, and Tyrants to disseize;
> Born for a World, that wants a *Hercules.*
> Monsters, and Monster-men he shall ingage,
> And toil, and struggle, through an Impious Age.
> Peace to his Labours, shall at length succeed;
> And murm'ring Men, unwilling to be freed,
> Shall be compell'd to Happiness, by need.
>   (V.i.412–421)

This is the third reference in the play to Hercules. The first, like this one, is brought forth by Jupiter in justification of his crime, and is, as we have seen, immediately and entirely deflated by Mercury's response. The second comes when Phaedra asks that Jupiter's union with Alcmena produce "Some Fool, some meer Elder-Brother, or some blockheadly Hero" (I.ii.157–158); and this view is confirmed when Phaedra later asks that her son by Mercury be a hero: Mercury replies, "That is to say, a Blockhead" (V.i.363–364). For Dryden and the Jacobites, William and his supporters seemed eager to pose as Protestant heroes, protecting the world from the Romanist monster Louis XIV; as at the beginning of the play, Dryden restates this view in such a manner as to display its preposterousness. The concluding couplet of Jupiter's prophecy promises "happiness" but dwells insistently on the idea of force: "murmuring," "unwilling," "compelled," "by need"—the redundancy here makes the future seem not only dubious, but positively malevolent. We can form some idea of this compulsory happiness from Sosia's comment on the prophecy: he will "produce a Squire to attend on young *Hercules*, when he goes out to seek Adventures; that when his Master kills a Man, he may stand ready to Pick his Pockets" (V.i.429–432). Dryden and the Jacobites felt William's union with England had produced the kind of military "heroism" that led to dangerous foreign entanglements and high taxation; and Dryden suggests that we can hardly hope much better from a reformer produced by the collusion of an unjust king with the very "impious age" his offspring is supposed to reform. The best possible result is the compulsory happiness predicted in the final line—such happiness as "this wonderful Revolution" had brought to Dryden himself, when the tyrant was "disseiz'd," the wrongs of murmuring Englishmen were redressed, and the country was compelled to accept whatever freedom William might in the end allow it.

3. "The Favour of Sovereign Princes": *King Arthur* and *Cleomenes*

In *Don Sebastian* and *Amphitryon* Dryden asserts an uncompromising Jacobitism. He measures the Revolution by both the conservative constitutional principles that all responsible Englishmen had claimed since the Restoration and by the transcendent moral and political values he claims to derive from classic literature, and he finds it in violation of both. In the Convention Parliament's attempt to change kings without altering the ancient constitution, he sees elements of both republicanism and absolutism; and in the behavior of the new monarchs and their followers, he sees uncontrolled ambition, duplicity, and ingratitude. Though centrally concerned with politics, these plays lack a clear polemic agenda; they are rather contemplative than persuasive. In his next two plays, Dryden is once again seeking an audience for his political reflections, and yet these reflections are more varied and ambiguous. The Revolution loses its place at the center of the action: in *King Arthur* Dryden ignores it altogether, and the version of it he provides in *Cleomenes* is comparatively innocuous, concerned rather with its personal effects than its political causes. The moral universe he presents in these two plays is based not as in the earlier plays on legitimacy and title, but rather on war and peace, engagement and detachment, action and resignation. And Dryden presents this universe in such a way as, without abandoning his loyalty to James and Catholicism, to appeal to the sympathies of all three major political parties: the Jacobites, the Court party, and the parliamentary opposition.

By 1691 the Williamites had begun to split into two opposed factions that were to emerge later in the decade as new Whig and

Tory parties. The Court party supported William in sacrificing immediate economic interests and even some civil liberties to the great war against France; the opposition resisted these aims. According to Keith Feiling in his *History of the Tory Party,*

> The abuses or dangers, of which the new Opposition complained, were enormous or misapplied taxes, diversion of expenditure to continental armies—thus starving the Navy, our proper weapon—the corrupt influence of placemen, the suspension of Habeas Corpus, the ruin of trade, and these topics were dinned in by a shower of pamphlets coming equally from Tory, Whig, and Jacobite quarters.[1]

In the year preceding the first performance of *King Arthur* in early summer of 1691, this party had found much to occupy its attention. William's success at the Boyne in July 1690 was qualified by the defeat of the navy at Beachy Head, a blow to the national pride that excited the contempt of, among others, Dryden's friend Sir Henry Sheeres:

> The Parliament may plague us with taxation,
> But till they cure the grievance of the nation,
> Monsieur will make the Narrow Seas his station;
> Then what becomes of all our ancient rule,
> Our right from Edgar and command from Thule?
> Believe me, Sirs, it will be then confessed
> Your flag's a dishclout, and your claim a jest.[2]

In October 1690 William asked Parliament for £1,800,000 to carry on the war. No record survives of the ensuing debate, but a contemporary satire ridicules the extravagance of William's demands, and the Tories Clarges and Seymour are known to have advocated a smaller army and a stronger fleet.[3] A record does survive of the debate held in November 1691 on a similar request. Opposition speakers argue against involvement in the continental war: "In the Rolls we find that, when money was asked by Edw. 3, to maintain what he had conquered in France, the parliament answered, 'They were concerned only to keep England, and not what was conquered in France' "; against the resulting decay of trade: "If we consider what merchants have lost, and money carried abroad, and that foreign merchants carry out your freight, I think it is a sign we are poor"; against a standing army: "Really

I am afraid of a Standing Army. We have the skeleton, though not the body, of the forces. I look upon the war with France to be merely a colour"; against heavy taxation: "If we maintain an army of 40,000 men abroad, I fear we shall have none left for common defence another year"; and in favour of a naval strategy: "As we are an island, we are to consider, that, if the French have all the seventeen provinces, and we are superior at sea, we may still be safe, and for what belongs to us."[4]

If in early 1691 Dryden had been seeking an intermediary between himself and this new opposition party, he could hardly have made a better choice than the dedicatee of *King Arthur*. George Savile, first marquis of Halifax, had earned a place in *Absalom and Achitophel* for his crucial role in the defeat of the exclusion bill. Yet he was also among the leaders of the Revolution and for the first year of William's government had served as his chief advisor. As such he had exposed himself to the vengeful attack of those who blamed him for the Tory revenge of the mid eighties and in February 1690 had resigned against William's wishes. He soon joined the opposition and by January 1691 had begun accepting conciliatory visits from James's agents.[5] As a prominent Williamite whose high principles had led him to change sides often and at last brought him to a sort of retirement, he was an unusually suitable candidate for the attentions of a Jacobite poet seeking public rehabilitation.

Halifax contributed heartily to opposition criticism of the danger and expense of the army and the neglect of the fleet. The abstract of a speech he made sometime between 1690 and 1694 shows his view of the army. He suspects William has provoked France only to provide himself with an excuse for building up a force he may later use against domestic opponents:

> Necessity is always a good arg^t if Reall but if hee that createth the necessity hath the benefit of it, the consequences are somewhat inconvenient. . . .
>
> A Maxime in Law, that no man is to have benefit from his own wrong Act; yet here there is power by declaring warre to provoke a stronger enemy by which the necessity of self p[re]servation ariseth and that carrieth every thing along with it. . . .
>
> It must in time make the Gov^t so strong that it can not bee resisted and the people so poor that they cannot resist. . . .

When ever the warre is done, Hee hath an Army at his devotion
loath to bee disbanded ready to support that power which keepeth
them on foot.[6]

Halifax's "Rough Draught of a New Model at Sea," published
anonymously in 1694, summarizes the opposition's view of the
fleet. He begins by establishing its importance to national security:

if allegiance is due to protection, ours to the sea is due from that rule,
since by that, and by that alone, we are to be protected; and if we have
of late suffered usurpation of other methods, contrary to the homage
we owe to that which must preserve us, it is time now to restore the
sea to its right.[7]

He goes on to make several suggestions for increasing the fleet's
size and efficiency.

Dryden does not directly appeal to any of these principles in his
Dedication, but some knowledge of them helps illuminate the
meaning and purpose of what he says about his patron and his
play.[8] He concludes the *Dedication* by reminding his readers of his
long association with Halifax:

I think I cannot be deceived in thus addressing to your lordship, whom
I have had the honour to know, at that distance which becomes me, for
so many years. It is true, that formerly I have shadowed some part of
your virtues under another name; but the character, though short and
imperfect, was so true, that it broke through the fable, and was discovered by its native light.[9]

Throughout Dryden emphasizes those parts of Halifax's career in
which his views coincide with Dryden's own. Now as during the
exclusion crisis, both can be said to stand together against the fury
of the mob; and a long passage celebrating Halifax's wise direction
of Charles's policy is followed by another in praise of retirement:

But, as a skillful pilot will not be tempted out to sea in suspected
weather, so have you wisely chosen to withdraw yourself from public
business, when the face of heaven grew troubled, and the frequent
shifting of the winds foreshowed a storm. There are times and seasons
when the best patriots are willing to withdraw their hands from the
commonwealth, as Phocion, in his latter days, was observed to decline
the management of affairs; or as Cicero (to draw the similitude more

home) left the pulpit for Tusculum, and the praise of oratory for the sweet enjoyments of a private life; and, in the happiness of those retirements, has more obliged posterity by his moral precepts, than he did the republic in quelling the conspiracy of Catiline. What prudent man would not rather follow the example of this retreat, than stay, like Cato, with a stubborn unseasonable virtue, to oppose the torrent of the people, and at last be driven from the market-place by a riot of a multitude, uncapable of counsel, and deaf to eloquence?

(Pp. 133–134)

None of this is inconsistent with the pure Jacobitism of *Don Sebastian*; but Dryden follows his attack on the government from which he and Halifax had fled with an assertion of sturdy English patriotism calculated to appeal to the parliamentary opposition:

A Roman soldier was allowed to plead the merit of his services for his dismission at such an age; and there was but one exception to that rule, which was, an invasion from the Gauls. How far that may work with your lordship, I am not certain, but I hope it is not coming to the trial.

(*Dedication*, p. 134)

This is an oblique attack on English naval failures: the French had followed up their victory at Beachy Head by landing troops on England's west coast and burning the village of Teignmouth; and until the battle of La Hogue helped restore allied control of the Channel in 1692, an "invasion of the Gauls" seemed possible. Dryden goes on, however, to make a profession of buoyant confidence in the navy:

In the meantime, while the nation is secured from foreign attempts by so powerful a fleet, and we enjoy, not only the happiness, but even the ornaments of peace, in the divertisement of the town, I humbly offer you this trifle.

(P. 134)

One of the principle complaints of the opposition was that the nation was not so protected;[10] and even the most dedicated court apologist might have hesitated to celebrate the blessings of peace within weeks of the loss to the French of the strategic Flemish town of Mons. Dryden praises the country for precisely those qualities it most obviously lacks; and this kind of irony recurs, as we shall see, in the play itself.

Another passage in the *Dedication* provides further hints of both the means and the objects of political commentary in *King Arthur*. In discussing Halifax's final triumph over the Whigs, Dryden makes a great show of restraint:

> I might dilate on the difficulties which attended that undertaking, the temper of the people, the power, arts, and interest of the contrary party, but those are all of them invidious topics,—they are too green in our remembrance, and he who touches on them, *Incedit per ignes suppositos cineri doloso.*
>
> (P. 131)

Yet he goes on to draw a lesson from those times which has at least as pointed an application to present events as would any condemnation of the exclusionists:

> But, without reproaching one side to praise another, I may justly recommend to both those wholesome counsels, which, wisely administered, and as well executed, were the means of preventing a civil war, and of extinguishing a growing fire which was just ready to have broken forth among us. So many wives, who have yet their husbands in their arms; so many parents, who have not the number of their children lessened; so many villages, towns, and cities, whose inhabitants are not decreased, their property violated, or their wealth diminished,—are yet owing to the sober conduct and happy results of your advice.
>
> (Pp. 131–132)

Such an encomium must have had an odd sound at a time when England was engaged in a military conflict on a greater scale than any since Cromwell's protectorate; yet it has several parallels in the opera itself, which, despite its heroic protagonist, is filled with catalogues of the evils of war and the blessings of peace.

The opposition political agenda, however, remains throughout the play as well as in the *Dedication* merely an undercurrent of irony and implication. The open support of a known Catholic Jacobite was more likely to undermine than aid the cause of the opposition; but there is another, and perhaps stronger, reason for Dryden's obliquity. He reminds us in the *Dedication* that

> Poets, who subsist not but on the favour of sovereign princes, and of great persons, may have leave to be a little vain, and boast of their patronage, who encourage the genius that animates them; and there-

fore, I will again presume to guess that her Majesty was not displeased to find in this poem the praises of her native country, and the heroic actions of so famous a predecessor in the government of Great Britain as King Arthur.

(P. 136)

Dryden does not want us to suppose that he has wavered in his loyalty to James: in claiming Mary's patronage he is careful to withhold the least hint of praise, and he introduces the subject by reminding us that he is acting out of a kind of financial necessity in mentioning the queen at all. Further, Arthur is merely her "predecessor in the government" and not, as he would no doubt have been in the original version, the type and example of the reigning monarch. Nonetheless, Dryden wants to exhibit his potential value to the present government, and his play is constructed to serve this end among others.[11]

It is generally recognized that the meaning of *King Arthur* is primarily political. Those who think otherwise have commonly claimed that it has no meaning at all, that it is "a mere fairy tale, as totally divested as possible of any meaning beyond extravagant adventure"; or "a fantastic account of Arthur's battles with the Saxons," from which "all the real substance of the story had been removed."[12] Dryden himself encourages this view: he tells us in the *Dedication* that "this poem was the last piece of service which I had the honour to do for my gracious master King Charles II," and that in order to stage it in 1691, he has "been obliged so much to alter the first design, and take away so many beauties from the writing, that it is now no more what it was formerly, than the present ship of the Royal Sovereign, after so often taking down and altering, is the vessel it was at the first building" (pp. 129, 135). Most who have examined the opera's political reference, also taking their cue from this passage, argue that Dryden meant some sort of compliment to William III or his party, yet they are not altogether comfortable in ascribing such sentiments to a professed Jacobite.[13] In the most recent and by far the most thorough analysis of politics in *King Arthur*, Curtis Price attempts to solve this problem by tracing through the opera two contradictory parallels—one in which Arthur is James and William Oswald; another in which Arthur is William, James Oswald, and the battle in Act I a parallel of James's defeat at the Boyne. In addition he points out several ironic gestures that undermine the opera's apparent meaning. He does not, however, reconcile his two parallels or explain their participation in a coherent whole, and it is not therefore clear just what these ironies are undermining.[14]

This confusion may be explained by the complexity, indeed the inconsistency, of Dryden's purposes. He wants at once to recommend himself to the court as a poet of patriotism, to protest the war in Flanders, and to reassert and justify his continuing loyalty to James. The first of these purposes is the most obvious and requires little attention. It is clear throughout in the play's cloying nationalism, and most pointed in the concluding masque. England is celebrated as the queen of islands, the envy of the world, abounding in fish, grain, and wool, stocked with hardy peasantry, and beloved of Venus. At the end of it all stands William, "Our Sovereign High," bestowing honors on his willing subjects.

Dryden's other purposes, though less immediately apparent, account, I think, more fully for his peculiar treatment of his subject. Though the play is ostensibly concerned with the successful wars for which Arthur was traditionally renowned, its battles are brief and ineffective, and Arthur's military talents rather obstruct than advance his purposes. He is introduced by his supporters in the first scene of the play and contrasted with his rival in a few pointed details. Oswald is "free and open-hearted," "Revengeful, rugged, violently brave" (p. 142); whereas Arthur, though brave, is also merciful and calm in battle (p. 143). His character is most completely described by Aurelius:

> His worth divides him from the crowd of kings;
> So born, without desert to be so born;
> Men, set aloft to be the scourge of heaven,
> And, with long arms, to lash the under-world.
>
> (P. 143)

Thus Arthur is notable not for his military prowess, which Oswald can match, but for his lack of the sort of indiscriminate bellicosity of which William and his party were accused.[15]

Further, though the business of Act I is the decisive triumph in battle of the Britons over the Saxons, its effect is to undermine the apparent glory of war. Whereas Arthur, the victor, spends his last moments before the battle bantering with Emmeline, the Saxons stage preposterously elaborate preparations made hollow by their coming defeat. First Oswald and Osmond solemnly implore the aid of the gods. Thor, Freya, and Woden are invited to revenge Hengist's death, to "spell you Saxons, / With sacred runic rhymes," to "edge their bright swords," but at this point Osmond interrupts the proceedings to hear Grimbald's report on the human sacrifices:

> I have played my part;
> For I have steeled the fools that are to die, —
> Six fools, so prodigal of life and soul,
> That, for their country, they devote their lives
> A sacrifice to mother Earth, and Woden.
>   (Pp. 147–148)

The grand solemnity of the invocation is irrecoverably dispelled by this plain comment on the value of dying for one's country. An ode follows, in which a chorus of priests sings the praises of these martyrs in absurdly inflated language:

> The lot is cast, and Tanfan pleased;
> Of mortal cares you shall be eased,
> Brave souls, to be renowned in story.
> Honour prizing,
> Death despising,
> Fame acquiring,
> By expiring;
> Die, and reap the fruit of glory,
> Brave souls, to be renowned in story.
>   (P. 150)

It is impossible to take this seriously. Of the two promises here, the first, that the martyrs will be eased of mortal cares, is a specious euphemism, and the second, that they will win fame and "be renowned in story," is quite clearly false: the six fools are not so much as named. The Ode completed, Oswald rushes into battle boasting emptily:

> Ambitious fools we are,
> And yet ambition is a godlike fault;
> Or rather 'tis no fault in souls born great,
> Who dare extend their glory by their deeds. —

> Now, Britanny, prepare to change thy state,
> And from this day begin thy Saxon date.
>
>   (P. 151)

He is immediately defeated.

The act ends with the Britons' song of victory, in which a great deal of daring and charging about is interrupted by an incongruous view of the battle from the perspective, not of the Britons, but of the gods:

> Now they charge on amain,
> Now they rally again:
> The gods from above the mad labour behold,
> And pity mankind, that will perish for gold.
>
>   (P. 151)[16]

From this authoritative perspective, the futility of war is clearly apparent. War is an unfortunate symptom of the human condition, as regrettable and as inevitable in modern as in ancient Britain. Dryden provides no specific condemnation of William's wars: any pointed details here would both endanger the patriotic air of the opera and compromise the Olympian perspective from which in his old age he so often preferred to view comtemporary politics. But these wars are clearly open to the general charge, just as William is open to the general condemnation of the "crowd of kings."

This Olympian perspective is established in *King Arthur* through what Dryden calls in the *Dedication* "that fairy kind of writing which depends only upon the force of the imagination," and which pleases its audience with "a true taste of poetry" (p. 136); and the play is indeed firmly anchored in literary tradition. The sources of *King Authur* have long been recognized. Philidel, Grimbald, and Merlin derive from *The Tempest*, the bathing sirens from *The Faerie Queene*, the enchanted forest from *Gerusalemme Liberata*, and various motifs concerning heaven and hell, the recovery of Emmeline's sight, and her deliverance from rape, from *Paradise Lost* and *Comus*. By emphasizing that which "depends only upon the force of the imagination," Dryden may claim to soar above history and politics to a realm of sweet visions and eternal truths; and these provide him with unquestioned standards by which he may justify his principles and condemn William's belligerent policies.

After the initial battle, the "fairy kind of writing" takes control of *King Arthur*. The war plot, which from its elaborate exposition in the first scene we might have supposed to have carried through the play, is suddenly suspended in the second act. The battle is over, the victorious Britons are soon "drunk or whoring" (p. 161), and the management of the action reverts to the magician Merlin and his assistant Philidel. The latter is introduced in the first scene of Act II, and his first speech is yet another condemnation of war:

> Alas, for pity of this bloody field!
> Piteous it needs must be, when I, a spirit,
> Can have so soft a sense of human woes!
> Ah, for so many souls, as but this morn
> Were clothed with flesh, and warmed with vital blood,
> But naked now, or shirted but with air!
>
> (P. 152)

War is again presented as a general affliction, as "human woes"; and here it is shown to be cruel as well as mercenary and futile. The validity of Philidel's judgment is confirmed by his account of himself as a fallen spirit whose tenderness and pity have raised him above his fellows and prevented him from participating in the battle. His view of war is reinforced by both speech and action throughout Act II. Merlin gives him an opportunity to redeem himself by rescuing the Britons from the marshes into which Grimbald, disguised as a homely shepherd, is endeavoring to lead them. In the ensuing contest between the two spirits, the conflict between Briton and Saxon gives way to that between good and evil, heaven and hell. Military prowess is of no avail here, as Philidel's advice to Arthur and his followers makes clear: " 'Tis a fiend, who has annoyed ye; / Name but heaven, and he'll avoid ye" (p. 154). Arthur is rescued, but greater danger awaits Matilda and Emmeline. Left alone and unprotected in the British camp, they are being entertained by "a crew of Kentish lads and lasses," whose song celebrates a condition of life that may be instructively compared with that of its hearers both on stage and in the audience:

> How blest are shepherds, how happy their lasses,
> 　　While drums and trumpets are sounding alarms!
> Over our lowly sheds all the storm passes;
> 　　And when we die, 'tis in each other's arms.

All the day on our herds and flocks employing;
All the night on our flutes, and in enjoying.

(P. 158)

The song exposes the emptiness of military glory, and the action immediately confirms this lesson: no sooner do the shepherds depart than Emmeline is abducted by Oswald and the Saxons. The victory of Act I has accomplished nothing at all: in his ensuing conference with Oswald, Arthur can only bluster. Arms are impotent; justice can be restored only through the interposition of heaven through Merlin and his agents.

This lesson is a particularly important one for Dryden in 1691, for not only does it condemn William's effort, it also justifies James's—and Dryden's—inaction. The future of England is in the care of Providence: James may therefore be excused for staying in France, and Dryden for reestablishing his literary position in England. Arthur's inability to learn this lesson gives Dryden frequent occasions in Act III of having it restated. At the end of Act II Arthur is shown rushing from the stage crying "To arms, with speed, to arms!" (p. 164); but the folly of such heroism is exposed a moment later. Act III begins with Conon's weary negation of this command: "Furl up our colours, and unbrace our drums; / Dislodge betimes, and quit this fatal coast" (p. 164). Aurelius explains that Osmond has protected the approach to Oswald's fortress with enchantments which arms cannot penetrate. Arthur, however, remains unconvinced and prepares to win glory against all odds:

Now I perceive a danger worthy me.
'Tis Osmond's work, a band of hell-hired slaves:
Be mine the hazard, mine shall be the fame.

(P. 165)

His rant is interrupted by Merlin, who instructs him to "wait heaven's time" (p. 165). Arthur is forced to use patience, to rely on time and providence. The moral of his story, though not specifically applied to contemporary events, is nonetheless appropriate to Dryden's view of them. It is surely no accident that a major theme of a Jacobite work written after the battle of the Boyne on the expulsion of foreign dominance from Britain should be that one must wait patiently for heaven's reassertion of justice.

The next two scenes are dominated by Grimbald and Osmond, and their behavior obliquely reflects upon that of Dryden's enemies. In the first, Grimbald berates Philidel for his disloyalty to hell:

Thou miscreant elf, thou renegado scout,
So clean, so furbished, so renewed in white,
The livery of our foes; I see thee through:
What mak'st thou here? thou trim apostate, speak.

(P. 167)

As a Catholic convert, Dryden was frequently berated as an apostate, and he must have enjoyed the irony that lies behind Grimbald's fury at Philidel for betraying his allegiance to hell. This is followed by the cure of Emmeline's blindness, achieved, like everything else of substance, by Merlin's power. Emmeline behaves like Milton's Eve after creation: she first falls in love with her own reflection, then with Arthur, who is "of a controlling eye, majestic make" (p. 173). The Miltonic allusions continue at Arthur's departure. He is reluctant to leave Emmeline in Osmond's power, but Merlin assures him that "the enchanter has no power on innocence." Osmond has other ideas. He conjures up a masque to seduce Emmeline, which concludes thus:

He's a grateful offender
    Who pleasure dare seize;
But the whining pretender
    Is sure to displease.

(P. 179)

Rape was a popular metaphor among Jacobites for William's usurpation and among the opposition for his designs against liberty.[17] Both parties may well have felt that he was, in the eyes of too many of their countrymen, a "grateful offender." Merlin, however, proves right in his prediction: Osmond is called away at the critical instant to aid Grimbald, and for the moment heaven reasserts its protection.

In Act IV, Arthur is sent to destroy the enchanted forest, and once again his success depends, not on martial valor, but on patience and the aid of heaven. Arthur himself recognizes the irony of his position as he flees the naked sirens who tempt him to bathe with them: "How dear this flying victory has cost, / When, if I stay

to struggle, I am lost" (p. 184). He withstands also a chorus of
dancing nymphs and sylvans; but unlike his counterpart Rinaldo
in *Gerusalemme Liberata*, he falls victim to the last temptation. He
strikes at a tree, it bleeds, and a vision of Emmeline emerges from
it, imploring his pity and offering her love:

> *Em.* They, only they, who please themselves, are wise.
> Disarm thy hand, that mine may meet it bare.
> *Arth.* By thy leave, reason, here I throw thee off,
> Thou load of life. If thou wert made for souls,
> Then souls should have been made without their bodies.
>
> (P. 187)

He is in the act of pulling off his gauntlet when Philidel appears,
strikes the image with his wand, and reveals it as Grimbald. Once
again, martial heroism alone is of no avail in the world Dryden has
constructed in *King Arthur*: only patience and trust in God, the
virtues Dryden had been teaching himself in the years since the
Revolution, are capable of success.

In the fifth act we return to history—to the history of ancient
Britain in the resolution of the conflict between Arthur and Oswald and to that of modern England in the prophecies with which
the play concludes. It has often been remarked that, despite his
claim to have consulted "Beda, Bochartus, and many other authors," Dryden makes little use either of historical accounts of
ancient Britain or legendary materials associated with Arthur. He
does, however, include in the speeches of Arthur and Oswald certain allusions to their past that clearly set his play in the frame of
British history as recounted by both Bede and Geoffrey of Monmouth. Oswald is the son of Hengist (p. 147), whose aid against
the Picts was purchased by Arthur's predecessor Vortigern with
the kingdom of Kent (pp. 161, 192). There has been some past
dispute about Oswald's importing Saxons to enlarge his territory
(p. 162). Oswald is now eager to avenge Hengist's death (p. 147).
Except for the last detail, which only Geoffrey mentions (Bede
notes the death of Hengist's brother Horsa), this follows the out-
line of both histories, which agree that Vortigern brought in Hengist and the Saxons to defend the Britons against the Picts, that
Hengist found the Britons weak, sent home for reinforcements,
and attacked them. The event of the conflict in both histories is,
however, very different from that in *King Arthur*. In Bede, who

makes no mention of Arthur, the Saxons "established a strangle-
hold over nearly all the doomed island. . . . Some fled overseas in
their misery; others, clinging to their homeland, eked out a
wretched and fearful existence among mountains, forests, and
crags, ever on the alert for danger."[18] Geoffrey describes a series
of glorious victories for Arthur at home and abroad, but at length
brings the island under Saxon rule. Indeed, that the aboriginal
Britons were driven out by the Angles, Saxons, and Jutes is the one
historical fact about ancient Britain that every learned Englishman
might be expected to know.

Dryden, however, though he links his story to these historical
accounts, concludes it with brazen disregard for the facts. Having
beaten Oswald in single combat (with Merlin's aid), Arthur orders
him to depart with his people:

> Thy life, thy liberty, thy honour safe,
> Lead back thy Saxons to their ancient Elbe:
> I would restore thee faithful Kent, the gift
> Of Vortigern for Hengist's ill-bought aid,
> But that my Britons brook no foreign power,
> To lord it in a land sacred to freedom,
> And of its rights tenacious to the last.
>
> (P. 192)

Price has noted the irony of this speech: the audience was indeed
brooking a foreign power on the English throne while the play was
being performed.[19] And if Dryden had been at liberty to construct
parallels at will, he might well have presented that of ancient Britain: the English invited William and the Dutch to fight for them
against the French and found themselves plundered by their pro-
tectors. This was a favorite parallel for Jacobite polemicists, and
Dryden's audience would have been aware of its potential reference to William.[20] But as in the *Dedication*, where he refuses to
cause offence by describing past quarrels between Whig and Tory,
Dryden is here exercising restraint. Rather than offend by telling
the true story of Britain's conquest, he will please by recounting
the Britons' victory, and so flatter the delusions of their modern
counterparts concerning their own political wisdom. Yet the omis-
sions and falsifications are so glaring, the Britons and English so
obviously celebrated for just those virtues that they lack, that the
apparent praise becomes veiled satire. Further, this satire is calcu-

lated to appeal to the mainstream opposition as well as to the Jacobites. There was a great deal of anti-Dutch feeling among those who competed with William's compatriots for important places in the government and the army; and many who favored William opposed Ginkel and Bentinck.

Merlin provides a different view of the future relations between Britons and Saxons; it is, however, no less preposterous:

> Britons and Saxons shall be once one people;
> One common tongue, one common faith shall bind
> Our jarring bands, in a perpetual peace.
>
> (P. 193)

This also falsifies historical fact: the Saxons did not return to Germany, they did not unite with the Britons; rather, they conquered the island and ruled it for themselves. Its inaccuracy is even more glaring if we take it as a metaphorical reference to England's future. No one who had like Dryden witnessed and at last fallen victim to a half century of violent religious struggle could have taken such a prophecy seriously. Again, by straining to conceal what might displease the court party, Dryden in fact suggests that the revolutionary government is illegitimate and unjust.

In the final series of songs celebrating England's future, Dryden employs the same strategy of praising his country for what it notoriously lacks. At the end of this series, and of the play, Arthur remarks candidly on Merlin's misrepresentation of the future:

> Wisely you have, whate'er will please, revealed:
> What would displease, as wisely have concealed:
> Triumphs of war and peace, at full ye show,
> But swiftly turn the pages of our woe.
> Rest we contented with our present state;
> 'Tis anxious to inquire of future fate.
>
> (P. 199)

Arthur may rest contented, but there is no reason why Englishmen of 1691 should have done so. Dryden's prettified version of the future, already undermined by the facts as he and his audience knew them, is here overtly contradicted. The series begins with a song announcing the rise of Britannia from the sea, which emphasizes England's character as an island. The contemporary significance of this is made clear as Pan and Nereid sing of its protected situation: "Round thy coasts, fair nymph of Britain, / For thy guard our waters flow" (p. 194). Like Dryden's remark on naval power in the *Dedication*, this is belied by the recent defeat at Beachy Head and its consequences. Further, it echoes the complaints of the contemporary opposition against William's continental wars: a country guarded by the sea need not squander its resources in expensive campaigns abroad.

The next song, in praise of England's profitable woolen manufacture, is also suspect. Since the beginning of the war, English trade had been crippled by the blockade against France and by the heavy losses to French privateers of merchant vessels which the navy was too weak to protect, and this also had crossed the opposition.[21] This song, filled with gentle rhythms and pastoral imagery, is followed by a rollicking chorus of drunken peasants, who "roar out" a mindless patriotism—Price has suggested the possibility of an ironic intention beneath this sudden shift in tone.[22] The next two songs, both celebrating love, are perhaps merely hyperbolic; but the allusion to William that ends the series, though superficially laudatory, may easily be construed as scathingly ironic:

> Our natives not alone appear
>   To court this martial prize;
> But foreign kings, adopted here,
>   Their crowns at home despise.
>   (P. 198)

This stanza clearly unites, in what appears to be a compliment, two of the most important charges against William. He was not "adopted," and he certainly did not despise his crown at home. For the Jacobites, he usurped his throne, and for a much larger proportion of the English public, he was all too fond of his native country. The opposition, as we have seen, regularly accused him of spending English money and English lives in the Dutch interest. If Dryden had truly meant a compliment, he might easily have celebrated his martial courage or his recent victories in Ireland. Instead he draws attention to precisely those points on which he was felt to be most open to condemnation by both the Jacobites and the parliamentary opposition. The last stanza continues the attack:

> Our sovereign high, in awful state,
>   His honours shall bestow;
> And see his sceptred subjects wait
>   On his commands below.
>   (P. 198)

Price interprets these "sceptred subjects" as Queen Mary during a
regency, or perhaps King James; but neither of these possibilities
seem likely. He is far nearer the mark when he analyzes a "perverse musical pun" in Purcell's setting of this line: "In this somewhat puffed-up chorus of public supplication to the 'Sovereign
High,' his 'Scepter'd Subjects' discreetly reveal a stubborn
independence."[23] By endowing William's subjects with scepters,
Dryden points up the great potential for conflict between the sovereign and his supporters. William no doubt hoped that his subjects would wait on his commands; but Dryden suggests that at the
Revolution, when lineal descent of the crown was interrupted by
the popular will, the subjects took the monarchical authority in
their own hands. Though very obliquely indicated here, it is the
same lesson he teaches in *The Hind and the Panther* and *Don
Sebastian*: a usurper lies at the mercy of those who have removed
his predecessor.

King Arthur may not be among the best of Dryden's postrevolutionary works. It has been accused of disunity and extravagance, unevenness of tone and infirmity of purpose. But it is not
the mere fairy tale that some of its critics have claimed; its miscellaneous character arises rather from a surplus than a deficiency
of serious purpose. He wants to write a patriotic drama that will
impress the court and so leavens his play with a loud and insistent
nationalism. He wants to appeal to the parliamentary opposition
and so makes his historic and panegyric materials fit so ill with the
reality as to expose the failures of the government they purport to
celebrate. Finally, he wants to define and justify his own position
as a Jacobite living in passive compliance with an illegal government and so emphasizes the importance of patience and the futility
of individual effort. Dryden was himself aware of the deficiencies
of the resulting combination: he warns us of them in the *Dedication*. But even in the course of this disclaimer he provides hints of
where we may look for value and meaning: the opera is "now no

more what it was formerly, than the present ship of the Royal Sovereign, after so much taking down and altering, is the vessel it was at first building" (p. 135). It seems likely that Dryden was attracted to this particular ship by its name as much as its appearance. So much taking down and altering of the sovereign of England had forced Dryden to make his opera appropriate to its subject, to substitute prettified history for truth, and condemnation of war for celebration of peace.

It may seem mere perversity to argue that in *Cleomenes* Dryden continues the campaign of conciliating the Williamites that he began in *King Arthur*. For in *Cleomenes* the parallel between the dispossessed and exiled kings of Sparta and England is glaringly obvious—far more so than the subtle resemblances that loom so large in my discussions of *Don Sebastian* and *Amphitryon*. Indeed, so obvious was its parallel that, whereas the earlier plays were performed to general applause, *Cleomenes* was very nearly banned from the stage. Apparently completed by October 1691, the play was twice scheduled and twice prohibited during the winter of 1692 and not finally performed until mid-April. According to Dryden's *Dedication* and *Preface*, it was redeemed only through the interposition of Lord Falkland, who brought evidence that Dryden had considered a dramatic treatment of its subject in prerevolutionary times; and the earl of Rochester, the queen's uncle and as of March 1692 a member of the Privy Council.[24]

Surely Dryden knew the risks involved in writing Jacobite parallels; and we may well ask why, after having so carefully guarded against these risks in *Don Sebastian* and *Amphitryon*, he chose to ignore them here. Further, his carelessness would seem the more puzzling if, as I have argued, he was seeking in 1691 to propitiate the court. Yet we have independent evidence that, even while finishing *Cleomenes*, he continued to hope for court favor. The day after receiving £30 from Tonson for the play, he wrote a letter to Dorset, his patron and William's Lord Chamberlain, begging a favor from Mary herself: "if I had confidence enough my Lord, I would presume to mind you of a favour which your Lordship formerly gave me some hopes of from the Queen."[25] Unless we are willing to accuse Dryden of the most calculated double-dealing—of trying to cash in on *King Arthur* before the appearance of the Jacobite *Cleomenes* could antagonize the court—we must conclude either that he saw no parallel at all in his new play, or that, though aware of the parallel, he felt it involved no attack on the court.

If we may trust Dryden's own assertion in his *Preface*, the former of these was in fact the case: "I dare assure you, that here is no parallel to be found: it is neither compliment, nor satire; but a plain story, more strictly followed than any which has appeared upon the stage" (p. 222). He prefixed Creech's translation of Plutarch's *Life of Cleomenes* to the first edition of the play to show how closely he had adhered to the facts. The closeness of a historical play to its source, however, is not in itself enough to disprove its function as a parallel; the Restoration parallelist normally presents the resemblances between present and past as the result of the natural and inevitable operation of historical laws, not as his own manufacture.[26] Throughout his long career, Dryden had repeatedly demonstrated his unequalled expertise at adapting literary and historical materials to contemporary political circumstances. It is inconceivable that he would have missed entirely the obvious correspondences between James and Cleomenes; and unlikely that, if he had nothing to say by manipulating these correspondences, he would have risked offending the government merely because he happened to like the story.

We are left, then, with the second possibility—that Dryden meant a parallel of some kind but no direct criticism of the Revolution or the current government; and this, I will argue, is corroborated by his treatment of the parallel in the play itself. Dryden's political aim in *Cleomenes* is, I think, to show how respect and admiration for James may be reconciled with obedience to William and patriotic devotion to English interests and institutions. Poets "subsist not but on the favour of sovereign princes": both claimants to the sovereignty of England come out of *Cleomenes* looking rather well. Dryden carefully constructs his parallel so as to exclude from it all points of dispute between Williamites and Jacobites: William/Antigonus is neither treacherous nor despotic; James/Cleomenes is neither the national enemy waiting to resume his tyranny at the head of a foreign army, nor the wronged monarch forced into exile by ambitious and ungrateful subjects. His political circumstances matter at all only insofar as they provide the stuff of high tragedy, the occasion for heroic fortitude and constancy.

Any attempt to read *Cleomenes* as straightforward Jacobite polemic must first encounter the obvious fact that, however similar in effect, the causes of Cleomenes's exile are strikingly different from those of James's. In *Don Sebastian* and *Amphitryon* Dryden directs his attack primarily against what he sees as the treachery and ingratitude of the English political nation and the ruthless ambition of the usurper. In *Cleomenes* there is not the least hint that Sparta is either responsible for Cleomenes's exile or able to effect his return. We are at first led to expect in Antigonus the evil foreign conqueror of Jacobite polemic; but when he is at last described at the end of Act I, he seems rather a liberator than a plunderer:

> think some king,
> Who loved his people, took a peaceful progress
> To some far distant place of his dominions;
> Smiled on his subjects, as he rode in triumph,
> And strewed his plenty, wheresoe'er he passed.
> Nay, raise your thoughts yet higher;—think some deity,
> Some better Ceres, drawn along the sky
> By gentle dragons, scattered as she flew
> Her fruitful grains upon the teeming ground,
> And bade new harvests rise.
> . . . .
> The soldiers marched, as in procession, slow;
> And entered Sparta like a choir of priests,
> As if they feared to tread on holy ground.
> No noise was heard; no voice, but of the crier,
> Proclaiming peace and liberty to Sparta.
> At that, a peal of loud applause rang out,
> And thinned the air, till even the birds fell down
> Upon the shouters' heads: the shops flew open,
> And all the busy trades renewed their tasks;
> No law was changed, no custom was controlled;
> That had Lycurgus lived, or you returned,
> So Sparta would have shown.
>
> (P. 284)

This is the only passage in which Antigonus and the conquest of Sparta appears; but it is enough in itself to disarm the parallel of any Jacobite sting and to justify its author in expecting government favor. The king has changed, but the ancient constitution of Sparta remains as Lycurgus left it. Further, Antigonus has no time to plunder: he is called away to defend his native Macedonia against foreign invaders; and having won a great victory, he dies in triumph. Dryden's Jacobite view of the Revolution is retained only in Antigonus's assumption of rule by conquest, and this single detail guarantees the sincerity of the rest. Unlike the "Sovereign High" at the end of *King Arthur*, this king is neither adopted nor indifferent to his "crown at home." William is praised here not for those qualities the lack of which brought him into public disfavor but for those which he genuinely possessed and for which he was generally admired.

Though Cleomenes loses his throne by conquest rather than revolution, Dryden nevertheless contrives to include a revolution of sorts in his play, and his portrayal of it is no less surprising than his portrayal of Antigonus. At the end of the play, Cleomenes and his friends attempt to rally the Egyptians against the tyrant Ptolemy, whom they hope to replace with his brave and honest brother Magas. The polemic of the rebels is rather English and Whig than Greek or Egyptian: they declare for "liberty," and Cleanthes begs his father to "Engage not for an arbitrary power, / That odious weight upon a free-born soul" (p. 355). Significantly, no Egyptian Tory rises up to remind the rebels that innovation is the blow of fate. Rather, the revolution fails because of the slavish fearfulness of the people, who disperse in comic terror at the first sound of the government's approach: "Every one for himself. The government is a-coming" (p. 354).[27] Here Dryden is clearly entertaining the possibility that under certain circumstances lawful monarchs may justly be dethroned in popular insurrections. A principled Jacobite could hardly go further than this in conciliating his opponents.

As Sparta lacks England's Revolution, so Egypt lacks France's continental war. The lazy and ineffective Ptolemy bears little resemblance to any contemporary English version of Louis XIV. Yet there is one suggestive similarity. James records in his *Memoirs* that in the months following his return to France after his defeat at the Boyne, he had tried to persuade Louis to help him in an invasion of England:

But his most Christian Majesty was dissatisfied with the King's late conduct, either of himself or the insinuations of his minister. He was averse to another expedition, which might, he thought be as hastily relinquished. He pretended an indisposition, and would not see the King, till in fact it was too late to do any thing. When the King observed this cause of delay, his patience never in his life underwent such another trial. . . . But he was destined to be a victim to patience by Providence; which his friends, as well as his enemies, exercised by turns. He even pressed to be permitted to go on board the fleet. This was denied, as nothing, they said could be done, without land-forces.[28]

There are several suggestive similarities here to Cleomenes's dealings with Ptolemy: in addition to the denial of aid, we have the underhand "insinuations" of a minister and the humble request "even to go on board the fleet." Whether or not some hint of this story had filtered through to Dryden, he clearly needed somehow to drive a wedge between Louis and James if he hoped to succeed in celebrating James's heroism in a manner acceptable to the Williamites. He thus constructs his play from a story that allows him to transfer the blame for James's misfortunes from England to England's great adversary. In the untroubled realm of art, William, James, and England could be presented in alliance against the tyrant Louis and his slavish subjects.

Dryden, then, depicts Sparta and Egypt, Antigonus and Ptolemy, in such a way as to clear from his path the obstacles presented by their contemporary counterparts to his celebration of the heroic fortitude of his king in exile. Even this, however, is not enough; before he can display Cleomenes's heroism, he must first define and qualify the admiration he feels for it. Cleomenes may be great, but he lacks private wisdom and public benevolence; and Dryden devotes Act I to the exhibition of these deficiencies. At the beginning of the play, Cleomenes is bemoaning his misfortunes. His mother enters and chides him for his grief, whereupon he grows boastful, though still convinced of his ruin. He compares his wife and mother to

Two twining vines about this elm, whose fall
Must shortly—very shortly, crush you both.
And yet I will not go to ground,
Without a noble ruin round my trunk:
The forest shall be shaken when I sink,

And all the neighbouring trees
Shall groan, and fall beneath my vast destruction.

(P. 277)

Cleomenes's fifteen-year-old son Cleonidas, inflated, despite his
age, with martial enthusiasm, applauds this resolution; declares his
father will triumph; huffs at his stepmother's doubts; and resolves
to fight at his side: "And though you say, I have but fifteen years, /
We Spartans take ten strides before our age, / And start beyond
dull nature" (p. 278). Cleomenes approvingly predicts his son will
"soon shoot up a hero" and remembers begetting him in "the
pride of conquest."

Such military ardor is clearly meant to seem admirable; but if
we find its expression cloying and its intermixture with the most
intimate domestic relations unnerving, we may take comfort in
Cleora's weak and Pantheus's much stronger protests against it.
The account of Cleonidas's begetting is interrupted by Pantheus's
arrival. He has spent the morning merrily walking "with myself, in
laughing at the world, / Making a farce of life, where knaves, and
fools, / And madmen, that's all humankind, were actors" (p. 279).
This is exactly the attitude toward life which Dryden himself had
been cultivating in his prose; most recently in the *Dedication* of
Amphitryon, where he finds "no disposition in my self to Cry,
while the mad World is daily supplying me with such Occasions of
Laughter." Pantheus goes on to express another of Dryden's recurring ideas, one with specific application to Cleomenes's circumstances. Cleomenes asks what part Pantheus acted; he answers,
"As little as I could; and daily would have less, / So please the
gods, for that's a wise man's part" (p. 279). Like Dryden in the
Preface to *Cleomenes*, he has learned to possess his soul in patience. He eschews the kind of heroic endeavor Jupiter fosters in
Amphitryon and, like Arthur, submits himself to the will of the
gods.

Cleomenes, however, is unable to achieve such detachment:

Cleom: Would I could share thy balmy, even temper,
And milkiness of blood.
Panth. You may.
Cleom. As how?
Panth. By but forgetting you have been a king.

> *Cleom.* Then must I rust in Egypt, never more
> Appear in arms, and be the chief of Greece?
>
> (P. 280)

He goes on to swear by his "great forefather, Hercules" that he would rather face defeat than cease to struggle. He is seconded by his excitable son, who also invokes Hercules, and calls for trumpets and charges. Pantheus remarks, "If fortune takes not off this boy betimes, / He'll make mad work, and elbow all his neighbours"; and Cleonidas answers, "My neighbours! Little: Elbow all the world, / And push off kings, like counters, from the board, / To place myself the foremost" (p. 280). Cleora invites her husband to view "as in a glass, your darling fault, ambition, / Reflected in your son"; and Cleomenes answers, "My virtue rather" (p. 280). Cleomenes, the "Spartan hero," thus placed between the wise Pantheus and the overeager Cleonidas seems marred by the defect that compromises heroism in *Amphitryon* and *King Arthur*: a willingness to foster ambition at the expense of others' peace and in defiance of fate. Yet here Dryden uses this defect, not to criticize William, but to qualify his praise of James.

Once this defect has been established in the exposition, it is confirmed by Cleomenes's reaction to the first important event in the plot. Informed that the merchant Coenus has come with news of Sparta, Cleomenes anticipates his arrival with apparent dread that he will hear "how proud Antigonus / Led o'er Eurotes' banks his conquering troops, / And first to wondering Sparta showed a king, / A king that was not hers" (p. 281). He clears the stage so that his family will not be "polluted with such ills," and when Coenus arrives, can hardly contain his grief.

> I pr'ythee, gentle Coenus, tell the story
> Of ruined Sparta; leave no circumstance
> Untold, of all their woes; and I will hear thee,
> As unconcerned, as if thou told'st a tale
> Of ruined Troy. I pr'ythee, tell us how
> The victors robbed the shrines, polluted temples,
> Ransacked each wealthy house: —No, spare me that;
> Poor honest Sparta had no wealth to lose.
> But [*Raises his voice*] when thou com'st to tell of matrons
>   ravished,

And virgins forced, then raise thy voice,
And let me hear their howlings,
And dreadful shrieks, as in the act of rape.

(P. 283)

When Coenus denies that this has happened, Cleomenes's loud grief gives way to a quieter but apparently deeper sorrow. Coenus tells him that his "sick imagination feigns all this"; Cleomenes declares that he knows "what follows victory"; and Pantheus suggests the real source of these fears, "You interrupt, as if you would not know." There follows Coenus's flowery account of Antigonus's merciful proclamation of peace and liberty to Sparta. In despair, Cleomenes remarks, "If this indeed be true, / Then farewell, Sparta" (p. 285). His eager anticipation of rapine and plunder has been disappointed; he seems sincerely sorry that his country has been preserved. Selfish ambition can hardly go further than this.

Cleomenes's heroism, then, however great in its kind, destroys his own peace, and threatens the world's. A wise man would retire with Pantheus to laugh at the folly of man, and a good one would never grieve to hear that Sparta's matrons remain unravished and her virgins unforced. In reminding us of this, Dryden suggests, I think, his willingness to follow himself the wisest and best course. James is the victim of a cruel destiny, and we can pity his condition and admire his fortitude. But James has also become the pawn of France, and any attempt to rectify the injustice done him is likely to bring about a purposeless destruction of life and property without achieving any political good. In Act I of *Cleomenes* Dryden isolates James's heroic qualities from their political causes and effects and having done so can devote the remainder of the play to uninhibited and, at times, perhaps excessive celebration of them. By placing James and his predicament within the transcendent structure of high tragedy, Dryden gives them a memorable and coherent meaning: James becomes not a blundering politician, but the victim of a tragic fate and so worthy of the respect and admiration of both poet and audience. Dryden says of Cleomenes in his *Preface* that "Even his enemy, Polybius, though engaged in the contrary faction, yet speaks honourably of him, and especially of his last action in Egypt" (p. 226). Dryden's Williamite audience should do the same for James.

Dryden's mood may have begun to change even before he had finished *Cleomenes*. In a letter dated August 13, 1691, about two months before Dryden turned the manuscript over to Tonson, William Walsh asks him whether the play is finished,[29] and Thomas Southerne, in his *Dedication* of *The Wives Excuse*, mentions that Dryden called on him to help complete the last act. In any case the *Dedication* and *Preface* of *Cleomenes*, written almost a year after Dryden must have begun the play, but within a few weeks of his struggles with the government over its suppression, employ a far less conciliatory tone than the *Dedication* of *King Arthur*. In their uncompromising defiance of the badness of the age and their rigorous subordination of the political to the literary, they resemble *Eleanora* and the *Discourse Concerning Satire*, both written in 1692. Like *King Arthur*, *Cleomenes* is dedicated to a prominent politician who was celebrated in *Absalom and Achitophel* for standing by Charles and who fell out with James before the Revolution; and, as in the earlier work, Dryden emphasizes his long association with the dedicatee. Here, however, that association is domestic and personal rather than political: he has read to his patron's family; and his daughter and wife have been especially kind to him (p. 216). Further, he barely mentions Rochester's political triumphs of either the past or the present; rather, he praises his literary accomplishments.

To describe his relation to Rochester, he employs an image of literary transcendence drawn from classic poetry: "Ariosto . . . has given us a fine allegory of two swans; who, when Time had thrown the writings of many poets into the river of oblivion, were ever in a readiness to secure the blest, and bear them aloft into the temple of immortality." He first associates Rochester with the swans, then supposes Ariosto "means only that some excellent writers, almost as few in number as the swans, have rescued the memory of their patrons from forgetfulness and time" (p. 214). In either case, Rochester and Dryden are safely placed in a realm beyond the merely temporal and upheld by literary merit. Further, despite Rochester's accomplishments as a politician, Dryden is careful to celebrate him for his apparently more important accomplishments as a reader and patron of poetry:

> to your experience in State affairs, you have also joined no vulgar erudition, which all your modesty is not able to conceal: for, to un-

derstand critically the delicacies of Horace is a height to which few of our noblemen have arrived; and that this is your deserved commendation, I am a living evidence, as far, at least, as I can be allowed a competent judge on that subject. Your affection to that admirable Ode, which Horace writes to his Maecenas, and which I had the honour to inscribe to you, is not the only proof of this assertion. You may please to remember that . . . you took me aside, and pleased yourself with repeating to me . . . the Ode to Barine, wherein you were so particularly affected with that elegant expression, *Juvenumque prodis publica cura.* There is indeed the virtue of a whole poem in those words; that *curiosa felicitas,* which Petronius so justly ascribes to our author. The barbarity of our language is not able to reach it; yet, when I have leisure, I mean to try how near I can raise my English to his Latin; though in the meantime, I cannot but imagine to myself, with what scorn his sacred *manes* would look on so lame a translation as I could make.

(P. 215)

Beneath this self-deprecation, Dryden clearly casts himself and Rochester as the English Horace and Maecenas, men whom the details of politics cannot reach.

A similar contempt for the merely local and topical can be felt throughout *Dedication* and *Preface.* Dryden begins the *Dedication* by thanking Rochester for "a just and honourable action, in redeeming this play from the persecution of my enemies" (p. 213). He is careful here to play down the political motive behind its suppression: it was banned only through the malice of personal enemies. In the *Preface,* he proclaims his indifference to these enemies:

I know it will be here expected, and I should write somewhat concerning the forbidding of my play; but, the less I say of it, the better. And, besides, I was so little concerned at it, that, had it not been on consideration of the actors, who were to suffer on my account, I should not have been at all solicitous whether it were played or no. Nobody can imagine that, in my declining age, I write willingly, or that I am desirous of exposing, at this time of day, the small reputation which I have gotten on the theatre. The subsistence which I had from the former Government is lost; and the reward I have from the stage is so little, that it is not worth my labour.

(Pp. 221–222)

Here Dryden combines professions of age and poverty with a tone of defiance: he makes no money from public approval, and therefore has no reason to seek it. Indeed, in the current political climate, concern for such approval is likely to destroy the literary value of one's work. Dryden complains that his play

> had been garbled before by the superiors of the play-house; and I cannot reasonably blame them for their caution, because they are answerable for anything that is publicly represented; and their zeal for the Government is such, that they had rather lose the best poetry in the world, than give the least suspicion of their loyalty. The short is, that they were diligent enough to make sure work, and to geld it so clearly in some places, that they took away the very manhood of it.
>
> (P. 222)

Political slavishness, Dryden suggests, emasculates poetry; he was later to develop this theme at length in the *Discourse Concerning Satire.* Here he implies that the proper attitude toward the public and its topical concerns is scornful indifference, and he ends his *Preface* with lofty disdain: "I have learned to possess my soul in patience, and not to be much disquieted with any disappointment of this nature" (p. 227). Dryden's experiment with conciliation had come to an end.

4. The Poet, Not the Man: Poetry and Prose, 1692– 1700

"To My Honour'd Kinsman" is one of the only works on the rhetorical purposes of which Dryden comments in his letters. In the poem he celebrates his cousin's (and by implication his own) scorn of public favor, beginning with a description of happy retreat from public cares:

> How Bless'd is He, who leads a Country Life,
> Unvex'd with anxious Cares, and void of Strife!
> Who studying Peace, and shunning Civil Rage,
> Enjoy'd his Youth, and now enjoys his Age.[1]

Effective political action is described not as heroic endeavor, but as untroubled stolidity: because he is "unwilling to be Great" Driden is unusually well qualified to serve in Parliament; and while there he urges the country to retreat from continental military entanglements as he himself has shunned public life.[2] At the end of the poem, Dryden briefly suggests his own indifference to the public: he is recording the actions of his kinsman for posterity, not urging his immediate readers to share his political views. Though in the *Preface* to *Fables* he mentions the poem only incidentally, as an "original paper" that is to be judged in comparison with his other poems on the basis of its literary merit, in his letters he is clearly worrying about its political content. He sent it to the Williamite official Charles Montague, so that it might be approved as free of political subversion: Dryden promises him that "nothing relateing to the publique shall stand, without your permission."[3] He declares his description of a parliament man "a Memorial of my own Principles to all Posterity"; but the defiance of contemporary judgment that such a characterization implies is rather weakened by the following sentence: "I have consulted the Judgment of my Un-byassd [presumably Williamite] friends, who have some of them the honour to be known to you; & they think there is nothing which can justly give offence."[4] During the ensuing months he seems to have worried a good deal about the public reception of the poem. He tells his cousin Mrs. Steward that he has shown the verses on Driden and the Duchess of Ormond to Montague and Dorset, who "are of opinion that I never writt better. My other friends are divided in their Judgments which to preferr: but the greater part are for those to my dear Kinsman; which I have Cor-rected with so much care, that they will now be worthy of his Sight: & do neither of us any dishonour after our death." In the same letter, Dryden implies that he intended in the poem a more immediate political effect: he expects that "My Cousin Driden, & the Country Party" will oppose a standing army, "for when a Spirit is raisd, 'tis hard conjureing him down again."[5] After the poem's publication in *Fables*, Dryden repeats that "I always thought my Verses to my Cousin Driden were the best of the whole; & to my comfort the Town thinks them so." In the same letter he mentions the commons' "Entire victory" over the king and lords: and quietly rejoices in the probability of further conflict "whensoever they next meet."[6]

Dryden's demonstrable concern with the rhetorical effect of "To My Honour'd Kinsman" might lead us to suspect a similar concern in other of his last works. However, in analyzing most of Dryden's work in the nineties, especially the translations and long prose treatises that dominate his work after 1692, most critics seem to accept without question Dryden's frequent professions of retirement from public life. The topical allusions that permeate these works are taken as more or less direct embodiments of Dry-den's personal feelings and principles, which serve an expressive rather than a rhetorical function. Thus Arthur W. Hoffman ob-serves that in the 1690s "Dryden expresses himself as looking back, reviewing, summing up, imbued with the attitude of a cap-tain at the end of a voyage"; and "to Dryden, in the last decade of his life, the king was nothing. He was, at the end of his career, more willing than ever to leave the world to Caesar; he saw more clearly that Caesar was beguiled." Reuben Brower finds in Dry-den's "latest phase" a "poetry of retirement" that anticipates the early Pope. Earl Miner claims that Dryden's conversion gave him "an increasing sense of isolation that led him . . . to a kind of private allusive style." George Watson finds in Dryden's last work a "secret language" that expresses a "stubborn and dedicated recusancy" more private than any "declaration of Jacobitism." Thomas H. Fujimura sees the Virgil translation as "a record of Dryden's own spiritual crisis and progress over a period of three difficult years."[7] Dryden himself does all he can to encourage this view: but his professions of retirement and isolation are, I think, themselves rhetorical, part of a deliberate and self-conscious presentation of himself and his materials in a certain way to a certain audience.

The methods and aims of Dryden's rhetoric are, however, quite different after 1692 from those that inform his work from *The Hind and the Panther* to *Cleomenes*. We have seen that after his conversion he attempts to repair his loss of political authority through an invocation of poetic tradition. This allows him to appear to examine contemporary politics with clear-sighted objectivity and according to standards derived from the heart of European culture. Thus in *King Arthur* the contemporary is enveloped in a pastiche of literary romance, in *The Hind and the Panther* in an elaborate and self-consciously traditional structure of fable and allegory. To be sure, in his last works he expresses his political principles no less frequently and deliberately: he praises the subjects of his complimentary verses for escaping the contamination of the age, he discusses purely literary principles and relations in pointed topical metaphors, and he finds ample scope even in his translations for miscellaneous observations on rebellion and revolution, prerogative and property, war and taxation, standing armies, usurpation, and tyranny. Further, his last works are, if anything, even more saturated in cultural and literary tradition: his prose consists primarily of discussion of the classics, his verse of translations of them. But the relation between the traditional and contemporary changes after 1692. In the works written between 1687 and 1692, the traditional functions as a norm against which the contemporary is to be measured: the supposed crimes of William and his party are exposed through romance, fable, farce, or tragedy as deplorable aberrations in the common pursuit of truth and justice. In the later works these crimes, though no less deplorable, come to seem inevitable and therefore less urgently in need of correction. Dryden provides for them a broad historical context that makes them appear not aberrant but lamentably normal, not avoidable violations of transcendent moral law, but contemporary manifestations of evils endemic to all human society. In this context the questions of right, legitimacy, and justice with which Dryden had been concerned since the Revolution are made almost irrelevant.

Dryden had not, however, abandoned the struggle; he had abandoned only the weapons that seemed to have proven ineffective against William and dangerous to himself, and taken up others in their place. By portraying politics as incorrigibly base and inevitably futile, he at once excuses his own arguably erratic political career and demonstrates his detachment as a poet. Throughout his last works he insistently portrays himself as exclusively concerned with literary matters; the notably discursive structure of these works is designed to suggest a random tour through a mind so richly cultivated that the reader is rewarded at every turn with fresh prospects of literary knowledge and insight. Having established his poetic credentials, Dryden is free to return to political criticism as a poet; the main focus of his attack on William's government is no longer its illegality and injustice, though these continue to appear in general remarks on the behavior of governments in all ages, but rather its failure to support the arts, which, Dryden claims, are alone capable of raising the nation and its rulers above the level of politics and so rescuing them from deserved oblivion.

I. Rhetorical Definition of Poet and Audience

The historical pessimism of Dryden's last works is well known;[8] it is most clearly expressed in the *Dedication* of *Examen Poeticum*: "No Government has been, or ever can be, wherein Time-Servers and Blockheads will not be uppermost. The persons are only chang'd, but the same juglings in State, the same Hypocrisie in Religion, the same Self-Interest, and Mis-management, will remain for ever. Blood and Money will be lavish'd in all Ages, only for the Preferment of new Faces, with old Consciences."[9] Of course, Dryden did not in 1692 suddenly renounce a progressive view of history for a cyclical or a static one. He had used various views in his earlier work for various rhetorical purposes. *Annus Mirabilis* concludes with a prophecy of English commercial empire, *The Medall* with a hypothetical prediction of a new cycle of civil war followed by restoration. The *Dedication* of *Don Sebastian* begins, as we have seen, with a vision of eternally recurring revolutions. In these works, however, Dryden is urging his audience to embrace the good or escape the ill he predicts by adopting a certain political policy—support for Charles or resistance to William. In *Examen Poeticum* we have neither progress nor hypothetical cycles but permanent stasis about which nothing can be done.

When he comes to praise the political behavior of his patrons, he is careful to place it in a historical context that confirms this view. In the *Dedication* of the *Georgics*, he compares Chesterfield to Scipio. The Roman retired when the public "began to grow restiff and ungovernable"; and the Englishman, knowing that "Ingratitude is not confin'd to Commonwealths," never entered public business at all.[10] The gesture is familiar from the *Dedication* of *King Arthur*, where Halifax is praised for retiring like Cicero in troubled times. But whereas in Halifax's case Dryden's language— "the torrent of the people," "the riot of a multitude"—suggests a specific parallel between the Roman Civil Wars and the English Revolution, here the reference includes a general "ingratitude" that afflicts all political systems in all ages. In the *Dedication* of the *Pastorals*, Clifford's constancy is compared with that of his ancestors of "the Ancient House of *Cumberland*" during the War of the Roses: "Your Forefathers have asserted the Party which they chose 'till death, and dy'd for its defence in the Fields of Battel" (p. 872). Again there is no specific parallel: the seventeenth century is similar to the fifteenth only in providing no less exacting trials of political constancy. Even the more conventional heroism of the duke of Ormond is presented in this dreary universal context: his military skills are praiseworthy "since the perverse Tempers of Mankind, since Oppression on one side, and Ambition on the other, are sometimes the unavoidable Occasions of War" (p. 1441).

Political parallel, Dryden's usual instrument for attacking William's government immediately after the Revolution, fades from his work after 1692. If all political systems are equally vicious, there can be no point in drawing specific comparisons between one's own and those of history, myth, or fable. Instead, Dryden favors general statements that suggest the congruence of politics in his own age with the universal condition. In "To My

Honour'd Kinsman," he remarks that private gentlemen take more pleasure in hunting than "Princes" who "once on slipp'ry Thrones were plac'd; / And chasing, sigh to think themselves are chas'd" (ll. 69–70). Levine sees in these lines an "attitude of near-exhaustion" that "cannot brook weighing the possible differences between reigns—all is of a piece, each age will run the same round."[11] Similarly general remarks are to be found throughout Dryden's late work. As the countess of Abingdon loved her husband and creatures love their god, "So Subjects love just Kings, or so they shou'd."[12] In the *Preface* to *Fables*, having anticipated certain points that he had meant to save for later, Dryden compares himself to "most Kings, *who love to be in Debt*, are all for present Money, no matter how they pay it afterwards" (p. 1450). There are dozens of such brief innuendos, all of which suggest that the crimes of William and his supporters are only contemporary examples of behavior typical of all kings and subjects. This typicality makes Dryden's opponents not less criminal but more contemptible.

Even the more extended passages of historical analysis in Dryden's prose have the same generalizing and belittling effect. His account in the *Dedication* of the *Aeneis* of the civil conflicts that led to the destruction of the Roman commonwealth and the rule of Augustus has, as Steven Zwicker has shown, a clear reference to similar conflicts between rebels and royalists, Whigs and Tories, which for Dryden led to the destruction of the English constitution and the usurpation of William.[13] It does not, however, form a political parallel. The civil wars begin when "*Marius* and *Cinna*, like Captains of the Mobb, under the specious Pretence of Publick Good, and of doing Justice on the Oppressours of their Liberty, reveng'd themselves, without Form of Law, on their private Enemies" (p. 1012); and Sylla, when he opposed them in the cause of the nobles, also "had nothing but Liberty and Reformation in his Mouth" and similarly "Sacrific'd the Lives, and took the Estates of all his Enemies, to gratifie those who brought him to Power" (p. 1012). Both sides bear some likeness to the rebels of the 1640s, the Whigs of the 1680s, and the Williamites of the 1690s, all of whom, for Dryden, pursued private ends under the pretence of public reforms. But since both sides are equally criminal, it is impossible to associate them with those recent conflicts in which Dryden had eagerly supported what he considered the better side.

He places specific topical allusions within a generalizing frame. After the wars, Pompey, Crassus, and Caesar "found the Sweets of Arbitrary Power" and ruled as "Patriots for their own Interest," until Caesar overthrew Pompey and "became a Providential Monarch" (p. 1013). The operative phrases here, "arbitrary power" and "providential monarch," apply equally to Cromwell and to William, since obedience to both was justified as concurrence in the will of heaven; but the series of events that led to Caesar's dictatorship lack any clear application. Dryden had often enough displayed his talent for adapting the details of history to the present: his failure to do so here is, I think, intentional. His purpose is not to trace correspondences between specific causes and results in the manner of *Don Sebastian*; it is rather to suggest that political systems inevitably rise and fall by the operation of the same human passions, are explained and excused by the same shifts and pretences, and so occupy a level far beneath that to which Dryden as a poet wishes to lay claim.

Perhaps the clearest indication of a change in Dryden's rhetorical concerns after 1692 is his last play, *Love Triumphant*, performed in 1694. Unlike *Don Sebastian*, *King Arthur*, and *Cleomenes*, the action involves no contested throne: Veramond, the cruel king of Arragon, seems to have a successive title. There is a competition between two princes for Veramond's daughter, but unlike the competition between Jupiter and Amphitryon for Alcmena, it is not given political meaning. The unworthy candidate, Garcia, is a relatively minor figure, and the worthy one, Alphonso, is blocked first by the supposition that the woman in question is his sister, then by Veramond's disapproval. Yet a number of passages contrasting the behavior of Veramond and Alphonso do have topical meaning. Veramond and Ramirez, king of Castile, went to war without good reason, and Ramirez has grown contrite:

> A trivial accident begot this war;
> Some paltry bounds of ill-distinguished earth,
> A clod that lay betwixt us unascertained,
> And royal pride, on both sides, drew our swords:
> Thus monarchs quarrel, and their subjects bleed.[14]

The lesson accords with opposition protest against the war between France and the allies, but it is generalized to include all monarchs and subjects. Alphonso, who has captured Ramirez in battle, pleads with Veramond for his release:

> Think on the slippery state of human things,
> The strange vicissitudes, and sudden turns
> Of war, and fate recoiling on the proud,
> To crush a merciless and cruel victor.
>
> (P. 385)

Veramond is inexorable. He retains over Ramirez

> The right of conquest; for, when kings make war,
> No laws betwixt two sovereigns can decide,
> But that of arms, where fortune is the judge,
> Soldiers the lawyers, and the bar the field.
>
> (P. 386)

Alphonso has allowed Ramirez to keep his sword as a "mark of sovereign justice" that should never "be wanting to a monarch"; Veramond again appeals to raw force: "Then, when he lost the power, he lost the claim, and marks of sovereign right."

The good Alphonso acts on a principle exactly opposite to this. When, later in the play, Ramirez advises him to make war on Veramond, he refuses, thus exposing himself to capture and execution:

> You've set an image of so vast destruction
> Before my sight, that reason shuns the approach,
> And dares not view the fearful precipice.
> . . . .
> What have the people done, the sheep of princes,
> That they should perish for the shepherd's fault?
> They bring their yearly wool, to clothe their owners;
> And yet, when bare themselves, are culled for slaughter.
> Should I do this, what could the wolf do more
> Than what the master did?
>
> (P. 446)

Many of William's crimes are involved in this contrast: his reliance on force over justice, his prosecution of an expensive, bloody, and unnecessary war; but they are presented within a universal context of kings and people, sovereigns, princes, soldiers, and subjects, the terms of political conflict in all ages.

So far this seems near enough to personal meditation: it may be argued that Dryden could not hope to inspire political opposition to William through a few incidental reflections on kings and subjects. It has, however, a public, rhetorical purpose: its effect is to excuse Dryden's apparently inconsistent political behavior, since *sub species aeternitatis* politics has little meaning, and more importantly to degrade politics in general and to elevate poetry, to portray the poet Dryden as one who sees all things, including current politics, clearly and completely from on high. Since 1687 Dryden had had to create an audience to replace what he had lost by his conversion and James's misdeeds. In *The Hind and the Panther, Don Sebastian,* and *Amphitryon* he writes in the fading hope that his principles will be vindicated by history; he warns the Williamites that their triumph will be brief and contrasts their inconstancy with his own firm adherence to the principles that preserved the nation and the monarchy during the exclusion crisis. In *King Arthur* and *Cleomenes* he attempts to regain a place in the national debate without compromising his politics or his religion. After *Cleomenes* he seems to have realized that as a political writer he was irreparably discredited, and to have abandoned the struggle. As a poet, however, he could still claim his audience's respect and attention; and therefore it is exclusively as a poet that he presents himself after 1692, even in such politically committed works as "To My Honour'd Kinsman." In the *Postscript* of the *Aeneis* he appeals directly to those who "without considering the Man, have been Bountiful to the Poet" (p. 1425); the same appeal runs through the whole of his late work. Repeatedly he suggests that his poetic achievement only is permanent and important: in his personal circumstances and political behavior he merely recapitulates patterns inherent in the human condition—as do also William III, his supporters, and his opponents. His pointed references to the crimes of the government are carefully placed within the universal vision that only a poet might claim.

In an interesting series of articles Thomas H. Fujimura has claimed that in his late works Dryden grew "strongly personal, and often private" and that he expressed his "personal anguish" in a "generalized and universalized" form because of his commitment to "neoclassical" literary strategies.[15] Fujimura's sense of Dryden's presentation of personal circumstances in a universalized form is, I think, quite accurate; but the purpose of this self-presentation is not expressive but rhetorical. Dryden avoids the confessional and invokes the universal not out of some neoclassical reflex, but as part of a deliberate rhetorical strategy. He assumes in his readers a knowledge of his personal circumstances and beliefs and encourages them to place that knowledge in the transcendent context he provides them, in the hope that they will consider the poet rather than the man. All of Dryden's postrevolutionary works are filled with references to his advanced age and broken health, his quixotic loyalty to James, his poverty and his sufferings; but in the works after 1692, these references are placed in a context that aligns all poets in all ages, and so deflects interest from the private man to the public poet. He offers to his patron Clifford "the wretched remainder of a sickly Age, worn out with Study, and oppress'd by Fortune: without other support than the Constancy and Patience of a Christian" (*Dedication* of *Virgil's Pastorals*, p. 869). This may seem mere personal complaint; it is, however, prefaced by an elaborate metaphor in which Charles II appears as Augustus, Clifford's father as Pollio, and Dryden as Virgil; and it is followed by a sort of inverted comparison of Dryden's career with Virgil's; Virgil wrote the *Pastorals* in youth, Dryden translates them at an age more advanced than that at which Virgil died. He places his relations with Clifford in a similarly broad context: among the Romans "Patronage and Clientship always descended from the Fathers to the Sons; and . . . the same *Plebeian* Houses, had recourse to the same Patrician Line, which had formerly protected them: and follow'd their Principles and Fortunes to the last. So that I am your Lordship's by descent, and part of your Inheritance" (p. 872). In the *Dedication* of the *Georgics*, Dryden again mentions his age; then describes the effects of Horace's and Virgil's age on their abilities; then the effects of age on the abilities of mankind in northern climates; and he concludes by applying this observation to Chesterfield, also an old man. These "confessional" passages are aggressively impersonal. Their effect is to correct any tendency in the reader toward considering Dryden as an individual with a particular past and a potentially objectionable set of beliefs: we are to see his life within a pattern that necessarily orders the lives of all poets and all men.

In the remarks on the inevitability of political corruption quoted above from the *Dedication* of *Examen Poeticum*, Dryden's main purpose is again to invite us to see him rather as a poet than a political agent. "Why am I grown Old," he asks, "in seeking so barren a Reward as Fame? The same Parts and Application, which have made me a Poet, might have rais'd me to any Honours of the Gown, which are often given to Men of as little Learning and less Honesty than my self." Dryden then launches his attack on government, and comments,

> These Considerations, have given me a kind of Contempt for those who have risen by unworthy ways. I am not asham'd to be Little, when I see them so Infamously Great. Neither, do I know, why the Name of Poet should be Dishonourable to me; if I am truly one, as I hope I am; for I will never do any thing, that shall dishonour it. The Notions of Morality are known to all Men: None can pretend Ignorance of those Idea's which are In-born in Mankind: and if I see one thing, and practise the contrary, I must be Disingenuous, not to acknowledge a clear Truth, and Base to Act against the light of my own Conscience. For the Reputation of my Honesty, no Man can question it, who has any of his own: For that of my Poetry, it shall either stand by its own Merit; or fall for want of it. Ill Writers are usually the sharpest Censors.
>
> (Pp. 363–364)

He proceeds with a lengthy attack on bad critics, who are described as rebels against and usurpers of poetic merit. Dryden suggests that he should be judged not by political standards, but by moral and poetic ones. His renunciation of politics is made to date not from the Revolution, but from his youth, when he chose the poetic vocation over the clerical.

But Dryden's presentation of himself as a poet does more than deflect our interest from his disastrous political career. It serves also to suggest the clarity of his vision and the permanent value of his ideals. His tendency in his earlier postrevolutionary work to claim as a poet a position outside and above the contemporary becomes even more pronounced after 1692. In the *Dedication* of *Eleanora*, for example, he presents himself as a sort of Homeric bard. He is one of the "Priests of Apollo" who "must wait till the God comes rushing on us, and invades us with a fury, which we are not able to resist: which gives us double strength while the Fit continues, and leaves us languishing and spent at its departure."[16] In *Eleanora* he claims to have "prophecy'd beyond my natural power"; he has been "transported by the multitude and variety of my Similitudes" and ignored the restraint of judgment, like "the inimitable *Pindar*, who stretches on these Pinnions out of sight, and is carried upward, as it were, into another World" (pp. 231– 232). This forthrightly vatic persona is, I think, unprecedented in Dryden's prose and very unlike his usual assumption of gentlemanly diffidence and ease. The same sense of elevation pervades the poem itself.[17] To describe something as apparently prosaic as Eleanora's "prudent Management" of her income, Dryden reaches toward the ultralunary:

> Thus Heav'n, though All-sufficient, shows a thrift
> In his Oeconomy, and bounds his gift:
> Creating for our Day, one single Light;
> And his Reflection too supplies the Night:
> Perhaps a thousand other Worlds, that lye
> Remote from us, and latent in the Sky
> Are lighten'd by his Beams, and kindly nurst;
> Of which our Earthly Dunghil is the worst.
>
> (ll. 75–82)

The countess of Abingdon's domestic economy is forgotten in this grand vision of transcendence. Indeed the poem gives us no clear idea of Eleanora's personality; the emphasis throughout is on the distance between the earthly and the celestial. Even when Dryden commands his muse to restrict itself to earth, it soon reascends:

> Muse, down again precipitate thy flight;
> For how can Mortal Eyes sustain Immortal Light!
> But as the Sun in Water we can bear,
> Yet not the Sun, but his Reflection there,
> So let us view her here, in what she was;
> And take her Image, in this watry Glass:
> Yet look not ev'ry Lineament to see;
> . . . .
> For where such various Vertues we recite,
> 'Tis like the Milky-Way, all over bright,
> But sown so thick with Stars, 'tis undistinguish'd Light.
>
> (ll. 134–145)

Though he later complains that "Distance and Altitude" conceal from him Eleanora's place in heaven (l. 269), the poetic vocation he describes in the *Dedication* allows him at least to define that altitude, and by it to measure the world's true littleness.

In the penultimate verse paragraph, Dryden comes down to earth with something of a jolt:

Let this suffice: Nor thou, great Saint, refuse
This humble Tribute of no vulgar Muse:
Who, not by Cares, or Wants, or Age deprest,
Stems a wild Deluge with a dauntless brest:
And dares to sing thy Praises, in a Clime
Where Vice triumphs, and Vertue is a Crime:
Where ev'n to draw the Picture of thy Mind,
Is Satyr on the most of Humane Kind:
Take it, while yet 'tis Praise; before my rage
Unsafely just, break loose on this bad Age;
So bad, that thou thy self had'st no defence,
From Vice, but barely by departing hence.
                              (ll. 359–370)

But despite the violence of attack here, Dryden is careful to preserve his purely literary persona. His diction—"muse," "sing thy
praises," "draw the picture of thy mind"—reminds us that this is
art rather than polemic; and the tone and subject of the passage
are derived, as Miner tells us, from Juvenal's *Satire I*, and from
Donne, whom Dryden cites as the precedent for the form of his
poem in his *Dedication*.[18] Dryden carefully labels this passage in
the margin with a piece of literary jargon: it is the "*Epiphonema:
or close of the Poem*." In Dryden's last works, even the most direct
indignation is carefully folded within several layers of literary tradition.

If the poet is privileged to soar into the celestial sphere, he is
capable also of looking back on humanity from the timeless perspective of the gods. In the *Preface* to *Fables* Dryden claims such
an ability for Chaucer. In his *Canterbury Tales* he provides us with
"God's plenty":

We have our Fore-fathers and Great Grand-dames all before us, as they
were in *Chaucer*'s Days; their general Characters are still remaining in
Mankind, and even in *England*, though they are call'd by other Names
than those of *Moncks*, and *Fryars*, and *Chanons*, and *Lady Abesses*,
and *Nuns*: For Mankind is ever the same, and nothing lost out of
Nature, though every thing is alter'd.

(P. 1455)

The poet, Dryden suggests, sees through the particular habits and customs to the unchanging truth that lies beneath; from his perspective, distinctions between Catholic and Protestant, Whig and Tory, simply do not matter. Further, the poet who sees the eternal beneath the ephemeral is himself eternal: Chaucer has lived to Dryden's time despite changes in language and customs, and Dryden expects the same for himself. He concludes "To My Honour'd Kinsman," the most topical poem of his last years, with an invocation of poetic immortality:

> Praise-worthy Actions are by thee embrac'd;
> And 'tis my Praise, to make thy Praises last.
> For ev'n when Death dissolves our Humane Frame
> The Soul returns to Heav'n, from whence it came;
> Earth keeps the Body, Verse preserves the Fame.
> (ll. 205–209)

One of the most striking features of Dryden's late works is their extreme allusiveness and digressiveness.[19] Dryden had never written systematic prose criticism, but in his last years his tendency to spontaneous effusions on matters unrelated to his ostensible subject becomes far more pronounced. The long prose treatises are put together seemingly at random, and most of the original poems are so loosely structured as to admit of considerable rearrangement without apparent loss of meaning. Even in the translations, where he must follow the structures of his authors, Dryden introduces his modifications and additions without system; and his arrangement of translated works in the miscellanies and *Fables* seems arbitrary and unplanned. Dryden himself frequently calls attention to this discursiveness and finds various means of explaining it. In the *Discourse of Satire* he asks that it be excused as "the tattling Quality of Age, which . . . is always Narrative";[20] and in the *Preface* to *Fables* he attributes it to the associative habits of the human mind as described by Hobbes (p. 1446). In the *Dedication* of the *Aeneis* he professes to write "in a loose Epistolary way . . . after the Example of Horace, in his First Epistle of the Second Book to *Augustus Caesar*, and of that to the *Piso's*, which we call his *Art of Poetry*. In both of which he observes no Method that I can trace" (p. 1009); and in the *Preface* to *Fables* he cites another precedent: "the Nature of a Preface is rambling; never wholly out of the Way, nor in it. This I have learn'd from the Practice of honest *Montaign*" (p. 1450). These explanations, however, do more to establish Dryden's presentation of himself (as typical of all men, or of men in old age) and his work (as part of a general literary tradition) than to account for his style.

In fact this style is an important part of Dryden's rhetorical strategy in these years. We are never allowed to forget that we are in the presence of a poet. His ability to wander effortlessly among the literary and historical monuments of all ages suggests the magisterial expertise of a mind enriched by years of literary study. He describes this expertise directly in the *Preface* to *Fables*:

> What Judgment I had, increases rather than diminishes; and Thoughts, such as they are, come crowding in so fast upon me, that my only Difficulty is to chuse or to reject; to run them into Verse, or to give them the other Harmony of Prose. I have so long studied and practis'd both, that they are grown into a Habit, and become familiar to me.
>
> (Pp. 1446–1447)

Repeatedly in his late work he describes himself as carried away by an inundation of poetic material. In *Eleanora* he "was transported, by the multitude and variety of my Similitudes; which are generally the product of a luxuriant Fancy; and the wantonness of Wit" (p. 232); in the *Dedication* of the *Aeneis*, he must stop himself from falling into a lengthy consideration of the unity of time in drama: "here, my Lord, I must contract also, for, before I was aware, I was almost running into a long digression" (p. 1005); in describing Chaucer's pilgrims in the *Preface* to *Fables* he complains of "such a Variety of Game springing up before me, that I am distracted in my Choice, and know not which to follow" (p. 1455). The "practiced ease" that Miner finds in the late poetry is deliberately constructed by Dryden himself.[21]

Further, Dryden invites us to suppose that his mind has been so long and so thoroughly cultivated that his random musings are more pregnant with interest than the comprehensive but plodding systems of scholarly commentators. In his criticism and translations he uses his acknowledged expertise as a poet to differentiate himself from those mere pedants who, while they have knowledge, lack judgment and inspiration. Thus in the *Dedication* of *Examen Poeticum* he claims to "have given my Author's Sense, for the most part truly: for to mistake sometimes, is incident to all Men: And not to follow the *Dutch* Commentatours alwaies, may be forgiven to a Man, who thinks them, in general, heavy gross-witted Fellows; fit only to gloss on their own dull Poets" (p. 371). Similarly, in comparing Juvenal, Horace, and Persius in the *Discourse of Satire*, Dryden adjudicates the claims of their scholarly champions:

> It had been much fairer, if the Modern Critiques, who have imbark'd in the Quarrels of their favourite Authors, had rather given to each his proper due; without taking from another's heap, to raise their own. There is Praise enough for each of them in particular, without encroaching on his Fellows, and detracting from them, or Enriching themselves with the Spoils of others.
>
> (P. 50)

He implicitly contrasts his own fairness and objectivity with the blind fondness of "Critiques, who, having first taken a liking to one of these Poets, proceed to Comment on him, and to Illustrate him; after which they fall in love with their own Labours . . . they defend and exalt their Author, not so much for his sake as for their own" (p. 49). Similarly, in the *Preface* to *Fables* he contrasts his own "common Sense" to the deluded favoritism of Chaucer's latest editor, who "would make us believe . . . that there were really Ten Syllables in a Verse where we find but Nine" (p. 1453).

In the *Dedication* of the *Aeneis* Dryden structures his attack on plodding commentators so as to take account of his known political principles. There is a hint of anti-Williamite patriotism in his mention of "Dutch commentators" in the *Dedication* of *Examen Poeticum*; and this hint is fully developed in the *Dedication* of the *Aeneis*: "I shall," he says, "continue still to speak my Thoughts like a free-born Subject as I am; though such things, perhaps, as no *Dutch* Commentator cou'd, and I am sure no *French*-man durst" (p. 1016). Later he contrasts his discursive manner with the style of the French critic Segrais: "his Preface is a perfect piece of Criticism, full and clear, and digested into an exact Method; mine is loose, and, as I intended it, Epistolary. Yet I dwell on many things which he durst not touch: For 'tis dangerous to offend an Arbitrary Master" (p. 1020). By following no one's plan and changing subjects at will, Dryden may assert—in contradistinction to the slavish compatriots of both William and Louis—the freedom from prejudice and restraint which he insists upon as the birthright of an Englishman and the prerogative of a poet.

If the digressiveness and allusiveness of the late work imply the mastery of the poet, they assume the same mastery in the readers who must follow him. In a single paragraph on epic poetry in the *Discourse of Satire*, he assumes in his readers a detailed knowledge of Homer, Virgil, Statius, Lucan, Ariosto, Tasso, Boiardo, Martial, Owen, Spenser, Fleckno, Waller, the Greek Anthology, LeMoyne, Chapelain, and Scudéry. He need only mention Lucan's "Heat, and Affectation," Ariosto's luxuriousness of style, Tasso's "Episodes of *Sophronia, Erminia,* and *Armida*"; his readers, he implies, will draw upon their own experience of these works to confirm Dryden's insights (pp. 13–14). Similarly, the reader of *Fables* is assumed to have some knowledge of Ovid, Homer, Virgil, and Boccaccio: Dryden's *Preface* purports not to introduce and explain them to the neophyte, but rather to compare them by alluding to characteristics with which the reader is already familiar. Thus he claims that "the Figures of *Chaucer* are much more lively [than Ovid's], and set in a better Light: Which though I have not time to prove, yet I appeal to the Reader, and am sure he will clear me from Partiality" (p. 1451). Throughout his late criticism Dryden implies that he and his reader share fluency in five languages and a thorough knowledge of the literature and history of Greece, Rome, Italy, France, and England, which may be brought to the surface by a few brief reminders. By his digressiveness he suggests that we have outgrown the need for systematic treatises and can follow him easily in his explorations of the whole of literary culture. By the subtlest of rhetoric, Dryden flatters us into sharing his implicit view of the irrelevance of his diastrous political affiliations and into recognizing the importance of his literary achievement.

Indeed, in his last works Dryden is no less interested in defining his audience than in defining himself. He had always sought to create for his more rhetorical works an audience capable of being convinced by them—the "more moderate sort," for example, in "To the Reader" of *Absalom and Achitophel*.[22] But in his last works he creates for his purely literary persona a purely literary audience, one whose learning and tastes place it above the ignorance, prejudice, and pedantry of Dryden's enemies. Despite his abstract critical purposes in the *Discourse of Satire* and the *Dedication* of the *Aeneis*, Dryden is always aware of their status as epistles, and frequently interrupts his criticism to compliment his fellow poets Dorset and Mulgrave on the insight and expertise that make them peculiarly well qualified to understand him. Less literary patrons also are praised for the breadth of their reading and the depth of their appreciation. Chesterfield enjoys "a foundation of good Sense, and a cultivation of Learning" (p. 917); Clifford has read Virgil "with pleasure, and I dare say, with admiration in the Latine, of which you are a Master. You have added to your Natural Endowments, which without flattery are Eminent, the superstructures of Study, and the knowledge of good Authors" (p. 872). Radcliffe is "a Critick of the Genuine sort, who [has] Read the best Authours, in their own Languages, who perfectly distinguish[es] of their several Merits" (p. 367).

Dryden is not, however, unaware of the potential market for his translations among the less deeply learned; he defines these readers against those plodding and pedantic commentators whose favoritism, ill nature, and subservience contrast with his own benign objectivity and patriotic freedom. Whereas the dully literal Barten Holiday translated Juvenal for scholars,

> We write only for the Pleasure and Entertainment, of those Gentlemen and Ladies, who tho they are not Scholars are not Ignorant: Persons of Understanding and good Sense; who not having been conversant in the Original, or at least not having made *Latine* Verse so much their business, as to be Critiques in it, wou'd be glad to find, if the Wit of our Two great Authors, be answerable to their Fame.
>
> (P. 87)

Similarly, he contrasts the readers of *Fables* to those "old *Saxon* Friends" whose superstitious "Veneration for Antiquity" may lead them to dislike his version of Chaucer: "Let them neglect my Version, because they have no need of it. I made it for their sakes who understand Sense and Poetry, as well as they; when that Poetry and Sense is put into Words which they understand" (p. 1459).

Dryden's insistence on the purely literary nature of his audience is not, however, the only rhetorical strategy through which he attempts to avert the potential interference of politics with a proper appreciation of his work. He associates learning and taste with transcendence of political faction, ignorance and pedantry with fanatical devotion to the worst aspects of William and the Revolution. We are familiar with the first of these strategies from the dedications of *Don Sebastian*, *Amphitryon*, and *King Arthur*,

each of which is addressed to a prominent Williamite who is willing to ignore political differences where they interfere with literary
merit. After 1692, this strategy is given added power by a new
emphasis on social as well as literary transcendence. Dryden repeatedly associates the noble lineage of his dedicatees with their
ability to recognize his merit. Abingdon "may stand aside" from
the bad age "with the small Remainders of the *English* Nobility,
truly such, and unhurt your selves, behold the mad Combat"
(p. 234). Clifford is descended from "the Ancient House of *Cumberland*," Ormond from the Plantagenets, and both have inherited
Dryden with their titles and estates (*Georgics*, p. 872, *Fables*,
p. 1439). In admiring Dryden's work, the less noble reader falls in
with "the most Ancient, most Conspicuous, and most Deserving
Families in *Europe*" (*Fables*, p. 1439).

The literary, the social, and the political are all involved in the
threefold division of readers of poetry adapted from Segrais in the
Dedication of the *Aeneis*. The lowest class of readers

> like nothing but the Husk and Rhind of Wit; preferr a Quibble, a
> Conceit, an Epigram, before solid Sense, and Elegant Expression:
> These are Mobb-Readers: If *Virgil* and *Martial* stood for Parliament-
> Men, we know already who wou'd carry it. But though they make the
> greatest appearance in the Field, and cry the loudest, the best on 't is,
> they are but a sort of *French Huguenots*, or *Dutch Boors*, brought over
> in Herds, but not Naturaliz'd: who have not Land of two Pounds per
> *Annum* in *Parnassus*, and therefore are not priviledg'd to Poll.
>
> (P. 1052)

William was widely resented for favoring Dutchmen and Huguenots as advisors and generals. In the *Preface* to *Fables*, Blackmore's poetic incompetence is associated with his social and political background. He is a "City Bard, or Knight Physician" with
"Fanatique Patrons," and so unworthy of serious attention. In the
Dedication of *Examen Poeticum* Dryden's pedantic critics are
given a no less damning social and political position. Modern critics (Dryden has Rymer in mind) have "become Rebels of Slaves,
and Usurpers of Subjects" (p. 364). Julius Scaliger, a type for Dryden of the pedant, "wou'd needs turn down *Homer*, and Abdicate
him, after the possession of Three Thousand Years" (p. 365).
Some critics, by their veneration of the Elizabethan dramatists,

"wou'd thrust out their Lawful Issue, and Govern us themselves, under a specious pretence of Reformation" (p. 366). Though Dryden's enemies resemble James's in their methods and origin, they differ in their success. In the *Dedication* of *Examen Poeticum* they evaporate before the judgment of the noble Radcliffe; and in the *Dedication* of the *Aeneis* the highest class of readers eventually defeats the mob by quietly attracting a majority: judicious readers "are few in number, but whoever is so happy as to gain their approbation, can never lose it, because they never give it blindly. Then they have a certain *Magnetism* in their Judgment, which attracts others to their Sense. Every day they gain some new Proselyte, and in time become the Church" (p. 1053). The literal and figurative levels of this social metaphor blur together as Dryden goes on to apply it to himself and his patron Mulgrave: "Such a sort of Reputation is my aim, though in a far inferiour degree . . . and therefore I appeal to the Highest Court of Judicature, like that of the Peers, of which your Lordship is so great an Ornament" (p. 1053). The common reader who rejects Dryden's poetic claims finds himself outclassed by the likes of Radcliffe and Dorset, and cast into a wilderness of foreigners and pedants, city bards, and party hacks.

Dryden does not in his last works abandon his interest in contemporary politics for abstract speculation on poetry and human nature. His insistence on generality and detachment is itself a rhetorical gesture designed to place him and his audience in a universal and therefore authoritative context that explains and justifies his beliefs and behavior and allows him to reenter politics as a poet. In the *Postscript* of the *Aeneis*—his last chance to court those readers upon whose approval the success of over three years of labor depends—Dryden reenacts in summary form the series of gestures that define his public persona throughout the mid- and late nineties. He complains of having undertaken the work in his "Declining Years: strugling with Wants, oppress'd with Sickness, curb'd in my Genius, lyable to be misconstrued in all I write; and my Judges, if they are not very equitable, already prejudic'd against me, by the *Lying Character* which has been given them of my Morals." Yet he has completed the work "steady to my Principles, and not dispirited with my Afflictions." He claims that he has added something to English literature "in the choice of my

Words, and Harmony of Numbers"; then delivers a brief attack on
bad poets, which he quickly interrupts: "Here is a Field of Satire
open'd to me: But since the Revolution, I have wholly renounc'd
that Talent. For who wou'd give Physick to the Great when he is
uncall'd?" (p. 1424). This is an odd transition from literary criticism to political satire, but it allows him to introduce the topic of
his political quietism (" 'Tis enough for me, if the Government will
let me pass unquestion'd") and to define himself again in purely
literary terms. There follows a list of prominent Williamites who
have been "Bountiful to the Poet" without "considering the Man":
"The Earls of *Darby* and of *Peterborough*"; "Sir *William Trum-
ball*, one of the Principal Secretaries of State"; "*Gilbert Dolben*
Esq, the worthy Son of the late Arch-Bishop of *York*"; and so
forth (p. 1425). There is a complex mixture here of bold self-
assertion and quiet apology; but it exactly suits Dryden's position
in the 1690s, when his enemies were equally willing to attack him
as a dangerous subversive if he condemned the government and as
an unprincipled opportunist if he did not.

II. The Political Rhetoric of the
Translations

Most of Dryden's verse between 1692 and 1700 is in his translations: the *Satires*, *Virgil*, and *Fables*, and two miscellanies, *Examen Poeticum* and *The Annual Miscellany: For the Year 1694*,
were published in these years. The political innuendos in these
works have already been extensively annotated;[23] I wish to comment only on their function, which has I think been often mistaken. Most critics have scanned *Fables* in search of unifying
themes, so that they may claim that Dryden has created from these
borrowed fragments an original "great work."[24] Judith Sloman
has taken this argument furthest, claiming that Dryden "imposes
his own personality" on the translations, and uses them as "a form
of oblique self-expression."[25] On the contrary, Dryden is, I think,
interested in rhetoric rather than self-expression and is attracted to
translation because it allows him the rhetorical advantage of ap-
pearing before his public as a poet and only a poet. Plot, character,
setting—everything that might be susceptible to a political interpretation, or imply a view of the world based on controversial
principles—was the work of another poet in another age; Dryden

ostensibly contributed only the diction and the versification, the purely stylistic qualities for which he was almost universally admired. He did sometimes alter his originals in such a manner as to make them appropriate to his own concerns, but with rare exceptions he is careful not to draw attention to himself: he consistently presents these poems as the work of others. In his prose Dryden admits that his translations are not literal, but in doing so he repeatedly assures us that his alterations are purely stylistic. The translators of the *Satires* have "follow'd our Authors, at greater distance" than Holiday and Stapylton, for "A Noble Authour wou'd not be persu'd too close by a Translator. We lose his Spirit, when we think to take his Body. The grosser Part remains with us, but the Soul is flown away, in some Noble Expression or delicate turn of Words, or Thought" (*Discourse*, pp. 87–88). Dryden's contribution consists of noble expressions and delicate turns. Similarly in the *Dedication* of *Examen Poeticum* he contrasts his translation of Ovid to that of Sandys, who "leaves him Prose, where he found him Verse" (p. 370). Of his *Virgil* he tells us that his additions "will seem (at least I have Vanity to think so,) not stuck into him, but growing out of him." They are necessary because "Modern Tongues, have more Articles and Pronouns, besides signs of Tenses and Cases" than the Latin. Dryden is forced to "forsake the Brevity" in order to "pursue the Excellence" of Virgil's poetry (p. 1054). The additions to Chaucer in *Fables* are to be explained by "want of Words in the Beginning of our Language" to give Chaucer's thoughts "their true Lustre" (p. 1457). Indeed, throughout the *Preface* he implies for his translations a transparency through which the originals are plainly visible: he invites the reader to confirm Chaucer's superiority to Boccaccio by comparing his own translations of a passage from each on the same subject.

Dryden, then, claims responsibility in his translations only for poetic style; social and political criticism is always the work of his originals. If his ideas happen to coincide with theirs, we may attribute the similarity to the fact that poets preserve the same function in all ages. Thus Chaucer's attack on the clergy is part of a general poetic responsibility:

> I cannot blame him for inveighing so sharply against the Vices of the Clergy in his Age: Their Pride, their Ambition, their Pomp, their Av-

arice, their Worldly Interest, deserv'd the Lashes which he gave them, both in that, and in most of his *Canterbury Tales*: Neither has his Contemporary *Boccace*, spar'd them. Yet both those Poets liv'd in much esteem, with good and holy Men in Orders: For the Scandal which is given by particular Priests, reflects not on the Sacred Function. *Chaucer*'s *Monk*, his *Chanon*, and his *Fryar*, took not from the Character of his *Good Parson*. A Satyrical Poet is the Check of the Laymen, on bad Priests.

(Pp. 1453–1454)

Dryden's translations invite us to see his views on politics in his own time as the views of all poets on politics in all ages. His topical innuendos against standing armies, mob rule, war and taxes, tyranny and usurpation, are almost always expressed as general observations applicable equally to Augustan Rome, Renaissance Italy, and ancient and modern England.

Further, these observations arise incidentally from works that vary widely in their subjects and purposes; whatever their immediate ends, Dryden's poets frequently find occasion for remarks on political subjects. In the *Virgil*, for example, the *Pastorals*, *Georgics*, and *Aeneis* all include versions of usurpation. Threatened with dispossession by army veterans, one of Virgil's shepherds asks,

> Or shall we mount again the Rural Throne,
> And rule the Country Kingdoms, once our own!
>   (I.95–96)

In the third *Georgic*, the behavior of a bull competing for a heifer is described in the same terms:

> Often he turns his Eyes, and, with a groan,
> Surveys the pleasing Kingdoms, once his own.
>   (ll. 353–354)

Aeneas finds in hell

> . . . They, who Brothers better Claim disown,
> Expel their Parents, and usurp the Throne.
>   (VI.824–825)

The mob that sells its allegiance appears in a wide variety of contexts:

How goes the Mob, (for that's a Mighty thing?)
When the King's Trump, the Mob is for the King
(Juvenal, *Satyr X*, ll. 112–113)

Hosts of Deserters, who their Honour sold,
And basely broke their Faith, for Bribes of Gold.
(*Aeneis* VI, ll. 832–833)

When Churls rebel against their Native Prince,
I arm their Hands, and furnish the Pretence;
And housing in the Lion's hateful Sign,
Bought Senates, and deserting Troops are mine.
(*Palamon and Arcite*, III.408–411)

So loyal Subjects often seize their Prince,
Forc'd (for his Good) to seeming Violence,
Yet mean his sacred Person not the least Offence.
(*The Cock and the Fox*, ll. 790–792)

This was the Way to thrive in Peace and War;
To pay his Army, and fresh Whores to bring:
Who wou'd not fight for such a gracious King!
(*Ovid's Art of Love*, Book I, ll. 153–155)

Whether concerned to describe the vanity of ambition, the tor-
ments of the damned, the blandishments of a flatterer, the powers
of a god, or the processes of courtship, Dryden's poets cannot help
but remark the venality of those who support illegitimate power
for pay.

This sense of universal agreement among poets on political subjects emerges most clearly in *Fables*, where very different poems
are thrown together without apparent order. Recent critics attempting to find thematic unity in this apparently random collection have, I think, missed the point entirely. The very miscella-
neousness of the collection has an important rhetorical purpose.
The thematic incoherence of *Fables* suggests even more powerfully
than the prose Dryden's communion with poets of all ages and all
kinds. Whatever their immediate object, Dryden's authors cannot
seem to avoid manifesting their common views on such matters as
tyranny and corruption. For example, we can trace through the
collection a series of related observations on kings and the use of
power that reflect clearly, though apparently by accident, on William and his supporters. *Palamon and Arcite* contains incidental
observations on court corruption, on the king's neglect of the wor-

thy, and on the illegitimate use of force. Arcite invites Palamon to compete with him for Emily "as Courtiers . . . justle for a Grant" (I.346); Dryden makes Chaucer contrast Theseus's patronage of the arts with "Princes" who "now their poets should regard, / But few can write, and fewer can reward" (II.661–662); Palamon's defeat occasions a reflection on power and virtue:

> The brave Man seeks not popular Applause,
> Nor overpow'r'd with Arms, deserts his Cause;
> Unsham'd, though foil'd, he does the best he can;
> Force is of Brutes, but Honour is of Man.
>
> (III.739–742)

The same three topics recur throughout *Fables* in the form of general observations suggested by the action. In *Sigismonda and Guiscardo*, Tancred has his guards murder his daughter's lover; and Dryden makes Boccaccio generalize on the acquisition of power through force and purchase:

> For, (Slaves to Pay)
> What Kings decree, the Soldier must obey:
> Wag'd against Foes; and, when the Wars are o'er,
> Fit only to maintain Despotick Pow'r:
> Dang'rous to Freedom, and desir'd alone
> By Kings, who seek an Arbitrary Throne.
>
> (ll. 596–601)

Achilles's attack on Agamemnon in *The First Book of the Illias* is also given a generalized application:

> 'Tis Death to fight; but Kingly to controul.
> Lord-like at ease, with arbitrary Pow'r
> To peel the Chiefs, the People to devour.
>
> (ll. 341–343)

In *The Cock and the Fox*, Chaucer is made to generalize from Reynard's flattery to all princes' patronage of unworthy poets and neglect of worthy ones:

> Ye Princes rais'd by Poets to the Gods,
> And *Alexander'd* up in lying Odes,
> Believe not ev'ry flatt'ring Knave's report,
> There's many a *Reynard* lurking in the Court;

And he shall be receiv'd with more regard
And list'ned to, than modest Truth is heard.

(ll. 659–664)

The processes of love in *Cymon and Iphigenia* are compared with those of conquering kings:

my Love disdains the Laws,
And like a King by Conquest gains his Cause:
When Arms take place, all other Pleas are vain,
Love taught me Force, and Force shall Love maintain.

(ll. 300–303)

All of these clearly reflect on William, but they are cast as general observations on the human condition that occur incidentally to various poets in various contexts. Dryden claims responsibility for them only as a poet, giving delicate turns and noble expression in his native language to a common store of political observation that transcends particular ages and nations.

III. The Relation Between Poetry and Politics

Through his general observations on important issues and principles in his own work and in his translations, Dryden reenters contemporary politics not as a representative voice in the political nation, but as a poet who sees such things from above. There is another way in which he uses his poetic status to participate in political debate. As a poet he is fully authorized to comment on matters relating to the perfection of genre or the improvement of language, and in his last years he finds that these literary issues are indivisibly interconnected with political ones. These connections arise from Dryden's view of literary culture as both permanent and progressive. Whereas political history has become meaningless iteration, poetry, though it may move forward in one age and backward in another, is always conceived as part of a continuing tradition in which progress is possible.

Dryden had, of course, advanced this view in his earlier work, most notably in the *Essay of Dramatic Poesie* and the *Defence of the Epilogue*, where he is concerned with defending the claims of his contemporaries to have surpassed in some respects the dramatists of the last age. But the poetry and criticism of the nineties is filled with detailed and elaborate accounts of the growth of literary genres; and these accounts are always organized geographically as well as temporally. Satire, epic, tragedy, and pastoral move from Greece through Rome, Italy, and France to England. Dryden's interest in the growth of national literatures is perhaps clearest in the *Preface* to *Fables*, where in comparing Chaucer, Ovid, and Boccaccio he is careful to place each within the literary history of his country: Boccaccio and Chaucer are alike in having "refin'd their Mother-Tongues," but Boccaccio was the heir of Petrarch, while Chaucer was the "Father of *English* Poetry" worthy to be held in "the same Degree of Veneration as the *Grecians* held *Homer*, or the *Romans Virgil*" (p. 1452). In comparing Chaucer and Ovid he remarks that "with *Ovid* ended the Golden Age of the *Roman* Tongue: From *Chaucer* the Purity of the *English* Tongue began" (p. 1450).

This theory of poetry has two important consequences. Since poetic endeavor leads to real progress and to achievements of permanent importance, it is inherently more noble than politics, which leads nowhere. The poet has a duty to improve the manners and morals of his age, and with this duty comes the privilege to direct the government's policies or censure its misdeeds. Further, literature contributes to national greatness and international reputation, and therefore those governments that encourage literature preserve their reputation for all time, whereas those that suppress or ignore it are lost in obscurity or descend to posterity as tyrannous and vile. As a poet, Dryden is necessarily a patriot. Though he supports one of the war aims of Louis XIV, as a poet he is obliged by his vocation to honor his country, to purify its language and to increase its reputation. Further, as a poet he can criticize court policy, but he judges it not, as in his earlier work, as a potential source of justice, right, and truth, but as a potential source of patronage, as a servant of poetic progress and achievement. All governments may be vicious, but some are more effective than others in cultivating the arts of peace. By this standard the tyrant Louis and the conqueror Augustus far outshine the usurper William, though his behavior is no more deplorable than the former's, and his title no more dubious than the latter's.

Original Verse

These topics are clearly developed in three of Dryden's most important poems in these years, "To My Dear Friend Mr. Congreve," "To Sir Godfrey Kneller," and *Alexander's Feast.* All three have received a good deal of excellent critical analysis separately;[26] but together they reveal a consistent approach to the relation between art and politics, an approach that also structures Dryden's late prose criticism. Both of the complimentary poems contain conflicting versions of this relation. On the one hand, art is independent of and superior to politics, the product of a continuous and noble tradition that transcends national boundaries and political disturbances. Thus Congreve is the culmination of two traditions in English drama: he unites the strength of the Jacobean period with the sweetness of the Restoration, or alternatively, the strength of Jonson and Wycherley with the sweetness of Fletcher, Etherege, and Southerne. At the end of the poem Dryden includes himself among the dramatists Congreve has surpassed and asks him to protect his reputation with posterity. Similarly, Kneller is presented as the culmination of a tradition Dryden traces from the prehistoric age through Greece and Rome to Italy: Kneller unites the design of Raphael with the color of Titian. All of this serves to place Dryden and his addressees above the contemporary.

On the other hand, Dryden portrays his addressees and himself as victims of contemporary neglect of the arts of peace. The laurel that should have descended from Dryden to Congreve has been usurped by Shadwell and Rymer. Dryden and Kneller have both lost Charles: they must be content "the first of these inferiour Times to be"; Kneller's genius is

> bounded by the Times like mine,
> Drudges on petty Draughts, nor dare design
> A more Exalted Work, and more Divine.
> (ll. 147–149)

What is described as actual achievement when Dryden is considering the place of his addressees in the great tradition becomes frustrated potential when he describes their place in contemporary England. The conflict is resolved in the Congreve poem by a prophecy that its subject will eventually wear not Dryden's laurel, but his own; but whatever the reference of this prophecy, it does nothing to counter the criticism of current government patronage implied throughout the poem. In the Kneller poem, the conflict remains unresolved: at the end Dryden predicts that time will mellow Kneller's color and increase his fame, but it cannot add to his design. Further, Dryden's criticism of the government appears in this poem at the expense of appropriateness as well as coherence: Kneller had no cause for complaint against the court. William retained him as court painter and knighted him in 1691.[27] Dryden's purpose in both poems is to present himself within an artistic tradition independent of and superior to contemporary politics and from that position to criticize William's government for its neglect of the arts. He appears before his public in the poetic role in which he knew them most willing to accept and admire him and then uses this role to castigate his political enemies.

The theme of the superiority of poetry to politics recurs throughout Dryden's late works; but it is expressed most directly and schematically in *Alexander's Feast*. On one side the emperor Alexander sits "Aloft in awful State," on the other the poet-musician Timotheus sits "high / Amid the tuneful Quire." Earl Miner describes their relation in the poem: "in each stanza Timotheus the musician plays upon Alexander, the instrument of his virtuosity. After the first stanza, only the fourth begins with consideration of Alexander . . . rather than Timotheus. The irony directed towards 'Phillip's warlike son' is apparent enough in his being an instrument manipulated at will. But Dryden enjoys making it clearer." Alexander "Assumes the God, / Affects to nod, / And seems to shake the Spheres"; he "grew vain, / Fought all his battails o'er again" until "At length, with Love and Wine at once oppress'd, / The vanquish'd Victor sunk" upon the breast of his mistress (ll. 39–40, 66–67, 114–115).[28] Howard Erskine-Hill suggests the topical relevance of this superiority of poet to ruler:

> In 1697 William III had just triumphed over Louis XIV who supported the fallen cause of James II; and James had, like Darius, been 'Deserted at his utmost Need, / By those his former Bounty fed.' The poem makes a general political allusion which is a part, but a part only, of its meaning; its full greatness lies in the way Dryden, like Timotheus, relentlessly brings out the moral truth behind the worldly triumph he purports to celebrate.[29]

This moral truth lies, I think, in the contrast between the power of art and the emptiness of political achievement. Again Dryden is writing as a poet on the subject of poetry and so entering politics from a position of strength. In the final stanza, Dryden gives another turn to this contrast. He asserts his distance from the action—it happened "long ago"—and elevates it to the eternal perspective that as a poet he enjoys. From this vantage point, Alexander is hardly visible: his heroic triumph means nothing at all. However, Timotheus gains added meaning and importance—he is enrolled in a transcendent artistic tradition. Cecilia's improvements on Timotheus's art do not diminish it: he is all the more admirable in having achieved such success within the "narrow Bounds" of his time, and thus he is able to "divide the Crown" with her. In the transcendent reaches of art to which Dryden declares his allegiance, progress and permanence are not incompatible; in politics, neither is even possible.[30]

Prose

In many ways, the *Discourse of Satire* and the *Dedication* of the *Aeneis* seem baffling and disappointing works. As dedications they are disconcertingly fulsome: in placing Dorset and Mulgrave at the peak of contemporary literature Dryden must ignore or pervert the literary standards that he claims as the basis of his criticism. As works of criticism they are almost entirely derivative: we miss in them the insights into satire and heroic verse that we might expect from one of the greatest practitioners of these forms. If we read this late prose only for its direct contribution to literary criticism, Dryden appears as the slave of his times, superior to Rymer and his kind only in the quality of his writing or in his occasional divergence from the narrow road of neoclassical precept. If, however, we read it with close attention to the social and political pressures against which he was forced to define his position, the prose appears as the work of the same complex and sensitive mind that produced the great poems of a decade before. Though rarely the sole object of his attention, the relation between poet and state is never far from Dryden's mind in his late prose: in one guise or another it makes its way into almost every topic of this notoriously miscellaneous body of work. And there emerges from its various manifestations a reasonably clear and unified view of that relation.

Dryden conceives of poetry as part of an unbroken and unassailable tradition, extending from the ancient Greeks to contemporary England and France; politics as a series of accidents and misfortunes—the scene of prosperous villainy and the toy of an inscrutable Providence. For Dryden, it follows that the poet is privileged to censure the state and that the state may to some extent redeem itself by supporting the poet. Throughout his late prose, Dryden carefully defines and redefines his position in contemporary England, suggesting where he can the venality of the victorious government and the ideal bases of his own principles, but never straying far from the purely poetic concerns that formed the basis of his authority with an audience that had rejected those principles.

In the panegyric on the Whig courtier Dorset, with which he begins the *Discourse of Satire*, Dryden prepares us for what follows by defining the nature and relative importance of poetry and politics. Throughout the first ten pages of the *Discourse*, Dorset is described by a series of monarchical metaphors that together establish poetry as an ideally stable kingdom.[31] Dorset is untouched by the quarrelsome spirit of his subjects—"There are no Factions, tho irreconcilable to one another, that are not united in their Affection to you, and the Respect they pay you" (p. 3)—and he is untroubled by enemies (p. 4). Or, if any rebels to his authority arise, they "must be like the Officer, in a Play, who was call'd Captain, Lieutenant, and Company. The World will easily conclude, whether such unattended Generals can ever be capable of making a Revolution in *Parnassus*" (p. 6). Nor is Dorset himself a quarrelsome ruler: his realm is so peaceful that his subjects urge him "like some Great Monarch, to take a Town but once a year, as it were for your diversion, though you had no need to extend your Territories" (p. 8). As his power is unopposed, so is his prerogative uncontested. It extends to "the petulant Scriblers of this Age," whom Dryden encourages him to banish or restrain; but he has also a "Prerogative to pardon ... those things, which are somewhat Congenial, and of a remote Kindred to your own Conceptions" (p. 5). In this he exemplifies a distinctly Jacobite notion of kingship—James was deposed in part for his too liberal interpretation of his prerogative to pardon like-minded subjects. The resemblance extends to the origins of their authority. Dorset's, like James's, is inherent. He is king of poets "by an undisputed Title," by which, Dryden says, "I mean not the Authority, which is an-nex'd to your Office: I speak of that only which is inborn and inherent to your Person: What is produc'd in you by . . . a Masterly and Commanding Genius over all Writers" (p. 9–10). In Parnassus, then, legitimacy is inherent and universally recognized and upheld. This provides an instructive contrast with revolutionary England: by defining literary affairs through political metaphors, Dryden delicately suggests the superiority of the literary to the political.

He is no less careful in defining his own relations with Dorset both within and without the terms of his metaphor. If Dorset is the king of poets, Dryden is his minister:

> As a Councellour bred up the knowledge of the Municipal and Statute Laws, may honestly inform a just Prince how far his Prerogative extends, so I may be allow'd to tell your Lordship, who by an undisputed Title, are the King of Poets, what an extent of Power you have, and how lawfully you may exercise it, over the petulant Scriblers of this Age.
>
> (P. 9)

If Dorset is the Messiah of poets, Dryden is his prophet:

> 'Tis true, I have one Priviledge that is almost particular to my self, that I saw you in the East at your first arising above the Hemisphere: I was as soon Sensible as any Man of that Light, when it was but just shoot-ing out, and beginning to Travel upwards to the Meridian. . . . I was Inspir'd to foretell you to Mankind, as the Restorer of Poetry, the greatest Genius, the truest Judge, and the best Patron.
>
> (Pp. 4–5)

By showing himself Dorset's loyal courtier and constant partisan, Dryden reminds us of his constancy to the real king Dorset resembles; the parallel suggests that this constancy is in both cases equally disinterested and equally justifiable. Dryden extends his allegiance to legitimate authority wherever he finds it, whether in the king of England or the king of Parnassus. If his literary constancy appears more clearly than his political, it is only because of the greater harmony and stability of the former realm.

This subject recurs when, after his digression on epic poetry, Dryden returns to his praise of Dorset; and here he explicitly draws attention to his unswerving loyalty both to James and to

Dorset. He acknowledges his patron's kindness "since this Revolution, wherein I have patiently suffer'd the Ruin of my small Fortune, and the loss of that poor Subsistence which I had from two Kings, whom I serv'd more Faithfully than Profitably to my self" (p. 23). His loyalty to the Stuart cause, though unrewarded, remains. Yet it is not inconsistent with loyalty to William's supporters: "I must not presume to defend the Cause for which I now suffer, because your Lordship is engag'd against it: But the more you are so, the greater is my Obligation to you: For your laying aside all Considerations of Factions and Parties" (p. 23). Further, the source of this mutual esteem, which on both sides transcends the quarrels of factions, is literary. In addition to gratitude, Dryden has "a more particular inclination" to honor and love Dorset:

> 'Tis no shame to be a Poet, tho' 'tis to be a bad one. *Augustus Caesar* of old, and Cardinal *Richilieu* of late, wou'd willingly have been such; and *David* and *Solomon* were such. You, who . . . are the best of the present Age in *England* . . . will receive more Honour in future Ages, by that one Excellency, than by all those Honours to which your Birth has intitl'd you, or your Merits have acquir'd you.
>
> (P. 24)

Though he uses his praise of Dorset to suggest the irreproachable basis of his loyalty to James, Dryden concludes it by again asserting the superiority of the literary over the political: kings and emperors have aspired to poetry without success; and Dorset will be remembered as a poet long after he has been forgotten as a statesman.

It follows from this that Dryden himself has deserved better treatment, and in his long digression on epic poetry, he suggests as much. This digression is framed by contrasting accounts of French and English patronage, which imply that the losses resulting from the neglect of Dryden's potential have fallen more heavily on the country than on the poet himself. He introduces the subject by claiming that "What has been, may be again: Another *Homer*, and another *Virgil* may possibly arise from those very Causes which produc'd the first" (p. 11). He remarks that certain ages — Augustan Rome, Renaissance Italy — "have been more happy than others in the production of Great Men" (p. 11). And he offers an English example: "In Tragedy and Satire . . . this Age and the last, particularly in *England*, have excell'd the Ancients: . . . and I wou'd instance in *Shakespear* of the former, in your Lordship of the latter sort" (p. 12). It is difficult to tell how sincere Dryden is in thus exalting Dorset above Horace and Juvenal; certainly his support of a more likely candidate for such an honor is more detailed and enthusiastic:

> Thus I might safely confine my self to my Native Country: But if I wou'd only cross the Seas, I might find in *France* a living *Horace* and *Juvenal*, in the Person of the admirable *Boileau*: Whose Numbers are Excellent, whose Expressions are Noble, whose Thoughts are Just, whose Language is Pure, whose Satire is pointed, and whose Sense is close: What he borrows from the Ancients, he repays with Usury of his own: in Coin as good, and almost as Universally valuable.
>
> (P. 12)

He follows this commendation with an explanation of Boileau's success:

> For setting prejudice and Partiality apart, though he is our Enemy, the Stamp of a *Louis*, the Patron of all Arts, is not much inferiour to the Medal of an *Augustus Caesar*. Let this be said without entring into the interests of Factions and Parties; and relating only to the Bounty of that King to Men of Learning and Merit: A Praise so just, that even we who are his Enemies, cannot refuse it to him.
>
> (Pp. 12–13)

Once again, literary judgments are able to transcend faction and party; and once again, through his use of the first-person plural and his redundant qualifications of his praise, Dryden reminds us of his patriotism. Indeed, he is so sure of his reputation as an English patriot, that he cuts short a later commendation of Boileau because "it might turn to his Prejudice, if 'twere carry'd back to *France*" (p. 84). Nonetheless, he cannot call attention to the bounty of the French king without implying the deficiency of his own, and he returns to this matter at the end of his history of epic.

Dryden uses this history both to assert again his patriotism and to place himself within a poetic tradition that transcends time and place: he makes these ends mutually dependent by defining himself as a potential English Horace or Virgil—as a poet who, given a chance, might have equalled the ancients, surpassed the moderns, and so covered in glory his native country. He reviews all considerable attempts at epic poetry since Virgil and finds them all lacking (though he devotes most time and admiration to his compatriots Spenser and Milton); then answers the claim that they have failed because Christianity is incompatible with the genre. He concedes that so far modern poets have indeed failed to use their religion properly in epic: "We cannot hitherto boast, that our Religion has furnish'd us with any such Machines, as have made the Strength and Beauty of the Ancient Buildings" (pp. 18–19). But he claims to have "an Invention of my own, to supply the manifest defect of our new Writers" and goes on to explain it in detail.

Dryden presents all this from the Olympian perspective appropriate to a review of seventeen centuries of literary history, dispensing praise and blame with an easy dogmatism that hardly admits the possibility of dispute. From such a perspective, he can speak to his Protestant patron of "our Religion"; political struggle throughout history within and between nations becomes, from the point of view of the guardian angels who, in Dryden's scheme, protect them, mere "Factious Quarrels, Controversies, and Battels." These are provoked ultimately by God's "Providential Designs for the benefit of his Creatures, for the Debasing and Punishing of some Nations, and the Exaltation and Temporal Reward of others" (p. 20). Such a perspective no doubt had its application for Dryden to contemporary events: if God could allow "the Rise of *Alexander* and his Successors, who were appointed to punish the Backsliding *Jews*, and thereby to put them in mind of their Offences" (p. 20), he could allow the rise of William over the English for a similar purpose. But it works primarily to suggest the futility of political effort, and the comparative importance of poetic tradition.

The poet is capable of taking such large views because his natural and acquired abilities place him above his contemporaries: he must be

> a Man . . . who to his Natural Endowments, of a large Invention, a ripe Judgment, and a strong Memory, has join'd the knowledge of the Liberal Arts and Sciences, and particularly, Moral Philosophy, the Mathematicks, Geography and History, and with all these Qualifications is born a Poet: knows, and can practice the variety of Numbers, and is Master of the Language in which he Writes; if such a Man, I say, be now arisen, or shall arise, I am vain enough to think, that I have propos'd a Model to him, by which he may build a Nobler, a more

Beautiful and more Perfect Poem, than any yet extant since the Ancients.

(P. 21)

Dryden had apparently considered himself just such a man—his failure to put his model to use was the result, not of his own deficiencies, but of his unfortunate circumstances. He had aimed to "put in practice" this scheme in an epic of his own, which he "had intended chiefly for the Honour of my Native Country, to which a Poet is particularly oblig'd" (p. 22). By casting this assertion in such general terms, Dryden makes it clear that he had chosen an English subject not because, as an Englishman, he found it particularly worthy of epic treatment, but because, as a poet, he is "oblig'd" to do so: the poet reflects honor upon his country, not the other way around. He names two possible subjects for this epic and then describes in further detail his intended method of celebrating his country. He would have interwoven "the Characters of the chiefest *English* Persons; wherein, after *Virgil* and *Spencer*, I wou'd have taken occasion to represent my living Friends and Patrons of the Noblest Families, and also shadow'd the Events of future Ages, in the Succession of our Imperial Line" (p. 23). He no doubt envisioned at that time a rather different succession than he found before him in the 1690s; and he goes on to imply some connection between the interruption of the Stuart line and the frustration of his plans:

> But being encourag'd only with fair Words, by King *Charles* II, my little Sallary ill paid, and no prospect of a future Subsistance, I was then Discourag'd in the beginning of my Attempt; and now Age has overtaken me; and Want, a more insufferable Evil, through the Change of the Times, has wholly disenabl'd me.
>
> (P. 23)

Dryden is as truthful in the first part of this explanation as in the second: we have abundant evidence that he was indeed ill paid under Charles; but he had found it rhetorically useful as early as 1687, in *The Hind and the Panther*, to remind his readers how little he had profited from his support of the Stuart cause, and his mention of it here serves as a convenient preface to his allusion in the next sentence to his loyal Jacobitism. The second part of the explanation points clearly to the deficiency of the present government: Boileau has been able to equal Horace and Juvenal through the largesse of Louis XIV; Dryden has received no such support for his far bolder attempt to equal Homer and Virgil. And the loss falls no more heavily on Dryden than on England. He thus presents himself, in his digression on epic, not as the displaced hireling of a discredited court, but as the rightful heir of a transcendent literary tradition. By neglecting him, William's England has, he suggests, not frustrated a potential traitor; it has rather robbed itself of the chance of standing in that tradition alongside Renaissance Italy and Augustan Rome.

Having established a context in which poetry transcends the accidental circumstances of its social and political surroundings, Dryden is at last ready to turn to satire itself, a genre notorious for its close engagement with those circumstances. He may seem, at first, to deny that engagement. He begins by distinguishing invective, which is "Nature, and that deprav'd," from satire, which though it arose from invective, "when it became an Art, it bore better Fruit" (p. 28); and most of his discussion of the genre's origin is directed toward the conclusion that the term "satire" is derived rather from the variety of its form than the lowness of its subject: he firmly rejects its traditional associations with that rustic, lecherous, and ill-natured being, the satyr (pp. 36–38). Along the way he traces its first beginnings to religious worship (p. 32), remarks on its superiority to mere parodies and attacks on individuals (p. 30), and excludes from it all "Wantonness and lubricity" (p. 36). We may sense the motivation behind this predominately formal and aesthetic definition of satire in Dryden's eagerness to distinguish it from libels and lampoons produced by ill-nature and political opportunism, and of which he had so often been the object. This eagerness shows itself quite early in the *Discourse*: Dryden interrupts his praise of Dorset for an attack on the "multitude of Scriblers, who daily pester the World with their insufferable Stuff":

> I complain not of their Lampoons and Libels, though I have been the Publick Mark for many years. . . . But these dull Makers of Lampoons, as harmless as they have been to me, are yet of dangerous Example to the Publick: Some Witty Men may perhaps succeed to their Designs,

and mixing Sence with Malice, blast the Reputation of the most Innocent amongst Men, and the most Virtuous amongst Women.
(Pp. 8–9)

Dryden promises to return to the subject "when I come to give the
Definition and Character of true Satires" (p. 9); and when he does
so return, he is no less eager to condemn lampoons and defend
himself against them: "that former sort of Satire, which is known
in *England* by the Name of Lampoon, is a dangerous sort of
Weapon, and for the most part Unlawful" (p. 59). He considers
two conditions under which personal attack may be excused—
when its object has attacked first, and when he is a "public nui-
sance." The second condition is appropriate to true satire; and I
will refer to it in a moment. The first is an offence against "Christian Charity," and Dryden claims to have therefore abstained from
revenging himself, despite his innocence.

All of this may seen unconvincing, coming as it does from the
author of *Absalom and Achitophel* and *MacFlecknoe*; yet Dryden
does not attempt in the *Discourse* to conceal his authorship of
these works. He refers quite proudly to both of them but in a
rather different context. They appear as modern examples of certain formal qualities of satire; and they serve once again to establish Dryden's place in a venerable literary tradition. After concluding his review of the origins of satire, Dryden promises to show
that "out of all these, sprung two several Branches of new *Roman*
Satire; like different Cyens from the same Root" (p. 42). The first
proceeds from Livius Andronicus and Ennius through Pacuvius,
Lucilius, Horace, Persius, and Juvenal. The second, Varronian satire, begins with Menippus and Varro, and includes the following
writers:

Petronius Arbiter, whose Satire, they say, is now Printing in *Holland*. . . . Many of *Lucian*'s Dialogues may also properly be call'd *Varronian* Satires; particularly his *True History*; And consequently the
Golden Ass of *Apuleius*, which is taken from him. Of the same stamp
is the Mock Deification of *Claudius*, by *Seneca*: And the *Symposium*
or *Caesars* of *Julian* the Emperour. Amongst the Moderns we may
reckon the *Encomium Moriae* of *Erasmus*, *Barclay's Euphormio*, and
a Volume of *German* Authors, which my ingenious Friend Mr. *Charles
Killigrew* once lent me. In the *English* I remember none, which are

mix'd with Prose, as *Varro*'s were; But of the same kind is *Mother Hubbard's Tale* in *Spencer*; and (if it be not too vain, to mention anything of my own) The Poems of *Absalom*, and *Mac Fleckno*.
(P. 48)

These works appear, then, not as invectives or polemics, but as the heirs of an unbroken tradition that extends back to ancient Greece. When he later considers *Absalom and Achitophel* in detail, he treats it again as an exclusively formal object, an example of the "fine Raillery" in which "the nicest and most delicate touches of Satire" consist and by which Horace is most distinguished:

How easie it is to call Rogue and Villain, and that wittily! But how hard to make a Man appear a Fool, a Blockhead, or a Knave, without using any of those opprobrious terms. . . . This is the Mystery of that Noble Trade: which yet no Master can teach to his Apprentice: He may give the Rules, but the Scholer is never the nearer in his practice. . . . I wish I cou'd apply it to my self, if the Reader wou'd be kind enough to think it belongs to me. The Character of *Zimri* in my *Absalom*, is, in my Opinion, worth the whole Poem: 'Tis not bloody, but 'tis ridiculous enough. And he for whom it was intended, was too witty to resent it as an injury. If I had rail'd, I might have suffer'd for it justly: But I manag'd my own Work more happily, perhaps more dextrously. I avoided the mention of great Crimes, and apply'd my self to the representing of Blind-sides, and little Extravagancies: To which, the wittier a Man is, he is generally the more obnoxious.
(P. 71)

Dryden's most overtly political poem becomes in the *Discourse* exclusively literary, the latest manifestation of a genre whose history reaches back to the beginning of civilization; and he himself appears as the modern counterpart of a Petronius or Horace.

Dryden is, then, eager to describe satire throughout the *Discourse* primarily as an aesthetic form, independent of the particular social and political conditions by which individual satires so often seem to have been provoked. Yet, though careful to provide for satire's greater dependence on higher inspiration than private quarrels or political factions, he nonetheless includes, as one of the formal requirements of the genre, a political program suited to the poet's times. Dryden advances as his principal innovation over other histories of satire his derivation of the genre not from the rude Roman farces, but from Greek Old Comedy, by way of the freed Greek slave Livius Andronicus:

> I will adventure . . . to advance another Proposition, which I hope the Learned will approve . . . that having read the Works of those *Grecian Wits*, his Countrymen, [Livius Andronicus] imitated not only the ground-work, but also the manner of their Writing. And how grave soever his Tragedies might be, yet in his Comedies he express'd the way of *Aristophanes*, *Eupolis*, and the rest, which was to call some Persons by their own Names, and to expose their Defects to the laughter of the People: the Examples of which we have in the foremention'd *Aristophanes*, who turn'd wise *Socrates* into Ridicule; and is also very free with the management of *Cleon*, *Alcibiades*, and other Ministers of the *Athenian* Government.
>
> (Pp. 40–41)

Andronicus's plays provided in turn a model for Ennius, the first Roman satirist, who in "abstracting" satire from the plays "preserv'd the Ground-work of their Pleasantry, their Venom, and their Raillery on particular Persons, and general Vices" (p. 42). Thus, attacks on public individuals are a distinguishing generic trait of the very first satires; later satirists, in attacking the "public nuisances" among their contemporaries, preserve the structure of a genre that transcends their times. Dryden returns to the subject of personal attacks in true satires when he considers the second of the two purposes for which they may be employed. The first of these, revenge, is not, as we have seen, justifiable; but the second, exemplary punishment, is not only justifiable, it is the satirist's moral duty:

> the second Reason, which may justifie a Poet, when he writes against a particular Person . . . is, when he is become a Publick Nuisance. All those whom *Horace* in his Satires, and *Persius* and *Juvenal* have mention'd in theirs, with a Brand of infamy, are wholly such. 'Tis an Action of Virtue to make Examples of vicious Men. They may and ought to be upbraided with their Crimes and Follies: Both for their own amendment, if they are not yet incorrigible; and for the Terrour of others, to hinder them from falling into those Enormities, which they see are so severly punish'd, in the Persons of others. The first Reason is only an Excuse for Revenge: But this second is absolutely of a Poet's Office to Perform.
>
> (P. 60)

Having once established the nobility of satire and its transcendence of the merely topical, Dryden gives it a political purpose that arises naturally from literary imperatives. Satirists are compelled to expose the crimes of public figures by both the formal requirements of the genre and the moral imperatives of their vocation.

This understanding of satire informs the comparison of Persius, Horace, and Juvenal with which Dryden follows his history of the genre. Of the three, Juvenal is the most successful in fulfilling his public duty; and this success accounts for the ability of his satires to give more pleasure than Horace's:

> The Meat of *Horace* is more nourishing; but the Cookery of *Juvenal* more exquisite; so that, granting *Horace* to be the more general Philosopher; we cannot deny, that *Juvenal* was the greater Poet, I mean in Satire. His Thoughts are sharper, his Indignation against Vice is more vehement; his Spirit has more of the Commonwealth Genius; he treats Tyranny, and all the Vices attending it, as they deserve, with the utmost rigour: And consequently, a Noble Soul is better pleas'd with a Zealous Vindicator of *Roman* Liberty; than with a Temporizing Poet, a well Manner'd Court Slave, and a Man who is often afraid of Laughing in the right place: Who is ever decent, because he is naturally servile.
>
> (P. 65)

The cookery metaphor suggests once again that the end of satire is primarily aesthetic; its use here reminds us that the genre's political engagement is one of the means to this end. The effect of this argument is to elevate satire above its political occasion; and Dryden goes on to present Domitian's tyranny not as provoking Juvenal's satire and therefore somehow limiting its meaning, but as presenting that poet with fortunate opportunities for increasing the purely aesthetic effectiveness of his satire:

> After all, *Horace* had the disadvantage of the Times in which he liv'd; they were better for the Man, but worse for the Satirist. 'Tis generally said, that those Enormous Vices, which were practis'd under the Reign of *Domitian*, were unknown in the Time of *Augustus Caesar*: That therefore *Juvenal* had a larger Field, than *Horace*. Little Follies were out of doors, when Oppression was to be scourg'd instead of Avarice: It was no longer time to turn into Ridicule, the false Opinions of Philosophers; when the *Roman* Liberty was to be asserted. There was more need of a *Brutus* in *Domitian*'s Day, to redeem or mend, than of

a *Horace*, if he had then been Living, to Laugh at a Fly-Catcher. This Reflection at the same time excuses *Horace*, but exalts *Juvenal.*

(Pp. 65–66)

By emphasizing the formal and aesthetic function of political engagement, Dryden does not entirely neglect its moral value. Later in the *Discourse*, he shows that Juvenal's attack on Domitian arises naturally from his moral purpose of exposing vice: "His was an Age that deserv'd a more severe Chastisement. Vices were more gross and open, more flagitious, more encourag'd by the Example of a Tyrant; and more protected by his Authority"(p. 69). Persius wrote against lewdness as "the Predominant Vice in *Nero*'s Court, at the time when he publish'd his Satires" (p. 69). The government, as the source of the nation's moral character, capable of encouraging and protecting vice, is the natural object of satiric attack. But again, the political is rigorously subordinated to the literary: the crimes of Domitian are mainly important insofar as they contribute to Juvenal's exquisite cookery.

The importance to satire of political engagement is rather confirmed than contradicted by Horace's lack of such engagement. As we have seen, Dryden at first excuses Horace, as denied by the virtue of his times the rhetorical opportunities and moral imperatives that enrich the work of Persius and Juvenal. Later, however, Dryden suggests that Horace's times were not altogether so innocent as they had been represented:

When *Horace* writ his Satires, the Monarchy of his *Caesar* was in its newness; and the Government but just made easie to the Conquer'd People. They cou'd not possibly have forgotten the Usurpation of that Prince upon their Freedom, nor the violent Methods which he had us'd, in the compassing of that vast Design: They yet remember'd his Proscriptions, and the Slaughter of so many Noble *Romans*, their Defendors. . . . His Adulteries were still before their Eyes, but they must be patient, where they had not power.

(P. 66)

Horace rather overlooked than wanted opportunities to write on subjects appropriate to satire: "*Horace*, as he was a Courtier, comply'd with the Interest of his Master, and avoiding the Lashing of greater Crimes, confin'd himself to the ridiculing of Petty Vices, and common Follies" (p. 68). For this reason, "the Subjects which

Horace chose for Satire, are of a lower nature than those of which *Juvenal* has written" (p. 69). The satirist has an active duty to direct his art against the vices of the government under which he lives; and when he fails to fulfill that duty, his work suffers both aesthetically and morally.

This account of Augustus's disguised tyranny brings up another relation between poetry and the state that is no less applicable to Dryden and his times, though he is necessarily less direct here than in his account of patronage. In his less attractive features, Augustus suggests Jacobite caricatures of William III. In William's times, as in Augustus's, "the Government had just been made easie to the Conquer'd People" who "cou'd not possibly have forgotten the Usurpation of that Prince upon their Freedom" (p. 66). From the Jacobite point of view, the English people were no less than the Roman "entertain'd with publick Shows, and Donatives, to make them more easily digest their lost Liberty" (p. 66). From this account of Augustus's usurpation, Dryden moves to a consideration of his repression of poetry:

> *Augustus*, who was conscious to himself, of so many Crimes which he had committed, thought in the first place to provide for his own Reputation, by making an Edict against Lampoons and Satires, and the Authors of those defamatory Writings, which my Author *Tacitus* . . . calls *Famosos libellos*.
>
> In the first Book of his Annals, he gives the following Account of it, . . . *Augustus* was the first, who under the colour of that Law took Cognisance of Lampoons; being provok'd to it, by the petulancy of *Cassius Severus*. . . . The Law to which *Tacitus* refers, was *Lex laesae Majestatis*; commonly call'd, for the sake of brevity *Majestas*; or as we say, High Treason. . . . *Augustus* was the first, who restor'd that intermitted Law. By the words, *under colour of that Law*, [Tacitus] insinuates that *Augustus* caus'd it to be Executed, on pretence of those Libels, which were written by *Cassius Severus*, against the Nobility; But in Truth, to save himself, from such defamatory Verses.
> (Pp. 66–67)

Persius and Juvenal must evade similar attempts at repression, Persius by obscurity (p. 51), Juvenal through a sort of parallel: "wheresoever *Juvenal* mentions *Nero*, he means *Domitian*, whom he dares not attack in his own Person, but Scourges him by Proxy" (p. 69). But the association of the subtlest and most effective means of repression with the usurper Augustus is a particularly appropriate one for the author of *Don Sebastian.*

Dryden uses his comparison of the three satirists to explore the potentially adversarial relations between poetry and state; at the end of the *Discourse* he turns again to those potentially harmonious relations that William's government has been unwilling to foster. He once again asserts his position in literary history and reminds us of the government's failure to support that position. In rejecting Heinsius's definition of satire, he claims that as Horace's manner is surpassed by Juvenal's, and Homer's by Virgil's, so Donne's is surpassed by that of Dryden and his contemporaries (p. 78). His review of versification meanders from Waller and Denham through Milton and Spenser, and their study respectively of Homer and Virgil, to examples from Virgil and Ovid. And, like his account of modern epic, it ends by dashing the hopes of equalling the ancients which it briefly arouses:

> we have yet no *English Prosodia,* not so much as a tolerable Dictionary, or a Grammar; so that our Language is in a manner Barbarous; and what Government will encourage any one, or more, who are capable of Refining it, I know not. But nothing under a Publick Expence can go through with it. And I rather fear a declination of Language, than hope an advancement of it in the present Age.
>
> (P. 86)

English poetry, advancing by such hopeful stages in recent times, is likely to regress under a government so little mindful of its obligations to literature as William's.

"A HEROICK Poem, truly such, is undoubtedly the greatest Work which the Soul of Man is capable to perform": thus Dryden begins his *Dedication* of the *Aeneis* with large claims for the importance of his subject. The soul of an epic poet must be "sent into the World with great advantages of Nature, cultivated with the liberal Arts and Sciences, conversant with Histories of the Dead, and enrich'd with Observations on the Living" (p. 1004). The moral responsibilities of such a poet are no less ponderous: he must "form the Mind to Heroick Virtue by Example." Dryden amplifies this point through a comparison of the moral operations of epic and tragedy. Both cure the moral distempers of mankind: epic corrects the manners, tragedy the passions. The medicinal metaphor is familiar from the preface to *Absalom and Achitophel*, but there is an important difference in Dryden's development of it here. The poet does not step in to perform an essential surgical operation during a crisis in the health of the body politic; instead he provides "Diet, good Air, and moderate Exercise" that harden the soul to virtue (p. 1007). In the *Dedication* of the *Aeneis* Dryden wants to advance his own set of morals, many of them pointedly topical; but he is careful always to advance them as a poet, as one concerned with the constant rules and conditions which govern mankind in all ages. This insistence on the nobility of his vocation and the generality of his concerns allows him to enter politics in a guise acceptable to his audience.

The relation between the poet and the state in Dryden's discussion of Homer's and Virgil's morals is somewhat different from that implied in the account of epic poetry in the *Discourse*. There the poet celebrates the achievements and improves the language of his country; in the *Dedication* the poet serves a specific political program. Though Homer's moral is more "noble" than Virgil's, both poets are concerned more with political utility than with nobility; thus *Virgil*'s moral "was as useful to the *Romans* of his Age, as *Homer*'s was to the *Grecians* of his." Homer recommends to his audience a strong defensive alliance: "*Homer*'s Moral was to urge the necessity of Union, and of a good understanding betwixt Confederate States and Princes engag'd in a War with a mighty Monarch" (p. 1101). He "liv'd when the *Median* Monarchy was grown formidable to the *Grecians*: and . . . the joint Endeavours of his Countrymen, were little enough to preserve their common Freedom, from an encroaching Enemy" (p. 1012). Virgil's moral is even more closely tied to the details of his audience's political concerns: it was "To infuse an awful Respect into the People" towards Augustus through a parallel with Aeneas, "By that respect to confirm their Obedience to him; and by that Obedience to make them Happy" (p. 1015). Both morals are derived from Le Bossu, but whereas the French critic writes generally of Greek disunity, and of the foundation of the Roman empire, Dryden provides a detailed set of historical conditions.[32]

His purpose in doing so may be explained by the relevance of both morals to contemporary English politics. Like the Greeks, the English were engaged in a military alliance against an encroaching monarchy; like the Romans they had recently received a new gov-

ernment. In general these resemblances suggest the potential use-
fulness of poetry to the court, of Dryden to William. But Dryden
soon dismisses Homer's moral as "not adapted to the times in
which the *Roman* poet liv'd" (p. 1012); and he so develops Virgil's
as to draw out a number of contrasts between poetry, politics, and
the relations among them in Virgil's time and his own. Dryden
describes Augustus's rise to power in much the same terms he had
employed in the *Discourse*. The Roman constitution was destroyed
by competing politicians under the guise of "Liberty and Reformation." Caesar "found the Sweets of Arbitrary Power" and made
himself "a Providential Monarch" (p. 1012–1013). But though
this account implies, as we have seen, a number of Jacobite lessons, Dryden is careful to preserve his rhetorical detachment: he
suggests that he is merely tracing in Roman history the inevitable
effects of universal laws. The destruction of the Commonwealth is
described as a necessary consequence of such laws: "So the Fab-
rique of consequence must fall betwixt them: And Tyranny must
be built upon their Ruines. This comes of altering Fundamental
Laws and Constitutions" (p. 1012). Dryden extracts from Roman
history the lesson of *Absalom and Achitophel*, *The Hind and the
Panther*, and *Don Sebastian*, but in doing so he stands at least as
far outside the history of his own country as that of Rome. His
rhetorical distance is so great that he appears not to be raising an
arguable political point; he is merely rehearsing matters long familiar to his learned readers: he introduces his account of Caesar's
dictatorship by promising "Not to trouble your Lordship with the
Repetition of what you know" (p. 1013).

This similarity between Rome and England forms the basis for
Dryden's main concern, which here as in the *Discourse* is the relation between poet and state. His most pointed criticism of contemporary England arises from his consideration of the bonds of
patronage and service that unite the greatest Roman emperor and
the greatest Roman poet.[33] Like Dryden's, Virgil's political principles differed from those of his government: "he was still of Republican Principles in his Heart"; but he supported Augustus because he "saw ... that the Commonwealth was lost without
ressource" (p. 1013–1014). Having stated the basic fact of Virgil's
relation to Augustus, Dryden provides for it (with very little sup-
portive evidence) a context that both generalizes to all writers and
points specifically to his own position. Virgil, Montaigne, and

Dryden all hold that "an Honest Man ought to be contented with
that Form of Government, and with those Fundamental Constitutions of it, which he receiv'd from his Ancestors, and under
which himself was Born" (p. 1014). We are invited to see Dryden's
political behavior as congruent with that of two great writers and
all honest men—the universal context adds meaning and importance to a futile and personally disastrous course of action. His
explanation of Virgil's deviation from this standard jusifies as well
Dryden's adherence to it:

> I say that *Virgil* having maturely weigh'd the Condition of the Times
> in which he liv'd: that an entire Liberty was not to be retriev'd: that
> the present Settlement had the prospect of a long continuance in the
> same Family, or those adopted into it: that he held his Paternal Estate
> from the Bounty of the Conqueror, by whom he was likewise enrich'd,
> esteem'd, and cherish'd: that this Conquerour, though of a bad kind,
> was the very best of it: that the Arts of Peace flourish'd under him: that
> all Men might be happy if they would be quiet: that now he was in
> possession of the whole, yet he shar'd a great part of his Authority with
> the Senate: That he would be chosen into the Ancient Offices of the
> Commonwealth, and Rul'd by the Power which he deriv'd from them;
> and Prorogu'd his Government from time to time: Still, as it were,
> threatning to dismiss himself from Publick Cares, which he exercis'd
> more for the common Good, than for any delight he took in greatness:
> These things, I say, being consider'd by the Poet, he concluded it to be
> the Interest of his Country to be so Govern'd.
> (Pp. 1014–1015)

The very length of this catalogue reinforces Dryden's suggestion
that the normal and commendable course is that of constancy to
fundamental constitutional principles which he himself pursued
and that any divergence from this constancy can be justified only
by very peculiar conditions. And every one of these conditions may
be pointedly contrasted with the Jacobite view of those of Dryden's own time. In England in 1697, a return to the ancient system
of government might be easily achieved by the restoration of
James; the "present Settlement" had no prospect of continuance in
the Nassau family, and the Jacobites, though at the moment dis-
couraged, might in the future dispossess the descendants of Anne
Hyde; Dryden himself was neither enriched, nor esteemed, nor
cherished by the conqueror; William, far from encouraging the
arts of peace, cultivated nothing but war; he shared as little au-

thority as he could with Parliament; and for the Jacobites he ruled only to promote his own greatness and that of his Dutch and Huguenot favorites.

For Dryden's purposes, the most important of Augustus's qualities was his promotion of the arts. His relations with Virgil and Horace suggest an ideal standard of patronage and service. The moral of Virgil's poem was "Honest in the Poet, Honourable to the Emperour, whom he derives from a Divine Extraction; and reflecting part of that Honour on the *Roman* People, whom he derives also from the *Trojans*; and not only profitable, but necessary to the present Age; and likely to be such to their Posterity" (p. 1015). In a well-ordered state, the poet reflects honor upon himself, his king, and his country and provides essential service to the people and their posterity. And as the poet serves his sovereign, so the sovereign preserves his poet: "I doubt not but it was one Reason, why *Augustus* should be so passionately concern'd for the preservation of the *Aeneis*, which its Author had Condemn'd to be Burnt . . . was, because it did him a real Service as well as an Honour; that a Work should not be lost where his Divine Original was Celebrated in Verse, which had the Character of Immortality stamp'd upon it" (p. 1015).

Dryden goes on to generalize the application of this point to patrons and poets in all ages and simultaneously to focus it specifically upon himself. The "great *Roman* families" of Virgil's time were "no less oblig'd by him than the Emperour" (p. 1015). He celebrates his favorite families as captains, leaders, and winners of games, and attacks his enemies as losers: "For *genus irritabile Vatum*, as *Horace* says. When a Poet is throughly provok'd, he will do himself Justice, however dear it cost him. . . . I think these are not bare Imaginations of my own, though I find no trace of them in the Commentatours: But one Poet may judge of another by himself. The Vengeance we defer, is not forgotten" (p. 1016). Virgil's praise of his countrymen is no less the common property of poets than his blame: Spenser derives the English from Aeneas; French poets derive their nation from Hector; "the Heroe of *Homer* was a *Grecian*, of *Virgil* a *Roman*, of *Tasso* an *Italian*" (p. 1016).

If we are in doubt about the place of Dryden and his age in this universal context, Dryden makes it sufficiently clear in the next paragraph. Augustus, he tells us, is "still shadow'd in the Person of Aeneas," and he will "prepare the Subject by shewing how dext'rously he mannag'd both the Prince and People, so as to displease neither, and to do good to both, which is the part of a Wise and Honest Man: And proves that it is possible for a Courtier not to be a Knave. I shall continue still to speak my Thoughts like a free-born Subject as I am; though such things, perhaps, as no *Dutch* Commentator cou'd, and I am sure no *French*-man durst" (p. 1016). The positioning here of Dutch and French, William and Louis on one side, and the English Dryden on the other, is itself polemical; and the sudden and apparently irrelevant assertion of political freedom alerts us to the topical implications of Virgil's courtiership: Dryden implies that only an audience familiar with William's government would be surprised that a courtier need not be a knave. Dryden continues by reiterating the main point of contrast between his relations with William and Virgil's with Augustus: "I have already told your Lordship my Opinion of *Virgil*; that he was no Arbitrary Man. Oblig'd he was to his Master for his Bounty, and he repays him with good Counsel, how to behave himself in his new Monarchy" (p. 1016).

This counsel is embodied in a series of parallels between Augustus and Aeneas that Dryden goes on to develop at some length. Aeneas has no claim to the Trojan crown except through his wife Creusa, the daughter of Priam, and this is barred by Helenus, a surviving son of Priam. Similarly, he has no claim on the Latin crown except through his wife Lavinia (pp. 1016–1017). In all this, as Zwicker and others have shown, Aeneas's title resembles William's to the English throne.[34] But, significantly, he differs from William in his behavior: he makes no claim to the Trojan crown, and he does not assume the Latin crown during the life of his father-in-law Latinus, a benevolent "King by inheritance." Dryden is careful, however, to embed these topical allusions within a discussion of the exemplary relations between Augustus and his poets: Virgil's portrait of Aeneas both advances Augustus's fame and checks his bad impulses by reminding him of defects in his title that can be overcome only by generous treatment of his people. Similarly, Horace wrote an ode "on purpose to deter" Augustus from his unpopular resolve to rebuild Troy: "by this, my Lord, we may conclude that he had still his Pedigree in his Head; and had an Itch of being thought a Divine King, if his Poets had not given him better Counsel" (p. 1018). Ideally, the poet encourages his sovereign's best qualities and restrains his worst ones.

In discussing Aeneas's manners, Dryden finds another parallel to Augustus which, while it continues his discussion of the relation between poetry and politics, directs us to a rather different, but no less important, set of topical applications. Whereas Aeneas's title refers to William's, his manners refer to James's: "Those Manners were Piety to the Gods, and a dutiful Affection to his Father; Love to his Relations; Care of his People; Courage and Conduct in the Wars; Gratitude to those who had oblig'd him; and Justice in general to Mankind" (p. 1018). Of these virtues, Dryden gives fullest treatment to piety, which "takes place of all, as the chief part of his Character" (p. 1018). This is, of course, the distinguishing trait of that other avatar of James, Don Sebastian; and there is much to suggest the parallel in both the preparations for and the substance of Dryden's discussion of Aeneas's manners. He promises "to vindicate my Divine Master to your Lordship, and by you to the Reader" (p. 1019), and prepares the ground by defining the character of his own patriotism. He will enlist the aid of the French critic Segrais, "For, impartially speaking, the *French* are as much better Criticks than the *English*, as they are worse Poets. Thus we generally allow that they better understand the management of a War, than our Islanders; but we know we are superiour to them, in the day of Battel. They value themselves on their Generals; we on our Souldiers" (p. 1019). The great general of the English forces was William himself: Dryden here reconciles his belief in the French cause against William with his love of his country and so justifies his appeal to French aid for the defense of his Master.

When he returns to Aeneas's manners, he has narrowed the issue in such a way as to emphasize the reference to James. "*Virgil* is Arraign'd for placing Piety before Valour; and making that Piety the chief Character of his Heroe" (p. 1020). He excuses Virgil first by reminding us of the political purpose of the *Aeneid.* Homer and Tasso were free to create imperfect heroes, "But *Virgil*, who design'd to form a perfect Prince, and would insinuate, that *Augustus*, whom he calls *Aeneas* in his Poem, was truly such, found himself oblig'd to make him without blemish; thoroughly Virtuous; and a thorough Virtue both begins and ends in Piety"

(p. 1020). He demonstrates the superiority of piety to valor in a paragraph that he twice insists is "Translated literally from *Segrais*":

> *Virgil* had consider'd that the greatest Virtues of *Augustus* consisted in the perfect Art of Governing his People; which caus'd him to Reign for more than Forty Years in great Felicity. He consider'd that his Emperour was Valiant, Civil, Popular, Eloquent, Politick, and Religious. He has given all those Qualities to *Aeneas*. But knowing that Piety alone comprehends the whole Duty of Man towards the Gods, towards his Country, and towards his Relations, he judg'd, that this ought to be his first Character, whom he would set for a Pattern of Perfection. In reality, they who believe that the Praises which arise from Valour, are superior to those, which proceed from any other Virtues, have not consider'd (as they ought,) that Valour, destitute of other Virtues, cannot render a Man worthy of any true esteem. That Quality which signifies no more than an intrepid Courage, may be separated from many others which are good, and accompany'd with many which are ill. A Man may be very Valiant, and yet Impious and Vicious. But the same cannot be said of Piety; which excludes all ill Qualities, and comprehends even Valour it self, with all other Qualities which are good. Can we, for example, give the praise of Valour to a Man who shou'd see his Gods prophan'd, and shou'd want the Courage to defend them? To a Man who shou'd abandon his Father, or desert his King in his last Necessity?
>
> (Pp. 1020–1021)

The application of this passage grows clearer as it proceeds. Dryden adds to Segrais only in the final phrase, which he expands from "à un homme qui abandonnerait son Roy & son pére."[35] James may have lacked Augustus's "perfect Art of Governing," but in the far more important virtue of piety, he was no less a pattern of perfection. William was for Dryden a sad proof that a valiant man might be vicious and impious. The two examples with which the passage concludes refer more pointedly to James and William. James lost his throne by his overeager defense of his gods; William abandoned his father-in-law, and his supporters deserted their king in his last necessity.

Throughout his discussion of Virgil's moral and Aeneas's manners, then, Dryden reflects upon the crimes of William and the virtues of James. He is, however, careful rather to allow these lessons to arise incidentally from his material than to arrange them in a coherent parallel. And he places this political commentary in the general frame of a discussion of the exemplary relations between the court poet Virgil and his imperial patron Augustus. In the remainder of his defense of the *Aeneid*, though specific topical references grow less frequent, he continues to reflect upon the general relation between poetry and politics in such a manner as to explain and elevate his own present position. He interrupts his account of the Dido episode to demonstrate the poet's superiority to the truths of history. A poet may be partial to the cause of his native country:

> for he is not ty'd to truth, or fetter'd by the Laws of History. *Homer* and *Tasso* are justly prais'd for chusing their Heroes out of *Greece* and *Italy*; *Virgil* indeed made his a *Trojan*, but it was to derive the *Romans*, and his own *Augustus* from him; but all three Poets are manifestly partial to their Heroes, in favour of their Country. For *Dares Phrygius* reports of *Hector*, that he was slain Cowardly; *Aeneas* according to the best account, slew not *Mezentius*, but was slain by him: and the Chronicles of *Italy* tell us little of that *Rinaldo d'Estè* who Conquers *Jerusalem* in *Tasso*. He might be a Champion of the Church; but we know not that he was so much as present at the Siege.
>
> (P. 1029)

As in the *Discourse*, Dryden elevates poetry and so himself above the unfortunate accidents of politics, by which a Mezentius triumphs over an Aeneas, and a William over a James. Poetry constitutes an ideal realm, where false pretenders are easily exposed, and real virtue wins out.

In discussing the freedom of poets from chronology, Dryden places the specific issues of James's reign within this general conception of poetry and politics. Virgil "might make this *Anacronism*, by superseding the mechanick Rules of Poetry, for the same Reason, that a Monarch may dispense with, or suspend his own Laws, when he finds it necessary so to do; especially if those Laws are not altogether fundamental" (p. 1031). Zwicker, explaining the allusion to James's use of his dispensing power to elude the Test Act, sees this as politics "under the guise of poetics."[36] But the discussion of poetics that occasions not only this allusion but the whole *Dedication* is crucial to Dryden's meaning. He is not merely conducting political commentary under cover of literary criticism, he is defining the relation between poetry and politics in such a way as to display the untroubled permanence and importance of the one, and the unredeemable and unending folly of the other, and so to advance both his political attack on William and the rehabilitation of his public image.

Though at the beginning of the *Dedication* the poet appears as the physician of the state, inculcating in the people important lessons and helping to establish political stability, the poetic duty that appears most frequently in Dryden's essay is patriotism. Patriotic celebration is for the poet more important than historic truth: "To love our Native Country, and to study its Benefit and its Glory, to be interested in its Concerns, is Natural to all Men, and is indeed our common Duty. A Poet makes a farther step; for endeavouring to do honour to it, 'tis allowable in him even to be partial in its Cause" (p. 1028–1029). Indeed, such partiality is for Dryden the most important source of poetic originality. In defending Virgil from the charge of imitating Homer, he employs an analogy of painters whose approach to the same subject—the fall of Troy—differs according to their nationality: "*Apelles* wou'd have distinguish'd *Pyrrhus* . . . because he was a *Grecian*, and he wou'd do Honour to his Country. *Raphael*, who was an *Italian*, and descended from the *Trojans*, wou'd have made *Aeneas* the Heroe of his piece" (p. 1035). This principle is repeated throughout the *Dedication*, and in Dryden's concluding discussion of his own translation it provides a means of understanding his place within classic and native literary tradition.

His relation to both traditions is apparent in the claim of unique appreciation of Virgillian diction and prosody that begins his account of the style of his translation: he may not have equalled Virgil, "but I have endeavour'd to follow the Example of my Master: And am the first *Englishman*, perhaps, who made it his design to copy him in his Numbers, his choice of Words, and his placing them for the sweetness of the sound" (p. 1046). He corroborates this claim with a technical discussion of Latin and English prosody which, however brief in itself, implies that he is drawing on vast resources of knowledge and experience; and he soon refers to the source of this expertise: "I have long had by me the Materials of an English *Prosodia*, containing all the Mechanical Rules of Versification, wherein I have treated with some exactness of the Feet, the Quantities, and the Pauses." This work would raise English verse above its competitors: "The *French* and *Italians* know nothing of the two first; at least their best Poets have not practis'd them"; and it would finally identify the source of sweetness in Denham's famous lines on the Thames. But for a number of reasons—the difficulty of the project, personal modesty, the weakness of his fellow poets, and Mulgrave's advice against it—Dryden will at present keep this work to himself (pp. 1047–1948).

This is not, as we have seen, Dryden's first mention of an English prosodia. In the *Discourse of Satire* he attributes the lack of such a work to governmental neglect (p. 86). In the *Dedication* of *Examen Poeticum* he is even more vehement. He claims that the faults of English poets

> with care and observation, might be amended. For after all, our Language is both Copious, Significant, and Majestical; and might be reduc'd into a more harmonious sound. But for want of Publick Encouragement, in this *Iron Age*, we are so far from making any progress in the improvement of our Tongue, that in few years, we shall Speak and Write as Barbarously as our Neighbours.
>
> (P. 372)

The same complaint about state patronage of the arts in William's England is implicit in his account of English prosody in the *Dedication*. He could hardly say that he was withholding his work on prosody until he could find sponsorship for its proposals in a government more favorable to him than William's, but the discussion of English and French poetry and patronage that follows suggests as much. The French, who lack genius, enjoy court patronage: "The want of Genius, of which I have accus'd the *French*, is laid to their Charge by one of their own great Authors. . . . If Rewards cou'd make good Poets, their great Master has not been wanting on his part in his bountiful Encouragements: For he is wise enough to imitate *Augustus*, if he had a *Maro*" (p. 1049). The reference to Augustus introduces a digression on the ideally reciprocal relations between poet and sovereign; and this serves to place Dryden's discussion of contemporary England and France within the universal context of such relations that he establishes at the beginning of the essay: "The *Triumvir* and *Proscriber* had descended to us in a more hideous form than they now appear, if the Emperour had not taken care to make Friends of him and *Horace*" (p. 1049). When he returns to England, he suggests the application of this lesson to the modern counterparts of Virgil and Augustus: "But

Heroick Poetry is not the growth of *France*, as it might be of
England, if it were Cultivated. *Spencer* wanted only to have read
the Rules of *Bossu*: for no Man was ever Born with a greater
Genius, or had more Knowledge to support it" (p. 1049). Dryden
has just traced his own descent from "*Virgil* in Latine, and *Spencer*
in English" (p. 1048). The French have patronage but lack genius;
the English have genius—and the implication is that they lack the
patronage with which to cultivate it, and that Dryden himself, as
the successor of Spenser and a follower of Bossu, is the genius who
might best have received such patronage. Further, the loss is not
only literature's, but the nation's and the king's. England will lose
an opportunity of surpassing its cultural rivals France and Italy,
and William will descend to posterity without the blessing of his
poets.

Throughout the remainder of the *Dedication*, Dryden continues
to define the English literary tradition; its continuity with the classics, its potential superiority to the continental, and his own important function in sustaining and advancing both these qualities.
He excuses his high opinion of his work as an expression of patriotism: "What I have said, though it has the face of arrogance,
yet is intended for the honour of my Country; and therefore I will
boldly own, that this *English* Translation has more of *Virgil*'s
Spirit in it, than either the *French*, or the *Italian*"(p. 1051). He
praises the accomplishments of other English poets who have attempted parts of Virgil—Mulgrave, Roscommon, Denham,
Waller, and Cowley—and hopes that he has equalled their success
despite having to bear "the weight of a whole Author on my shoul-
ders." He has followed the great English writers of the past by
imitating the Romans: "*Spencer* and *Milton* are the nearest in English to *Virgil* and *Horace* in the Latine; and I have endeavour'd to
form my Stile by imitating their Masters" (p. 1051). He finds
evidence for the superiority of English verse to continental in the
former's use of triplets and alexandrines:

> *Spencer* is my Example for both these priviledges of *English* Verses.
> And *Chapman* has follow'd him in his Translation of *Homer*. Mr.
> *Cowley* has given in to them after both: And all succeeding Writers
> after him. I regard them now as the *Magna Charta* of Heroick Poetry;
> and am too much an *English*-man to lose what my Ancestors have

gain'd for me. Let the *French* and *Italians* value themselves on their Regularity: Strength and Elevation are our Standard.

(P. 1055)

All of this has a clear application to Dryden's political position in the nineties. By claiming to uphold his country's greatness, he counteracts the taint associated with Jacobitism of treasonous correspondence with the French, and by connecting poetic irregularity with English liberty, exactitude with foreign domination, he not only appropriates the libertarian language of the Williamites but suggests their own association with foreign power and their surrender to William of those native privileges their ancestors had gained.

It is, however, important to remember that Dryden is talking about poetry as well as politics; and he repeatedly suggests that the poetic tradition that sustains English greatness is repressed by malign political influences. The poetry of Cowley, for example, is marred by impurity of diction, "For through the Iniquity of the times, he was forc'd to Travel, at an Age, when, instead of Learning Foreign Languages, he shou'd have studied the Beauties of His Mother Tongue" (p. 1056). Dryden's diction in his translation forms the basis of an extended metaphor that explores the relative value to the nation of contemporary poetic and political achievements:

> Words are not so easily Coyn'd as Money: And yet we see that the Credit not only of Banks, but of Exchequers cracks, when little comes in, and much goes out. *Virgil* call'd upon me in every line for some new word: And I paid so long, that I was almost Banckrupt. . . . What had become of me, if *Virgil* had tax'd me with another Book? I had certainly been reduc'd to pay the Publick in hammer'd Money for want of Mill'd; that is in the same old Words which I had us'd before: And the Receivers must have been forc'd to have taken any thing, where there was so little to be had.
>
> (P. 1058)

Zwicker has fully described the reference here to the coinage crisis and the public debt caused by William's expensive continental wars.[37] In comparing his own lack of words to England's lack of money, Dryden suggests the consequences for literature of the government's neglect of the arts of peace. When he resumes the metaphor, he gives it a rather different turn:

> If sounding Words are not of our growth and Manufacture, who shall hinder me to Import them from a Foreign Country? I carry not out the Treasure of the Nation, which is never to return: but what I bring from *Italy*, I spend in *England*: Here it remains, and here it circulates; for if the Coyn be good, it will pass from one hand to another. I Trade both with the Living and the Dead, for the enrichment of our Native Language.
>
> (P. 1059)

Dryden combines an assertion of his own place in poetic tradition with one of the superiority of his poetry, which enriches the nation, to William's policies, which impoverish it. He concludes the discussion with an observation by which he contrasts his patriotic Jacobitism with the treason of the Williamites: poets should "use this License very sparingly, for if too many Foreign Words are pour'd in upon us, it looks as if they were design'd not to assist the Natives, but to Conquer them" (p. 1060). Dryden uses foreign assistance to advance the glory of England; his opponents bring it into inglorious subjection.

The set of topics that inform the *Discourse* and *Dedication* make a final appearance in the *Preface* to *Fables*, where the presence of Chaucer allows Dryden to display even more clearly his poetic status and his place in the English tradition. He claims to have given Ovid's fables

> the same Turn of Verse, which they had in the Original; and this, I may say without vanity, is not the Talent of every Poet: He who has arriv'd the nearest to it, is the Ingenious and Learned *Sandys*, the best Versifier of the former Age; if I may properly call it by that Name, which was the former Part of this concluding Century. For *Spencer* and *Fairfax* both flourish'd in the Reign of Queen *Elizabeth*: Great Masters in our Language; and who saw much farther into the Beauties of our Numbers, than those who immediately followed them. *Milton* was the Poetical Son of *Spencer*, and Mr. *Waller* of *Fairfax*; for we have our Lineal Descents and Clans, as well as other Families: *Spencer* more than once insinuates, that the Soul of *Chaucer* was transfus'd into his Body; and that he was begotten by him Two hundred years after his Decease. *Milton* has acknowledg'd to me, that *Spencer* was his Orig-

inal; and many besides my self have heard our famous *Waller* own, that he deriv'd the Harmony of his Numbers from the *Godfrey of Bulloign*, which was turn'd into *English* by Mr. *Fairfax.*
(P. 1445)

Dryden appears only at the beginning of this account, as the superior of Sandys; but he would surely forgive us for seeing him as the rightful heir of both the traditions he describes.

His repeated expressions of admiration for Chaucer emphasize again his participation in native tradition and the patriotism to which he is obliged as an English poet. He translates Chaucer "to promote the Honour of my Native Country" and confesses partiality for "my Country-man, and Predecessor in the Laurel" (p. 1445). He holds Chaucer "in the same Degree of Veneration as the *Grecians* held *Homer*, or the *Romans Virgil*" (p. 1452). He protests that "no Man ever had, or can have, a greater Veneration for *Chaucer*, than my self" (p. 1459). He considers the *Knight's Tale* "perhaps not much inferiour to the *Ilias* or the *Aeneis*" (p. 1460). His modifications of Chaucer, far from suggesting any disrespect, are the effect of his close identification with his great predecessor:

> I have not ty'd my self to a Literal Translation; but have often omitted what I judg'd unnecessary, or not of Dignity enough to appear in the Company of better Thoughts. I have presum'd farther in some Places, and added somewhat of my own where I thought my Author was deficient, and had not given his Thoughts their true Lustre, for want of Words in the Beginning of our Language. And to this I was the more embolden'd, because (if I may be permitted to say it of my self) I found I had a Soul congenial to his, and that I had been conversant in the same Studies. Another Poet, in another Age, may take the same Liberty with my Writings; if at least they live long enough to deserve Correction.
> (P. 1457)

Despite the humility of the last clause, Dryden clearly asserts his place in an English tradition extending far into both the past and the future.

Further, he brings Chaucer into the same system of patronage and service that Virgil enjoyed and from which Dryden had been wrongfully excluded:

He was employ'd abroad, and favour'd by *Edward* the Third, *Richard* the Second, and *Henry* the Fourth, and was Poet, as I suppose, to all Three of them. In *Richard's* Time, I doubt, he was a little dipt in the Rebellion of the Commons; and being Brother-in-Law to *John of Ghant*, it is no wonder if he follow'd the Fortunes of that Family; and was well with *Henry* the Fourth when he had depos'd his Predecessor. Neither is it to be admir'd, that *Henry*, who was a wise as well as a valiant Prince, who claim'd by Succession, and was sensible that his Title was not sound, but was rightfully in *Mortimer*, who had married the Heir of *York*; it was not to be admir'd, I say, if that great Politician should be pleas'd to have the greatest Wit of those Times in his Interests, and to be the Trumpet of his Praises. *Augustus* had given him the Example, by the Advice of *Maecenas*, who recommended *Virgil* and *Horace* to him; whose Praises help'd to make him Popular while he was alive, and after his Death have made him Precious to Posterity.

(P. 1453)

Augustus and Henry IV, conscious that their titles were not sound, entrusted their reputations to Virgil and Chaucer; William III had ignored Dryden's conciliatory gestures in *King Arthur* and *Cleomenes*, and so missed an opportunity that his wiser predecessors had eagerly cultivated. The loss falls more heavily on William than on Dryden; as a poet of established reputation writing in the great tradition, as the English Virgil, the modern Chaucer, his position with posterity is assured, and his view of English politics will survive when the shams of William's supporters are forgotten.

Epilogue

It is difficult to gauge the effect of Dryden's rhetorical campaign in his last works. What evidence we have, however, suggests that his reputation as a poet increased in the 1690s even among those who opposed his politics. The *Virgil* was a financial success: 351 prominent Englishmen subscribed to the translation, and the first edition sold out within six months.[1] We may imagine that some of the five-guinea subscribers were willing to overlook Dryden's political reputation in order to accompany the poet in his assured march toward posterity by means of engraved plates inscribed with their coats of arms.

The best testimonies to Dryden's success are the protests of his enemies and competitors. Dryden's view of contemporary politics did not in fact survive. His party was repeatedly and decisively defeated, and his version of the Revolution fell victim to the retrospective appropriation of that event by the Lockean Whigs in the eighteenth century and has only recently been given extensive study. But Dryden's contemporaries could no more foresee this contingency than Dryden himself, and there is a noticeable political animus behind the attempts of such writers as George Powell, Luke Milbourne, and Jonathan Swift to circumvent Dryden's potential appropriation of cultural authority in the eyes of a credulous posterity. In the *Preface* to *The Fatal Discovery*, Powell describes Dryden's "To Mr. *Grenville*, on his Excellent Tragedy called *Heroique Love*" as "a true *Dryden* Composition, in all his own celebrated perfections of *Pride, Fancy,* and *Scandal*":

This Poem, though designed a Caress to the Honourable Author, however, makes the top Compliment at home: the main flourish is upon himself: when with his own long and laudable Vanity, all true *Drydenism*, he gives the Reader to understand, That *J. Dryden* is the very Father of the Muses, the Source, Fountain, and Original of Poetry, nay,

the *Apollo* himself; when all the Address he has to make this Ingenious
and Honourable Author, is, the Resignation of his own Lawrels.

But here, I am afraid, he makes him but a course Compliment, when
this great Wit, with his Treacherous Memory, forgets, that he had
given away his Lawrels upon Record, no less than twice before, *viz.*
once to Mr. *Congreve*, and another time to Mr. *Southern*.[2]

In his attack on the *Dedication* of the *Aeneis*, Milbourne also
derides Dryden's self-presentation as transparent vanity. Dryden's
comparison of himself to "Dutch commentatours" sends Milbourne into paroxysms of rage:

> But what a Happiness is it, that Mr. *D.* can speak so freely as no *Dutch*
> Commentator could? Poor Scoundrels, filthy illiterate Fellows they!
> What were the *Heinsius*'s and *Emmenessius*'s to Mr. *Dryden*? But *one*
> *Poet may judge of another by himself*. Excellent! *Poet Squab*, endued
> with *Poet Maro*'s Spirit by a wonderful *Metempsychosis*.[3]

Dryden's claim to have discovered the source of sweetness in Denham's lines on the Thames has a similar effect on Milbourne:

> And why must not others have observ'd both the *Sweetness* and the
> *Reason of the Sweetness* of that *Couplet*. Is Mr. *D.* the only Man of
> Ear? . . . I must believe, that no Man living can teach *him* to make
> *smooth well-running Verses*, who has not a *Musical Ear*: unless Mr. *D.*
> or some like *him*, would give us a new *English Parnassus*.
>
> (P. 24)

Milbourne reacts with the same defensive sarcasm to Dryden's
discussion of the dependence of historical fame on poetic patronage:

> *The Triumvir and Proscriber had descended to us in a more hideous*
> *Form, if the* Emperor *had not taken care to make Friends of* Virgil *and*
> Horace. Well, I can't but tremble at our *present King's* Fate: Boast not,
> *Great Prince*, of all thy *Martial Acquisitions*; boast not of having given
> Check to the *Grand Louis*; talk not of *Namure*, nor *Ireland* reduced,
> nor pretend to *Thanksgivings* for a *Glorious Peace*, for *the terrible Mr.*
> *Bays is disobliged!* What an unlucky thing was it to give *his Lawrel* to
> a *Shadwell* or a *Tate*, whose drawn Pen is more fatal than that of
> *Hipponax*, and more terrible than a *Lüxemburg* or *Boufflers in the*
> *Head of a French veterans Army*. Well, how *his Majesty*'ll come off I
> know not.
>
> (Pp. 25–26)

Swift's attack, though more clever than these, depends on ridicule of the same rhetorical strategies. Dryden's implied presentation of himself as the English Virgil is made ridiculously explicit in
the *Battel of the Books*:

> *Dryden* in a long Harangue soothed up the good *Antient*, called him
> *Father*, and by a large deduction of Genealogies, made it plainly ap-
> pear, that they were nearly related. Then he humbly proposed an Ex-
> change of Armor, as a lasting Mark of Hospitality between them. *Vir-
> gil* consented . . . tho' his was of Gold, and cost a hundred Beeves, the
> others but of rusty Iron.[4]

In *A Tale of a Tub* Swift inflates Dryden's professions of retirement from politics to ridiculous proportions:

> THESE Notices may serve to give the Learned Reader an Idea as well
> as a Taste of what the whole Work is likely to produce; wherein I have
> now altogether circumscribed my Thoughts and my Studies; and if I
> can bring it to a Perfection before I die, shall reckon I have well em-
> ploy'd the poor Remains of an unfortunate Life. This indeed is more
> than I can justly expect from a Quill worn to the Pith in the Service of
> the State, in *Pros's* and *Con's* upon *Popish Plots*, and *Meal-Tubs*, and
> *Exclusion Bills*, and *Passive Obedience*, and *Addresses of Lives and
> Fortunes*; and *Prerogative*, and *Property*, and *Liberty of Conscience*,
> and *Letters to a Friend*: From an Understanding and a Conscience,
> thread-bare and ragged with perpetual turning; From a Head broken
> in a hundred places, by the Malignants of the opposite Factions, and
> from a Body spent with Poxes ill cured, by trusting to Bawds and
> Surgeons, who, (as it afterwards appeared) were profess'd Enemies to
> Me and the Government, and revenged their Party's Quarrel upon my
> Nose and Shins. Fourscore and eleven Pamphlets have I written under
> three Reigns, and for the Service of six and thirty Factions. But finding
> the State has no farther Occasion for Me and my Ink, I retire willingly
> to draw it out into Speculations more becoming a Philosopher, having,
> to my unspeakable Comfort, passed a long Life, with a Conscience
> void of Offence.
>
> (Pp. 69–71)

The modern author of *A Tale* claims to have been honored with
Dryden's confidences on the subject of his self-presentation: "He
has often said to me in Confidence, that the World would have
never suspected him to be so great a Poet, if he had not assured
them so frequently in his Prefaces, that it was impossible they

could either doubt or forget it" (p. 131). If Dryden were as fla-
grantly self-promoting as these parodies suggest, there would be
little need for parodies. Swift, writing as an unknown in the late
1690s, is reacting to a masterly rhetoric of self-definition that
seems not only to have deflected criticism from Dryden's political
behavior but to have dominated the literature of his times.

Notes

Introduction

1. Earl Miner, *Dryden's Poetry* (Bloomington: Indiana University Press, 1967), p. 289; Michael West, "Dryden's Ambivalence as a Translator of Heroic Themes," *Huntington Library Quarterly*, 36 (1973), 347–366, p. 365.

2. Jay Arnold Levine, "John Dryden's Epistle to John Driden," *JEGP*, 63 (1964), 458–474, pp. 470–471; Thomas H. Fujimura, "The Personal Element in Dryden's Poetry," *PMLA*, 89 (1974), 1007–1023, p. 1021.

3. Fujimura, " 'Autobiography' in Dryden's Later Work," *Restoration*, 8 (1984), 17–29.

1: "Echoes of Her Once Loyal Voice"

1. Phillip Harth, in *The Contexts of Dryden's Thought* (University of Chicago Press, 1968), claims that in *The Hind and the Panther* Dryden is able to keep politics and religion separate from one another: "at any given moment in the poem he is dealing with 'Matters either Religious or Civil,' to use his own words, never with both topics simultaneously" (p. 229). Yet Harth's own version of Dryden's rhetorical purpose throughout the poem suggests a close connection between the two: "Dryden was attempting to persuade his Anglican readers to grant religious tolerance as well as political toleration to the members of his new church" (p. 49). If the Anglicans had not been threatening to rebel against a Catholic monarch, Dryden would have been less troubled by their unwillingness to concede that Catholic doctrine was "not unreasonable." Throughout the poem he insists upon a close relation between political and religious rebellion against just authority.

2. Thomas Babington Macaulay, *The History of England from the Accession of James the Second*, ed. Charles Harding Firth (London: Macmillan, 1914), pp. 845–855. For more recent manifestations of this theory see C. V. Wedgwood, *Poetry and Politics Under the Stuarts* (Cambridge: Cambridge University Press, 1960), p. 178; Donald R. Benson, "Theology

and Politics in Dryden's Conversion," *Studies in English Literature*, 4 (1964), 393–412, pp. 406–407; William Myers, "Politics in *The Hind and the Panther*," *Essays in Criticism*, 19 (1969) 19–33, *passim*.

3. Earl Miner, ed. and Vinton A. Dearing, textual ed., *The Works of John Dryden*, vol. 3 (Berkeley and Los Angeles: University of California Press, 1969), p. 350.

4. All citations to *The Hind and the Panther* are to Miner, ed., *Works*, 3.

5. Harth (p. 261) notices this rhetorical strategy and finds analogues in contemporary Catholic apologetics.

6. Miner, *Dryden's Poetry* (Bloomington: University of Indiana Press, 1967), p. 192, briefly notes the significance of the order in which Dryden introduces his beasts and argues that the Panther is even worse than her fellows: "The introduction of the Panther only after the sectarian beasts . . . adversely affects our opinion of her. As the Wolf was worse then the Fox, the Panther is fiercest of all." But Dryden intends not only to compare bad parties with worse ones but also to taint popular parties with the reputation and principles of universally condemned ones.

7. *The Rhetoric of Aristotle*, trans. Lane Cooper (Englewood Cliffs, N.J.: Prentice-Hall, 1932), 3.15.2. In attacking the Anglicans for Whiggish rebelliousness Dryden was in line with polemicists both before and after the Revolution. See for example *A New Test of the Church of England's Loyalty* (London, 1687) p. 8:

> For my business is, to set forth in its own Colours the extraordinary Loyalty of these Men, who obstinately maintain a *Test*, contriv'd by the *Faction* to usher in the Bill of Exclusion. . . . And it is much admir'd even by some of her own Children, that the Grave and Matron-like Church of *England*, which values her self so much for her Antiquity, should be overfond of a new Point of Faith lately broach'd by a Famous *Act of an Infallible* English *Parliament* conven'd at *Westminster*, and guided by the Holy Spirit of *Shaftsbury*.

And *A Lord's Speech without Doors* (London, 1689; reprinted in *An Answer to Two Papers*, London, 1689, p. 6):

> Believe me, My Lords, it is the boldest bid that ever Men made; I see Forty One was a Fool to Eighty Eight; and that we Church of *England* Protestants, shall cancel all the merits of our Fathers, overthrow the ground and Consequence of their most *Exemplary Loyalty* to King *Charles* the First and Second; render their Death, the Death of *Fools*; trample their *Memories* and *Blood* under our Feet; subject our selves to the just Reproach of the

Phanaticks, whose Principles and Practices we have out-done, even to that King, that we forced upon them, and by our Example, had brought them to live well withal.

Dryden's attackers were well aware of his objects: see for example *The Revolter* (London, 1687); *A Poem in Defence of the Church of England Written in Opposition to the Hind and the Panther* (London, 1688); both are epitomized by Hugh Macdonald in *John Dryden: A Bibliography* (Oxford: Clarendon Press, 1939), item nos. 242, 253.

8. Miner, ed., *Works,* 3:383, thinks this a reference to the Anglican reaction to persecution under Mary. It would seem, however, inconsistent with the Hind's purposes to taunt the Panther with a change in the right direction and to describe her royal daughter as a "butcher."

9. This strategy has been remarked by Myers. He cites the allusion to Monmouth (II.281–282), argues that the Hind compares the Panther's jury of apostles to Shaftesbury's jury of City Whigs (II.242–243), and, rather inconsistently, compares the Panther's "attempt to mollify the Sects" to "Charles II's attempts to control Parliament" (II.272–274); and justly observes that "This is all calculated to make the Panther feel ill at ease. It is obviously disorienting for Tory High-Churchmen to be told that theologically they think like Whigs, that Anglican authority is as specious as Monmouth's legitimacy" (p. 26). He does not, however, seem to recognize its function in the poem, the purpose of which was, he thinks (before its author was surprised by the Declaration of Indulgence), "to demonstrate the practical good sense of the Church allying herself with the Royal Party" (p. 25). In fact the references to Tory polemic in part II argue the political no less than the theological Whiggery of the contemporary Anglicans. Dryden had more political sense than to expect a triumphant alliance between the Anglicans and the court; and if he had expected such an alliance, he certainly had more polemic ability than to have supposed he could abuse the Anglicans into joining it.

10. See Steven N. Zwicker, *Politics and Language in Dryden's Poetry,* pp. 144–145.

11. All citations to *The Medall* are to *The Works of John Dryden,* vol. 2, ed. H. T. Swedenberg, Jr. and Vinton A. Dearing (Berkeley, Los Angeles, London: University of California Press, 1972).

12. See, for example, *Poems on Affairs of State,* vol. 3, ed. Howard H. Schless (New Haven: Yale University Press, 1968), pp. 408–409.

13. See note 1, above. Harth provides a rather more complex account of Dryden's rhetorical purpose: "to isolate the Dissenters, renounce the actions of the more extreme Catholics, and question the motives of the more intransigent Anglicans in the expectation of arriving at some kind of accommodation between men of good will in the Anglican and Catholic

camps" (p. 50). If this was Dryden's purpose, his decision to represent the entire Anglican church as a single beast was unfortunate.

14. See Zwicker, p. 150.

15. For an analysis, to which I am much indebted, of Dryden's attitude towards his work in his later poetry, see Zwicker, chapters 5–7.

16. Donald Wing, *Short-Title Catalogue of Books Printed in England ... 1641–1700*, 3 vols. (New York: Columbia University Press, 1945–1951), lists, under the heading "Aesop," eighteen Latin editions and as many editions of English translations, published between 1660 and 1700. For the generic status of fable in this period, see Thomas Noel, *Theories of the Fable in the Eighteenth Century* (New York: Columbia University Press, 1975), and Annabel Patterson, "Fables of Power," in *Politics and Discourse*, ed. Kevin Sharpe and Steven N. Zwicker (Berkeley, Los Angeles, London: University of California Press, 1987), pp. 271–296.

17. *Aesop's Fables with His Life in English, French, and Latin*, 2nd ed. (London, 1687).

18. See Caroline F. E. Spurgeon, *Five Hundred Years of Chaucer Criticism and Allusion* (Cambridge, 1925; rpt. New York: Russell and Russell, 1960), 1:238–272, *passim*.

19. The generic precedents of *The Hind and the Panther* have been the object of much excellent but rather confusing scholarly attention. The two fullest accounts are in Miner, *Dryden's Poetry*, pp. 144–175, and Sanford Budick, *Dryden and the Abyss of Light* (New Haven: Yale University Press, 1970), pp. 191–237. Miner places the poem in a number of traditions of which the most important are sacred zoography, beast fable, and discontinuous tropology; Budick thinks it "an adaptation of allegorical Holy Writ—of the complex beast fable of Daniel" (p. 227). Both offer excellent support for their conflicting views, and the controversy between them has not much clarified matters (see *The Times Literary Supplement*, 3 April 1969, p. 371; 1 May 1969, p. 466; 22 May 1969, p. 559; 3 July 1969, p. 730). Both, further, have contributed to our understanding of the poem; and Budick's work, by showing how Dryden turns against the Protestants antipapist polemic based on Daniel, advances our knowledge of its polemic strategies. Dryden himself, however, establishes the genre within which he means the poem to be read at the beginning of part III: whatever his sources, he wants his audience to see the poem not as discontinuous tropology or Old Testament prophecy but as Aesopian fable in the tradition of Chaucer and Spencer.

20. See Zwicker, pp. 150–153.

21. See Miner, ed. *Works*, 3:449, 456.

22. "An Apology for the Church of England, with Relation to the Spirit of Persecution, for Which She Is Accused," in *A Collection of Scarce and Valuable Tracts*, ed. Walter Scott (London, 1813), 9:175. On the

same page Burnet remarks that the papists' "little finger must be heavier than ever our loins were" (cf., *The Hind and the Panther*, part III.691).

23. See, for example, *Poems on Affairs of State*, 3:183–206, and *passim*.

24. *Reasons Against Repealing . . . the Test*, p. 4.

25. *The Spanish Fryar*, in *The Works of John Dryden*, ed. Walter Scott and George Saintsbury (Edinburgh: William Paterson, 1883), 6:442.

26. This explains the "confusion over imagery of flight" that D. W. Jefferson finds in the poem ("The Poetry of *The Hind and the Panther*," *MLR*, 79 (1984), 32–44, p. 42). It is appropriate to Dryden's polemic purposes that the Catholics be seen as victims of forces they cannot control.

27. Anne Barbeau Gardiner, in "Dryden's *Britannia Rediviva*: Interpreting the Signs of the Times in June 1688," *HLQ*, 48 (1985), 257–284, concentrates on this aspect of Dryden's poem. She justly remarks that lines 267–303 constitute an appeal to the country "to support the king's toleration"; but the heavy emphasis throughout the poem on divine intervention strongly suggests that Dryden has despaired of a human solution to England's political woes. His account of politics is cast entirely in general terms of sin and repentance, justice and mercy.

2: "Adhering to a Lost Cause"

1. For a bibliography of such attacks, see Hugh Macdonald, *John Dryden: A Bibliography* (Oxford: Clarendon Press, 1939), nos. 199 ff.

2. Macdonald, nos. 248 ff.

3. *The Works of John Dryden*, vol. 15, ed. Earl Miner and George R. Guffey (Berkeley, Los Angeles, London: University of California Press, 1976). All references are to this edition.

4. Several critics have found political meaning in *Don Sebastian*. John Robert Moore, "Political Allusions in Dryden's Later Plays," *PMLA*, 72 (1958), 36–42, lists, often quite accurately, several such allusions in the play but does not deal with their relation to one another or participation in a coherent whole. He identifies Dryden's Mobile with the London populace, Dorax with James's deserters, Benducar with Sunderland, the Mufti with the Anglican clergy, and Muley-Moloch with "the infatuated James." William Myers, *Dryden* (London: Hutchinson University Library, 1973), repeats many of Moore's discoveries, notes the similarity of Sebastian's subjects to the Jacobites, but then dismisses these political allusions as only pointing to "symptoms of deeper, more distressing confusions at the heart of the human condition," p. 130. John Loftis, *The Spanish Plays of Neoclassical England* (New Haven: Yale University Press, 1973) has ex-

plored the play's similarities to Calderon's *El principe constante*, and so remarked its Catholicism. Miner finds in the play only a general "exploration of the uncertainty attendant on man as a political creature" (p. 406), and discounts any specific contemporary application. Irvin Ehrenpreis, in *Acts of Implication* (Berkeley, Los Angeles, London: University of California Press, 1980), p. 49, observes the similarity between Sebastian and James. Others have attempted to interpret the play's themes and structure without reference to its political application: John A. Winterbottom, "Hobbesian Ideas in Dryden's Tragedies," *JEGP*, 57 (1958), 665–683; Bruce King, "*Don Sebastian*: Dryden's Moral Fable," *Sewanee Review*, 70 (1962), 651–670; Eric Rothstein, *Restoration Tragedy* (Madison: University of Wisconsin Press, 1967).

  5. See Arthur Mainwaring, "Tarquin and Tullia," in *Poems on Affairs of State*, 5:47–54, for a similar list of James's virtues, which ends with the couplet, "In sum, how godlike must his nature be / Whose only fault was too much piety."

  6. As Miner remarks in his commentary on the play in *Works*, 15:389.

  7. In two articles to which I am much indebted, "Dryden and History: A Problem in Allegorical Reading," *ELH*, 36 (1969), 265–290, and " 'Examples Are Best Precepts': Readers and Meanings in Seventeenth Century Poetry," *Critical Inquiry*, 1 (1974), 173–190, John Wallace traces the effect on seventeenth-century poetry of contemporary habits of reading history for lessons that might be applied to current politics. Dryden is here making use of these habits to sharpen his readers' association of Sebastian with James. I now believe that my disagreement with Wallace in a note to the original version of this chapter ("Dryden and the Revolution of 1688: Political Parallel in *Don Sebastian*," *JEGP*, 85 (1986), 346–365, pp. 348–349) is based on a misreading of his articles. Wallace does indeed allow for the possibility (which in this note I reserve to myself) that writers may control their reader's political applications, as Dryden does here and throughout his late career.

  8. So called by the Convention Parliament. For Jacobite ridicule of this view of James's departure, see the poems cited by William J. Cameron in *Poems on Affairs of State*, vol. 5 (New Haven: Yale University Press, 1971), pp. 57–60.

  9. "Dryden and History," p. 281.

  10. *The Dear Bargain* (n.p., n.d.), p. 24. For other examples, see *An Address to the Nobility, Clergy, and Gentlemen of Scotland*: "it will entail a War upon posterity" (p. 3); *Some Reflections upon His Highness the Prince of Orange's Declaration* (n.p., 1688): "for if they change Masters, they Entail Blood upon their Children about the Title of the Crown" (p. 2); *A Lord's Speech Without Doors*: "God defend us and our Children after us from the ill Consequences of what has been done, and prevent the

rest" (p. 3); *Reflections upon our Late and Present Proceedings*, in *A Tenth Collection of Papers Relating to the Present Juncture of Affairs in England* (London, 1689): "What we do now will transmit its good or ill Effects to after Ages, and our Children yet unborn, will in all probability, be happy or miserable, as we shall behave our selves in this great Conjuncture. . . . But if we do ingage in wrong Counsels, and build upon false Foundations, instead of a Blessing we may leave a Curse to our Posterity" (p. 1).

11. For examples of Jacobite censure of the deserters of James, see *Poems on Affairs of State*, 5:52–99.

12. In *The Poems of John Dryden*, ed. James Kinsley (Oxford: Clarendon Press, 1958), p. 1012.

13. In his note on these lines, Miner remarks the "similarity to the presentation of the Jews in *Absalom and Achitophel*," and refers us to lines 45–66. He goes on to say, however, that "The similarity suggests no particular attack on the English of 1689; it reflects Dryden's estimate of the mass of people everywhere" (p. 441). The genius of the Moors, however, is presented as national character, not human nature, and we have within the play itself a mass of people of which this is not true: the Portuguese. I do not know why we should suppose that Dryden would have hesitated to attack the English in 1689 for having done what he attacks them in 1681 for merely threatening to do.

14. *Works*, 3:134, 373.

15. *A Collection of Scarce and Valuable Tracts*, vol. 3 (London, 1748), p. 363; "A Dialogue Between the Ghosts of Russell and Sidney," in *Poems on Affairs of State*, 4:139–143. See also *The Dear Bargain* (n.p., n.d.): "If [William] doe these things in the Infancy of his Power, against those who set him up, what may we expect from him, should his Reign continue?" (p. 24); *A Remonstrance and Protestation . . . against Deposing . . . King James the Second* (London, 1689): "It is evident to the whole World, that the present State of the Kingdom is a *State of Force*; and that after all the pretence of *Property*, there is no *Law* in England but the *Long Sword*; and that upon this Foundation our present *Architects* are raising the Fabrick of their *New Government*" (p. 5).

16. Miner finds no source for this character; see *Works*, 15:429.

17. "Tarquin and Tullia," ll. 1–4.

18. See, for example, "Tarquin and Tullia," "The Coronation Ballad," and "The Female Parricide," in *Poems on Affairs of State*, 5. The lack of filial piety of which both William and Mary might be accused was a favorite topic of Jacobite polemicists. William "undertakes a War against his Unkle, and Father-in-Law, whom he knows to have as undoubted a Right to his Crown, as any King in Christendom" (*The Dutch Design Anatomiz'd*, London, 1688, p. 9); James's "Nephew and Son in Law, and

His own Daughter, without any Remorse are placed in his Throne" (*An Address to the Nobility, Clergy, and Gentlemen of Scotland*, n.p., n.d., p. 3); William's "Design is to be King. Now how this is practicable, and a Rightful King alive, his Uncle and his Wives Father, through whom only he can pretend any Interest; And besides this an Heir apparent, the *Prince of Wales*, who hath a Prior and Incontestable Title, I leave" to the gentry, clergy, and lawyers (*Some Reflections upon His Highness the Prince of Orange's Declaration*, n.p., 1688, p. 2);

> *King Lear* and his Daughters is perhaps but a Fable, and *Tullia*'s Father was but a Slave by Birth, and an Intruder into the Royal Family; but the paternal Love of King *James* towards his Daughters is as true as it is unparallel'd; his Care in their Education, Marriages, and Provisions for them are Demonstrations of it. The Honours conferred by him, upon their Mother's House, and their Proximity to the Throne, deserved some Returns of Gratitude; but how they have been made, and what was expected from Obligation and filial Duty, the World now seeth and judgeth. I need say no more, let Nature speak the rest in all who read this. (*The Dear Bargain*, p. 20)

James himself fell in with this view: he asks his subjects to consider "what Treatment they shall find from him, if at any time it may serve his Purpose, from whose Hands a Sovereign Prince, an Uncle, and a Father could meet with no better Entertainment" (*His Late Majesty's Letter to the Lords and Other of his Privy Council*, in *A Ninth Collection of Papers Relating to the Present Juncture of Affairs in England*, London, 1689, p. 12).

19. See John Wallace, "John Dryden's Plays and the Conception of a Heroic Society," in *Culture and Politics from Puritanism to the Enlightenment*, ed. Perez Zagorin (Berkeley, Los Angeles, London: University of California Press, 1980), pp. 113–134, for a discussion of the importance in this scene, in *Don Sebastian*, in Dryden's plays, and in Restoration society, of gratitude and the flow of benefits between the king and his subjects. The topic of ingratitude also appears frequently in Jacobite polemic, sometimes in language similar to Dorax's. See, for example, *The Lord's Speech without Doors*, in which the author censures the deserters of James for having broken "our warm and repeated Vows, to take his Fate, and dye at his Feet" (p. 6).

20. "Tarquin and Tullia," ll. 22–23.

21. "Pandora's Box," quoted in *Poems on Affairs of State*, 5:62.

22. Miner supposes that the Buzzard here represents William rather than Burnet. Nothing in these lines is, however, inconsistent with Burnet's

character or actions except the words "prince" and "king," and these are easily explained as part of the satire: the clergy act as "kings" and "princes" when they ought to act as clergy and leave politics to the court, here represented by the Landlord (*Works*, 3:454-55).

23. Burnet's vindictiveness and self-interest, and his habit of slandering and betraying his patrons, are frequently described in satiric poems of 1689. See, for example, "Tarquin and Tullia," "Suum Cuique," and "Burnet's Character," and the notes on these poems, in *Poems on Affairs of State*, 5.

24. See J. P. Kenyon, "The Earl of Sunderland and the Revolution of 1688," *Cambridge Historical Journal*, 11 (1955), 272–296, for a discussion of the origin, progress, and inaccuracy of this interpretation of Sunderland's behavior.

25. Macaulay, *History*, pp. 1206–1208, provides a full account of these riots. This was a popular topic of Jacobite polemic, though various writers drew various conclusions about the ultimate effect of the counterrevolutionary forces that must inevitably confront a usurper. The closest to Dryden is perhaps the author of *A Letter to a Member of the Convention*, who both remarks on the number of recent revolutions and hints at the possibility of a restoration brought about by the treachery of William's supporters:

> The Revolutions of State have been so quick and sudden of late, that all prudent Men will be cautious how they try Experiments, which are commonly dangerous and uncertain, but especially in matters of Government, which depend on the good liking of free and moral Agents, and when so many Hundred Thousands are to be satisfied, you can never guess at the prevailing Opinion, by the major Vote of a Convention.

> How many Discontents, think you, may arise between the Nobility and Gentry, who attend the new Court? Every Man will think he has some Merit, and expect some marks of Favour to have his share of Honour, and Power, and Profit, and yet a great many more must miss, than those who speed, and many of those who are Rewarded, may think they han't their Deserts, and be discontented to see others preferred before them; and those whose expectations are disappointed, are disobliged too, and that is a dangerous thing when there is another, and a rightful King to oblige; for Duty and Discontent together, to be revenged if a new King, and to be reconciled to an old One, will shake a Throne which has so sandy a Foundation.

These comments were reprinted in *A Second Collection of Papers Relating to the Present Juncture of Affairs*, (London, 1689) pp. 20, 22. Some expect a military dictatorship: "We are inevitably in a *State of Force*; for what is gotten by Force, must by Force be maintained; and let us flatter our selves what we will, it is not a Vote of Parliament, but the nature of the thing that will prevail: They that make the Change, must and will use Force for own Security, whatever becomes of Ours" (*A Remonstrance and Protestation*, p. 13).

> It is to be hoped I am not alone, but that the Eyes of all seeing Men are opened by the Smart of what they feel; and I appeal to their Consciences to judge which is most reasonable, or is likely to be most beneficial to us; To keep a Government built upon the most destructive Principles to the Peace and Tranquility of the Nation, that ever was contrived by the most pernicious *Machiavels* in the world; *viz.* the Original Contract with the People; a Government raised by Parricide and Usurpation, entred into by Violation of his own Declaration, supported by the Overthrow of all our Laws Sacred and Civil, and the Perjury of the Nation. A government . . . which drives furiously on arbitrary Principles, and cannot long subsist without breaking into that Tyranny we suffered under the Rump and *Cromwell*. (*The Dear Bargain*, London, n.d., p. 24)

Others expect anarchy: the revolutionaries would "undermine the Government both in Church and State, and reduce us to a state of Nature, wherein the People are at Liberty to agree upon any Government, or none at all" (*Reflections upon Our Late and Present Proceedings*, in *A Tenth Collection of Papers Relating to the Present Juncture of Affairs in England*, London, 1689, p. 4).

> Sir, the Horror & Amazement every thinking man must fall under, in his Reflections on the confusion & consternation the Kingdom of *England* was reduced to, upon the King's being necessitated to withdraw himself in *January* 1688, is certainly unexpressible, No age having produced so sudden a change from a Regular Government to an uncontrouled *Liberty*, and *Anarchy*. An Ominous presage of the dissolution of our ancient Hereditary Monarchy, and the inevitable ruine and fatallity following on it. (*An Old Cavalier Turned a New Courtier*, n.p., n.d., p. 1)

26. A production scheduled for 30 April 1690 was for some reason delayed. See Earl Miner's brief discussion of the date of the play in *The Works of John Dryden*, vol. 15, ed. Miner and George R. Guffey (Berkeley, Los Angeles, London: University of California Press, 1976), p. 460.

27. *Works*, 15:223–224. All citations of *Amphitryon* are to this edition.

28. Miner, citing Malone, refers us to Tom Brown's *The Late Converts Expos'd: Or The Reasons of Mr. Bays's Changing his Religion* (1690), in *Works*, 15:473.

29. Quoted in Miner, *Works*, 15:473.

30. Ehrenpreis (*Acts of Implication*, pp. 39–42) briefly discusses these allusions, and on the strength of them introduces, as "larger possibilities" over which he is "tempted to brood," the similarities between the competition in the play for Alcmena and in politics for the throne.

31. William Cameron, in *Poems on Affairs of State*, vol. 5 (New Haven: Yale University Press, 1971), notes the public reaction to "William's baffling refusal to trust any but a few chosen men with his political or private opinions" (p. 38); and the absoluteness and illegitimacy of William's rule were of course the bases of contemporary attack on his government and are in evidence throughout this volume.

32. Margaret Kober Merzbach, in "The Third Source of Dryden's *Amphitryon*," *Anglia* 73 (1955), 213–214, has shown that Dryden adapted this discussion from a scene in Heywood's *The Silver Age*.

33. See J. R. Jones, *The Revolution of 1688 in England* (London: Widenfield and Nicolson, 1972), pp. 313–314. Compare the protests in contemporary polemic:

> When so many, out of Zeal for the preservation of the *Protestant Religion*, either actually Contributed their Assistance to the Prince, or tamely yeilded to the common Inclination of the Multitude; it was out of confidence, that the Prince designed nothing, but what he had published in his Declaration . . . to Solicite the King to Call a *free Parliament*, & by it to secure our *Religion* and *Properties*. (*An Address to the Nobility*, p. 10)

> Had his *Highness* only pretended to come to deliver the *King* from *Evil Counsellor*, and to Engage him further into the Interest of *England* and *Europe*, that he might not seem a Property to a few ill Men of narrow ends, the *Prince of Orange* had less needed an Apology with some others; But to over-look the King, a Lawful King, the Father of his Princess, in whose Right he can only pretend to come, and instead of the Kings Name, to use in

England the Style of *WE* and *US, Commanding, Preferring, Advancing, Rewarding, Punishing, having of Parliaments,* and *setling the Nation; And last* of all, that *he will then send back his Army,* which sheweth he intends to stay behind himself, Can declare nothing else to us, but that his Design is to be King. (*Some Reflections upon his Highness the Prince of Oranges Declaration,* pp. 1–2)

[William's] *Errand* (as we are told) *was to Preserve our Religion and Laws, and Just Succession of the Royal Line.* This only could have made us endure an Action we should else have hated; presuming our *Kings Loss, should have been His Gain; and our Yielding, our Victory:* But since we behold, to our unspeakable Grief, that our Condescension is *Treacherously* abused to private Ends; and that *shew* of our *Disloyalty* not made a *Remedy* to the Government, but a *Ruine* to our King, and an *Infamy* to our selves, to serve the turn of some Mens Avarice and Ambition. (*A Remonstrance and Protestation,* pp. 6–7)

34. See Gerald M. Straka, "The Final Phase of Divine Right Theory in England, 1688–1702," *English Historical Review,* 77 (1962), 638–658: "The theory of providential delivery, full of biblical and historical precedent and imagery, became the favorite theme of Revolution church oratory, casuistry, and biblical exegesis, and during William's reign assumed as much importance in church writings as the subject of nonresistance enjoyed after the overthrow of Cromwell's Commonwealth in 1660" (p. 642).

35. See *Poems on Affairs of State,* 5:238–258.

36. Cited in Straka, *Anglican Reaction to the Revolution of 1688* (Madison, State Historical Society of Wisconsin, 1962), p. 74:

We ought in most profound prostration, to magnify the goodness of God to us in it: to him belongs the Glory of it, for his hand has wrought this Salvation for us. Some may mention their Chariots, and some their Horses, but we ought only to mention the name of the Lord our God. It will not at all derogate from the Honour of our Great Deliverer, to consider him as the Instrument, whom God has so highly exalted, in bringing about so great a work by his means, and so to direct our Homage and Adoration to the Original of this and all our other Blessings.

From *A Sermon Preached . . . before His Highness the Prince of Orange, the 23rd of December, 1688, by Gilbert Burnet* (London, 1689), pp. 18–

19. Burnet's sermon was notorious enough to have been mocked in a Jacobite Pamphlet: "And that any of us should be *Sainted* for his Treachery, and numbred among the *Heroes* for our running away, cannot surely *be the Lord's doing*, let Dr. *Burnet* say what he will," *The Lord's Speech Without Doors*, p. 3. But Williamite polemic of the months between the Revolution and the probable date at which Dryden completed *Amphitryon* is filled with references to Providence: see *A Sermon Preached at St. Paul's Covent Garden on the day of Thanksgiving Jan. XXXI 1688. For the Great Deliverance of this Kingdom by the Means of His Highness the Prince of Orange from Popery and Arbitrary Power*. By Simon Patrick (London, 1689); *A Sermon preached at Lincolns-Inn Chappel on the 31th of January, 1688, Being the Day Appointed for a Publick Thanksgiving to Almighty God for having made his Highnes the Prince of Orange the Glorious Instrument of the Great Deliverance of this Kingdom from Popery and Arbitrary Power*. By John Tillotson (London, 1689); *Seasonable Reflections, on a Late Pamphlet, Entituled, a History of Passive Obedience since the Reformation* (London, 1689): "God had delivered us from our dangers, and the dismal miseries which hung over our heads, he has given us a Deliverer, an excellent Prince, under whom our Laws, our Rights, our Fortunes, our Lives, our Religion are all secure" (pp. 2–3); *The Case of Allegiance in our Present Circumstances Consider'd* (London, 1689):

> If, lastly, we consider that the *Protestant Interest* in *Christendom*, and the *Civil* Interests of our own *Nation*, and some of our best *Neighbours* are at present in most *imminent* and *extraordinary* Danger, which in Human Probability is not to be *avoided* but by the *Prowess* and *Conduct* of this *Illustrious Prince*, whom God hath by *a Special Providence* raised up among us; we cannot but conclude, that the *Series of Providence*, and the *Necessity* of *Affairs*, have detrmin'd our *Allegiance* to His *Majesty*. (P. 24)

Salus Populi Suprema Lex (n.p., 1689): "God from Heaven presents [William and Mary] to us, and the highest necessity determines us to acquiesce in his good pleasure" (p. 6).

37. Lines 117–120, in *The Poems of John Dryden*, ed. James Kinsley (Oxford: Oxford University Press, 1958), vol. 4. For comment on the political reference of these lines see Kinsley, *Poems*, 4:2080, and "Dryden's *Character of a Good Parson* and Bishop Ken," *RES*, n.s. 3 (1952), 155–158.

38. The clearest instance is "To my Honour'd Kinsman," in which Dryden identifies himself with his country gentleman cousin; but he

makes similar gestures as early as 1687, in *The Hind and the Panther*, III.235–244.

39. James D. Garrison, "Dryden and the Birth of Hercules," *SP*, 77 (1980), 180–201. This is, to be sure, only one part of a complex and interesting argument about the play. Garrison rightly calls our attention to the play's satire and invites us to look for its objects in English politics of the 1690s. Indeed, he makes some approach toward finding them there. Noting II.ii.83–87 and V.i.144 (see above, pp. 84–85), he says, "For a moment, then, we are invited to see in the Jupiter-Alcmena-Amphitryon triangle an allusion to the political struggle between William (false Amphitryon) and James (true Amphitryon), vying to occupy the bed of England (Alcmena)" (p. 194). But he does not remark Dryden's careful preparation for and manipulation of this parallel in I.i, and he soon draws back from the implications of his discovery: "the context that invites us to see the topicality of the triangle in the first place also provides the key to its meaning. In the public poetry of James II's reign, Dryden had identified the true monarch with the virtue of justice and the loyal subject with the virtue of faith, and it is by emphasis on these specific human qualities that the topical allusions become meaningful in the play" (p. 194). Garrison goes on to apply this system of faith and justice—which is drawn, significantly, not from the politics of the 1690s, but from "the public poetry of James II's reign" (specifically *Threnodia Augustalis* and *Brittania Rediviva*)—to Jupiter's adultery and Phaedra's self-interested dealings, at length arriving at the conclusion that Dryden has rejected the "optimistic vision" of the 1660s.

40. "On the Late Metamorphosis" (1690), ll. 52–57, in *Poems on Affairs of State*, 5:151. Joined with the theory of providential deliverance in the writings of Burnet, Lloyd, and other prominent Williamites was the theory derived from Grotius of a "just war": see Mark Goldie's "Edmund Bohun and *Jus Gentium* in the Revolution Debate, 1689–93," *Historical Journal*, 20 (1977), 569–586, esp. pp. 582–585.

41. " 'Tis the way to be Popular, to Whore and Love. For what dost thou think old *Saturn* was depos'd, but that he was cold and impotent; and made no court to the fair Ladies" (I.i.235–237). These lines have occasioned considerable speculation on Dryden's topical satire. Frank Harper Moore, in *The Nobler Pleasure* (Chapel Hill: University of North Carolina Press, 1963), pp. 198–199, constructs upon them, and upon Jupiter's philandering, a parallel with Charles II, which Garrison rightly questions as "decidedly irrelevant to 1690" (p. 192). Nevertheless, it hardly seems appropriate to the Jupiter/William parallel, for however James may have been "cold and impotent" in his later years, William was not known for making "court to the fair Ladies" (I.i.237): indeed, he was

regularly satirized as a homosexual. If there is a reference to Charles here, the most recent monarch known to "whore and love" on a notable scale, it may perhaps serve as a contrast to William, who, as he is no more "popular" than James, may share his fate.

42. Howard Erskine-Hill, "Literature and the Jacobite Cause," in *Ideology and Conspiracy: Aspects of Jacobitism, 1689–1759*, ed. Eveline Cruickshanks (Edinburgh: James Donald Publishers, 1982), pp. 49–69, notes (p. 49) that the Jacobite view of William as a conqueror "found early expression in the polemical and sensational image of rape."

43. Garrison makes note of many of these allusions; however, he does not connect them with the Revolution or the Jupiter/William parallel. Rather he presents Gripus as "the perversion of ideal justice" and Phaedra as "the perversion of Alcmena's ideal faith" (p. 197), and so fits them, not without some strain, into his system.

44. Molière's Sosie declares that "Le véritable Amphitryon/Est L'Amphitryon où l'on dine" (III.v); but Dryden's "Lawfully begotten Lord" hints at his political purpose here.

45. Quoted in William Cobbett, *Parliamentary History of England* (London, 1806–20), 4:10, 15.

3: "The Favour of Sovereign Princes"

1. *A History of the Tory Party 1640–1714* (Oxford: Clarendon Press, 1924), p. 288. See also Gilbert Burnet, *History of His Own Times*, 6 vols. (Oxford University Press, 1833), 4:151–152. For a brief but representative list of Jacobite grievances, see *An Old Cavalier Turned a New Courtier* (n.p., n.d.): At the Revolution,

> It was not . . . consider'd what an entailed War was like to succeed even after the death of the King, betwixt the Prince of *Wales* and the issue of the Princesses, which can have no termination, without restoring him the Crown, to whom of right it doth belong. They foresaw not the strength of *France*, nor what a Thorn *Ireland* would be in our side, or that the *Dutch* would rob us of our Trade, and that Transportation and Pestilential Diseases, would sweep away so many Thousands of our Sea-men and Souldiers, nor could divine that our Merchants should lose so many Millions by Storm and Surprise. They had no apprehensions that the Country should not onely be Fleeced by quarter and Taxes, but be reduced to a very Skeleton, and the Forreign Beare-skins and Thrum Caps should suck the marrow out of our Bones. (P. 3)

2. *Poems on Affairs of State*, vol. 5, ed. William J. Cameron (New Haven: Yale University Press, 1971), p. 234. Dryden wrote his "Character of Polybius" for Sheeres's 1693 translation of that historian.

3. *Poems on Affairs of State*, 5:232; Henry Horwitz, *Parliament, Policy, and Politics in the Reign of William III*, p. 62.

4. *The Parliamentary History of England*, ed. William Cobbett (London, 1809), 5:659–662.

5. H. C. Foxcroft, *The Life and Letters of Sir George Savile, Bart. First Marquis of Halifax*, 2 vols. (London: Longmans, 1898), 2:143.

6. Foxcroft, 2:138–139.

7. Foxcroft, 2:456.

8. *King Arthur* is called a "dramatic opera" on its title page and has been described with other works of its age and genre as a "semi opera" and a "play with music." In calling it simply a "play," I advance no theory of its genre; I mean merely to use the least cumbersome of available terms.

9. *The Works of John Dryden*, ed. Sir Walter Scott, rev. ed. George Saintsbury, vol. 8 (Edinburgh: William Paterson, 1882), p. 137. All citations to *King Arthur* and *Cleomenes* are to this edition.

10. For the reaction to Beachy Head see *Poems on Affairs of State*, vol. 5, ed. William Cameron (New Haven: Yale University Press, 1971), pp. 226–230, especially "A Long Prologue to a Short Play," a poem critical of naval management written about October 1690 by Dryden's friend Sir Henry Sheeres. For a satire written in 1691 on the impotence of the navy, see "The English Triumphs at Sea," pp. 392–394. Even William's supporters recognized the inadequacy of the fleet. See for example *Reflections upon the Occurences of the Last Year* (London, 1689), p. 8:

> If . . . we take a Prospect of the Progress of our *Affairs at sea*, we shall find . . . the two famous Nations for Action at Sea, not onely baffled by the sole Power of *France*, but our losses in Men by *Sickness* and *Mortalities* greater than by *Fight*, and in our Merchandise and Trade, not less than our Expences: And, as if the Power of our Enemies were not enough to annoy us, after all, (if the Complaints of our Merchants and their Mariners be true,) our Ships have been made a Prey by those who should have been their Guard and Convoy, and were imployed for that Purpose.

See also *The Management of the Present War against France Consider'd* (London, 1690); *A Modest Enquiry into the Causes of the Present Disasters in England. And who they are that brought the French Fleet into the English Channel* (London, 1690): "To see the *French Masters at Sea*, and the *English* Glory thus sunk in the eyes of all *Christendom* by a

Complication of *Disasters*, cannot but raise the Curiosity of all true Lovers of their Countrey to enquire into the Source and Cause of so important Events" (p. 1); Henry Maydman, *Naval Speculations* (London, 1691): England must "reassume her ancient *Glory* and *Prowess*, in her *Naval Affairs*, and command of the *Narrow- Seas*, which we have lost in a great degree; or at least eclipsed . . . the which, if not gained speedily, I fear it may prove too late afterwards" (sig. A).

11. This humble submission to authority was originally countered by a parenthetical reference to the commendable manner in which Dryden surrendered the laureateship rather than alter his principles. See Fredson Bowers, "Dryden as Laureate: the Cancel Leaf in 'King Arthur'," *TLS*, 10 April 1953, p. 244.

12. Sir Walter Scott, in *The Works of John Dryden*, vol. 8 (Edinburgh: William Paterson, 1884), p. 127; Roberta F. Brinkley, *Arthurian Legend in the Seventeenth Century* (Baltimore: Johns Hopkins Press, 1932), p. 144. The most extreme expression of this view is James D. Merriman's, in *The Flower of Kings: A Study of Arthurian Legend in England Between 1485 and 1835* (Lawrence: University of Kansas Press, 1973), p. 63: "The final effect of the whole—to use the word loosely—with its compounding of sentimentalized blindness and exposed innocence, rhetorical passions and febrile eroticism, resembles a slightly sticky marshmallow sundae laced with absinthe and sprinkled with cantharides." In "The Impossible Form of Art: Dryden, Purcell, and *King Arthur*," *Studies in the Literary Imagination*, 10 (1977), 125–144, Michael W. Alssid attempts with dubious success to apply to the opera various New Critical notions of thematic manipulation and self-reflexiveness.

13. Samuel Kliger, in *The Goths in England: A Study of Seventeenth and Eighteenth Century Thought* (Cambridge: Harvard University Press, 1952), pp. 192–193, sees the Britons as Royalists and the Saxons as Democrats, and suggests that the opera recommends a reconciliation of the two parties. Robert E. Moore, in *Henry Purcell and the Restoration Theatre* (London: Heinemann, 1961), p. 72, and Franklin B. Zimmerman, in *Henry Purcell, 1659–1695: His Life and Times* (London: Macmillan, 1971) agree that Arthur represents William, though Zimmerman casts some doubt on Dryden's sincerity. Eugene M. Waith, in "Spectacles of State," *SEL*, 13 (1973), 317–330, places *King Arthur* in the masque tradition of compliment to the reigning king. Joanne Altieri, in "Baroque Hieroglyphics in Dryden's *King Arthur*, *PQ*, 61 (1982), 431–451, finds in the conclusion of the opera a celebration of mercantile values, in which she suspects some undercurrent of irony.

14. *Henry Purcell and the London Stage* (Cambridge University Press, 1984), pp. 289–319. Price lists five "humorous juxtapositions" in *King Arthur*, and together they make up a rather miscellaneous set. First is the

juxtaposition of the Saxon chorus of sacrifice with the song "I call ye all," in which the Saxons are invited to drink in Woden's Hall—Price remarks that "the solemn sacrifice becomes a bacchanal" (p. 299). There may well be some intentional deflation here; certainly there is quite a lot in the sacrifice itself. However, Ethel Seaton, in *Literary Relations of England and Scandinavia in the Seventeenth Century* (Oxford: Clarendon Press, 1935), p. 257, has shown that "I call ye all" is an imitation of "the Death Song of Rangnar Lothbrok" in Aylett Sammes *Britannia Antiqua Illustrati*; it is therefore perhaps merely a display of Dryden's antiquarian learning. Next Price finds that "The Arcadian vision of guiltless pleasure" presented before Emmeline and Matilda by the Kentish shepherds "is blurred by a reminder of the possible consequences of pre-marital sex" (p. 299). Next, in the famous Frost Scene, Purcell's music makes us feel the suffering of the cold genius, which is then ridiculed by Cupid's response. The remaining ironies occur in the prophetic masque at the end of the opera, and they are, I think, certainly crucial to Dryden's meaning. Price remarks that the "holy composition ['For Folded Flocks'] is followed by the Jolly, blasphemous folk-song 'Your hay it is mowed' " (p. 314), and that William's authority is undercut in the Grand Chorus by Dryden's reference to his "Scepter'd Subjects" (p. 316). In his new biography of Dryden, published since I wrote my own account of the play, James A. Winn follows Price in finding contradictory parallels; and adds much of his own. I coincide with Winn in seeing in Philidel a reflection of Dryden, and in finding opposition protest against the war in the *Dedication* and the play. See *John Dryden and His World* (New Haven: Yale University Press, 1987), pp. 448–451.

15. See for example *Some Reflections upon His Highness the Prince of Orange's Declaration* (n.p., 1688): War "is his Passion; his Education has been under that Discipline, and his Skill is in Martial Affairs. He told his Father (he now Invades) nine years ago, *This his Army had cost him 1300 Lives to bring it to that Discipline it was in.* A story that we, who talk of *Magna Charta's*, *Trials by Juries*, and *Habeas-Corpus-Laws*, may at leisure think upon" (p. 12).

16. For Alssid (p. 135), this stanza shows that "the Britons are sceptical . . . of their small achievements." The Britons do indeed sing the stanza, but that it does not express their point of view is clear from a change in pronouns—"we" in the first stanza becomes "they" in the second—and from the contrast between the second stanza and the fourth, in which the Britons' view is clearly expressed: "Now the victory's won, / To the plunder we run: / We return to our lasses, like fortunate traders, / Triumphant with spoils of the vanquished invaders" (*Works*, 8:151).

17. See Howard Erskine-Hill, "Literature and the Jacobite Cause," in *Ideology and Conspiracy: Aspects of Jacobitism, 1689–1759*, ed. Eveline

Cruickshanks (Edinburgh: James Donald Publishers, 1982), p. 49. In the speech quoted above, Halifax warns that "No Prince can bee so chast as that it is adviseable to tempt him to committ a rape," Foxcroft, p. 139.

18. *A History of the English Church and People*, trans. Leo Sherley Price, rev. ed. R. E. Latham (Harmondsworth: Penguin, 1968), p. 58.

19. *Henry Purcell*, p. 312.

20. The author of *The Dutch Design Anatomized* (London, 1690), for example, thus illustrates his assertion that William will bring in "a medley of Nations" that will "ravage and despoil our Country": "When *Vortigern* called in the *Saxons* to his aid, for a while they seemed content with Pay, and some Portion of Quarters; but finding the pleasure and riches of our Country so far exceed their own Habitations, they soon opened a passage for new recruits, and not only expelled the *Britains* the Country, but after an Infinite effusion of Blood, laid all the Cities, Burghs, Castles, and Fortresses in Ashes" (pp. 14–15); the author of *The Dear Bargain* (n.p., n.d.) claims of the Dutch:

> Doubtless we shall find them equally Conservators of our Properties, and of our Religion, such as the *Normans* were to the *Saxons*, and the *Saxons* in their turn had been to the *Britons*: The first under the Conquerour of this Man's fatal Name, had but one landing place, and made all *England* his own; the other under *Hengist* and *Horsa*, with but the sixth part of the number of our present Invaders, having got Possession of the Isle of *Thanet*, yet by little and little brought over so many from the same Shoar from whence our new Recruits are coming, that they entirely reined the British Monarchy (p. 23).

21. In addition to Feiling, Horwitz, and Burnet, cited above, see David Ogg, *England in the Reigns of James II and William III* (Oxford: Clarendon Press, 1955), pp. 297–303.

22. *Henry Purcell*, p. 314.

23. *Henry Purcell*, pp. 316–317.

24. See Charles Ward, *The Life of John Dryden* (Chapel Hill: University of North Carolina Press, 1961), pp. 253–254 for a full account of these events.

25. See Ward, p. 254, and *The Letters of John Dryden*, ed. Charles Ward (Durham, NC: Duke University Press, 1942), p. 49. Winn also mentions this request and remarks briefly that in view of it Dryden "acted inprudently" in writing *Cleomenes* (*Dryden*, pp. 451–452).

26. This is not entirely true of the most famous parallel of the age, *Absalom and Achitophel*; but this poem is in many ways a special case.

For a more representative use of overt parallel see Dryden and Lee's *The Duke of Guise.*

27. Anne Barbeau Gardiner, in a paper delivered at the MLA Conference on 27 December 1986, reads *Cleomenes* in light of contemporary Jacobite poetry, in which the English are portrayed as ingrates and degenerates; and thus identifies Dryden's Egyptians with them. It is not, however, likely that Dryden would depict his countrymen as backward during a Revolution. In all his works since the exclusion crisis, he had described them as inconstant to their leaders, and in the Dedication of *Eleanora*, written soon after *Cleomenes*, he makes a point of protesting this inconstancy. J. Douglas Canfield, in a paper delivered at the ASECS Conference on 24 April 1988, also considers *Cleomenes* an expression of unambiguous Jacobitism. The only dissent from this view is Judith Sloman's, who suggests, in a work published since I wrote my own account, that "The play salvages James as an object of personal admiration and loyalty while admitting the virtual impossibility of seeing him as a focus of concrete political action" (*Dryden: The Poetics of Translation*, Toronto: University of Toronto Press, 1985), pp. 45–46.

28. James Macpherson, *Original Papers Containing the Secret History of Great Britain* (London, 1775), I:233.

29. Letters, p. 252.

4: The Poet, Not the Man

1. Quoted from *The Poems of John Dryden*, ed. James Kinsley (Oxford: Clarendon Press, 1958). Further citations to *Fables* are to this edition: poetry is cited by line number, prose by page number.

2. For full analysis of the political meaning of this poem see Jay Arnold Levine, "John Dryden's Epistle to John Driden," *JEGP*, 63 (1964), 450–474, p. 471; and Elizabeth Duthie, " 'A Memorial of My Own Principles': Dryden's 'To My Honor'd Kinsman'." *ELH*, 47 (1980), 682–704.

3. *The Letters of John Dryden*, ed. Charles E. Ward (Durham, N.C.: Duke University Press, 1942), p. 121.

4. Letters, p. 120.

5. Letters, pp. 123–124.

6. Letters, p. 135.

7. Arthur W. Hoffman, *John Dryden's Imagery* (Gainesville: University of Florida Press, 1962), pp. 130–131; Reuben A. Brower, "Dryden and the Invention of Pope," in *Restoration and Eighteenth-Century Literature: Essays in Honor of Alan Dugald McKillop*, ed. Carroll Camden (Chicago: University of Chicago Press for William Marsh Rice University, 1963), 211–233, p. 211; Earl Miner, *Dryden's Poetry* (Bloomington: Indiana University Press, 1967), p. 226; George Watson, "Dryden and the

Jacobites," *TLS*, 16 March 1973, 301–302, p. 302; Thomas H. Fijimura, "Dryden's Virgil: Translation as Autobiography," *SP*, 80 (1983), 67–83, p. 83. Brower justly observes that "the figure of the 'retired' poet . . . was a cultural metaphor, not a simple fact" (p. 212), but he does not speculate on Dryden's purpose in invoking this metaphor. William J. Cameron, in "John Dryden's Jacobitism," in *Restoration Literature: Critical Approaches*, ed. Harold Love (London: Methuen, 1972), 277–308, is unusual in giving the late Dryden a public message. He argues that Dryden's purpose in the late work, especially the *Aeneis*, was to urge passive obedience to William on the Jacobites.

8. See, for example, Levine, pp. 470–471, and Achsah Guibbory, *The Map of Time* (Urbana: University of Illinois Press, 1986), pp. 245–247. Guibbory provides an interesting analysis of changes in Dryden's view of history throughout his career, with which I am in substantial agreement, though I see these changes as rhetorical rather than ideological.

9. Quoted from *The Works of John Dryden*, vol. 4, ed. William Frost, A. P. Chambers, and Vinton Dearing (Berkeley, Los Angeles, London: University of California Press, 1974), p. 363. All citations of the *Dedication* of *Examen Poeticum* are to this edition.

10. *Poems*, ed. Kinsley, l. 916. All citations to Dryden's *Virgil* are to this edition: poetry is cited by line number, prose by page number.

11. Levine, p. 471.

12. *The Works of John Dryden*, vol. 3, ed. Earl Miner and Vinton Dearing (Berkeley and Los Angeles: University of California Press, 1969), l. 181. All citations of *Eleonora* are to this edition.

13. Steven N. Zwicker, *Politics and Language in Dryden's Poetry: The Arts of Disguise* (Princeton University Press, 1984), pp. 181–182.

14. *The Works of John Dryden*, ed. Sir Walter Scott, rev. ed. George Saintsbury, vol. 8 (Edinburgh: William Paterson, 1882), p. 427. All citations of *Love Triumphant* are to this edition.

15. Thomas H. Fujimura, "The Personal Element in Dryden's Poetry," *PMLA*, 89 (1974), 1007–1023, pp. 1007–1008. See also "Dryden's Virgil" (cited above) and " 'Autobiography' in Dryden's Later Work," *Restoration*, 8 (1984), 17–29.

16. *Works*, 3:231. All citations of the *Dedication* of *Eleonora* are to this edition.

17. Donald R. Benson, in "Space, Time, and the Language of Transcendence in Dryden's Later Poetry," *Restoration* 8 (1984), 10–16, notes Dryden's emphasis on transcendence but sees it as the effect of a "general ontological shift" in progress during Dryden's age. For a more detailed and rather different reading of politics in *Eleonora*, see Anne Barbeau Gardiner, "Dryden's *Eleonora*: Passion for the Public Good as a Sign of the Divine Presence," *SP*, 84 (1987), 95–117.

18. *Works*, 3:501.

19. Dryden's late digressiveness has been remarked by Zwicker, who explains it as a strategy of disguise and a principle of aesthetics. See *Politics and Language*, pp. 62–63.

20. *Works*, 4:65. All citations of the *Discourse of Satire* are to this edition.

21. Miner, *Dryden's Poetry*, p. 287.

22. For a discussion of Dryden's definition of audience and other rhetorical strategies in his prefaces, see Zwicker, pp. 35–69.

23. Extended discussions of topical allusions in the translations are to be found in the works cited above by Watson, Cameron, Fujimura, Zwicker, Sloman, and Roper. Several such allusions are noted in Kinsley's edition.

24. There have been several attempts to find thematic and structural coherence in *Fables*. See Miner, *Dryden's Poetry*, pp. 287–323, Sloman, *Dryden*, and "An Interpretation of Dryden's *Fables*," *ECS*, 4 (1971), 199–211, and James D. Garrison, "The Universe of Dryden's *Fables*," *SEL*, 21 (1981), 409–423. Cedric D. Reverand II, in *Dryden's Final Poetic Mode: The Fables* (Philadelphia: University of Pennsylvania Press, 1988), also reduces *Fables* to a kind of unity: he finds in them systematic self-contradiction that neatly advances "subversion" as the final value for Dryden in the 1690s.

25. Judith Sloman, in *Dryden: The Poetics of Translation* (Toronto: University of Toronto Press, 1985), pp. 3–25. Sloman's contention that the translations somehow embody Dryden's own thought on a wide array of political, religious, philosophical, and aesthetic subjects cannot be disproven, but it is too dependent on arbitrary interpretation of evidence to be convincing. For example, to construct her argument about the philosophical coherence of *Fables*, Sloman must argue that we read Homer ironically, Ovid straightforwardly, and Boccaccio metaphorically: we are to reject the values of epic (p. 165), accept Ovid's version of Pythagoras's beliefs on time as a direct expression of Dryden's own view (p. 155), and understand Guiscardo's heart in *Sigismonda and Guiscardo* as symbolic of the eucharist (p. 185).

26. Alan Roper, in *Dryden's Poetic Kingdoms* (London: Routledge and Kegan Paul, 1965), pp. 165–184, provides an excellent discussion of politics in "To Congreve." The fullest analysis of "To Kneller" is Earl Miner's in "Dryden's *Eikon Basilike: To Sir Godfrey Kneller*," in *Seventeenth-Century Imagery: Essays on Uses of Figurative Language from Donne to Farquhar*, ed. Miner (Berkeley, Los Angeles, London: University of California Press, 1971), 150–167. The longest discussion of politics in *Alexander's Feast* is Bessie Proffitt's in "Political Satire in Dryden's *Alexander's Feast, TSLL*, 11 (1970), 1307–1316: a briefer but more

likely account is Howard Erskine-Hill's in "John Dryden" in *History of Literature in the English Language, Vol. 4 Dryden to Johnson*, ed. Roger Lonsdale (London: Barrie and Jenkins, 1971), 23–59, pp. 50–51.

27. See Miner's commentary in *Works*, 4:748. Some critics, most notably Cedric D. Reverand in "Dryden on Dryden in 'To Sir Godfrey Kneller'," *PLL*, 17 (1981), 164–180, argue that Dryden accuses Kneller of compromising his artistic integrity to serve the court. But in the poem, Dryden places the blame squarely on the court; indeed, it is impossible to tell from the poem alone that Kneller enjoys more court favor than Dryden.

28. *Dryden's Poetry*, pp. 268–269.

29. "John Dryden," p. 51.

30. John Dawson Carl Buck, in "The Ascetic's Banquet: The Morality of *Alexander's Feast*," *TSLL*, 17 (1975), 573–589; Ruth Smith, in "The Argument and Contexts of Dryden's *Alexander's Feast*," *SEL* 18 (1978), 465–490; and Robert P. Maccubin, in "The Ironies of Dryden's 'Alexander's Feast; or the Power of Musique': Texts and Contexts," *Mosaic* 18 (1986), 34–47, all suggest that Timotheus is meant to appear morally irresponsible in his manipulation of Alexander. I do not find this argument convincing: nowhere in the poem is Timotheus's moral standing presented for judgment; at the end he is clearly judged according to aesthetic standards and found worthy.

31. Unlike the *Dedication* of the *Aeneis*, the politics of which has been discussed at some length in the works cited above by Watson, Cameron, and Zwicker, the *Discourse of Satire* has been treated almost exclusively as a critical treatise. Michael Seidel, in *Satiric Inheritance: Rabelais to Sterne* (Princeton: Princeton University Press, 1979), pp. 143–144, notes that in discussing Horace as a court poet Dryden is thinking both of his opposition to William and his former service to Charles; and Edward P. Nathan, "The Bench and the Pulpit: Conflicting Elements in the Augustan Apology for Satire," *ELH*, 52 (1985), 375–396, suggests that in describing Augustus' extension of *Lex laesae Majestatis* Dryden is attacking contemporary censorship of literature.

32. See George R. Noyes, ed. *The Poetical Works of Dryden*, 2d ed. (Boston: Houghton-Mifflin, 1950), p. 1011, and *Poems*, ed. Kinsley, p. 2040, for Dryden's borrowing here from Le Bossu.

33. The analogy between Dryden-Virgil and Augustus-William has been analyzed by Cameron, Fujimura, in "Personal Element," and, most notably, by Zwicker, to whose account I am much indebted.

34. Several critics have discussed the application of the Augustus-Aeneas parallel to William. Watson and Cameron suggest that Dryden is advocating obedience to William; Zwicker argues more plausibly that Dryden condemns Aeneas for William's crimes. I think that contrast is at

least as important here as resemblance: Dryden follows Virgil in celebrating Aeneas and condemns William by enforcing the difference between the pious Trojan and the English parricide.

35. Jean Regnauld de Segrais, *Traduction de l'Énéide de Virgile* (Paris, 1668), 1:38.

36. *Politics and Language*, p. 188.

37. *Politics and Language*, p. 188.

Epilogue

1. Charles Ward, *The Life of John Dryden* (Chapel Hill: University of North Carolina Press, 1961), p. 292.

2. Reprinted in *Drydeniana X: Late Criticism, 1688–98* (New York: Garland, 1975).

3. Luke Milbourne, *Notes on Dryden's Virgil* (London, 1698; rpt. New York, Garland, 1974), p. 11. All citations are to this reprint.

4. *A Tale of a Tub* and *The Battel of the Books*, ed. A. C. Guthkelch and D. Nichol Smith (Oxford: Clarendon Press, 1958), p. 246. All citations of these works are to this edition.

Index

Abingdon, James Bertie, earl of, 122
Address to the Nobility, Clergy, and Gentlemen of Scotland, An, 172 n. 10, 174 n. 18, 177 n. 33
Aesop, 5, 22–24
Aesop Explained (1682), 23–24
Aesop Improved (1673), 22–23
Aesop's Fables with His Life (1687), 23
Alssid, Michael W., 183 n. 12, 184 n. 16
Altieri, Joanne, 183 n. 13
Andronicus, Livius, 143
Anglicans, Dryden's presentation of, 4, 9–33 passim, 42–44, 61–62, 169 n. 9
Apuleius, 141
Ariosto, Ludovico, 101, 120
Aristophanes, 143
Aristotle, 14
Athlone, earl of. *See* Ginkel
Atticus, Titus Pomponius, 36–37
Augustus Caesar, 113, 130, 137, 144–147, 148–155, 157, 162, 164

Barclay, John, 141
Beachy Head (naval battle), 76, 80
Bede, 88
Benson, Donald R., 167–168 n. 2, 187 n. 17
Bentinck, Hans Willem, earl of Portland, 90
Blackmore, Sir Richard, 122–123
Boccaccio, Giovanni, 125, 126, 128, 130
Bochart, Samuel, 88

Boileau, Nicholas Despreaux, 137, 140
Bossu, René le, 148, 158
Bowers, Fredson, 183 n. 11
Boyne, Battle of the, 76, 86
Brinkley, Roberta F., 81, 183 n. 12
Brower, Reuben A., 105, 187 n. 7
Brown, Tom, 177 n. 28
Buck, John Dawson Carl, 189 n. 30
Buckingham, George Villiers, second duke of, 142
Budick, Sanford, 170 n. 19
Burnet, Gilbert, 25, 49–52, 61, 170–171 n. 22, 178–179 n. 36, 180 n. 40, 181 n. 1
"Burnet's Character," 175 n. 23
Butler, James. *See* Ormond

Cameron, William, 177 n. 31, 187 n. 7, 188 n. 23, 189 nn. 31, 33, 34
Canfield, J. Douglas, 186 n. 27
Case of Allegiance, The (1689), 179 n. 36
Catholics, Dryden's presentation of, 9–33 passim, 40
Catiline, 79
Cato, 79
Cervantes, Miguel de, *Don Quixote,* 58, 63
Chapman, George, 158
Charles II, 52, 78, 81, 101, 113, 131, 139–140, 180 n. 41
Chaucer, Geoffrey, 5, 24, 116, 120, 121, 125, 128, 130, 160–162, 170 n. 19

Chesterfield, Philip Stanhope, second earl of, 108, 113, 121
Cicero, 35, 36, 78, 108
Clarges, Sir Thomas, 76
Clifford, Hugh, lord, 108, 113, 121, 122
Congreve, William, 131–132, 164
"Coronation Ballad, The," 174 n. 18
Cowley, Abraham, 158
Creech, Thomas, 94
Cromwell, Oliver, 36, 110
Cromwell, Richard, 36

Dear Bargain, The, 41–42, 172 n. 10, 173 n. 15, 185 n. 20
Declaration of Indulgence (1687), 9, 10–12, 32, 169 n. 9
Deists. *See* Socinians
Denham, Sir John, 148, 158, 164
Denmark, prince of. *See* George
Dialogue Between the Ghosts of Russell and Sidney, A (1689), 45, 173 n. 15
Dissenters, Dryden's presentation of, 4, 10–15
Domitian, 144, 146
Donne, John, 117
Dorset, Charles Sackville, sixth earl of, 48, 93, 121, 123, 133, 134–136
Driden, John, of Chesterton, 105
Dryden, John: attacks on, 2–3, 34, 87, 140–141, 163–166, 169 n. 7; conversion of, 9, 87; letters of, 9, 93, 101, 104–105
Works:
Absalom and Achitophel, 6, 12, 26, 43, 76, 101, 120, 141–142, 148, 149, 185 n. 26
Albion and Albanius, 37
Alexander's Feast, 131, 132–133
Amphitryon, 1–2, 4, 5–6, 34, 56–74, 75, 93, 95, 98, 99, 112, 121–122
Annual Miscellany: For the Year 1694, 123
Annus Mirabilis, 5, 107
Aureng-Zebe, 45
Britannia Rediviva, 33, 180 n. 39

"The Character of Polybius," 182 n. 2
Cleomenes, 4, 6–7, 75, 93–103, 106, 110, 112, 162
The Conquest of Granada, 45
Defence of the Epilogue, 129
The Discourse of Satire, 4, 101, 103, 117, 119, 120, 125, 133–147, 148, 149, 155, 157
Don Sebastian, 1–2, 4, 5–6, 33, 34–56, 64, 66, 71, 75, 79, 93, 95, 108, 110, 112, 121–122, 147, 149, 153
The Duke of Guise, 43, 186 n. 26
Eleanora, 1–2, 101, 109, 114–116, 118, 122
Essay of Dramatic Poesie, 129
Examen Poeticum, 124; *Dedication,* 107–108, 113–114, 118, 122, 125, 157
Fables Ancient and Modern, 2, 4, 117, 124, 127–129; "The Character of a Good Parson," 61; *Dedication,* 108, 122; *Preface,* 104, 109, 116–117, 119, 121, 122, 125, 130, 160–162; "To My Honour'd Kinsman," 104–105, 108–109, 112, 117, 170 n. 38
The Hind and the Panther, 4–5, 9–33, 34, 40, 43, 44, 49–51, 53, 55, 66, 106, 112, 139, 149, 180 n. 38
Juvenal and Persius, The Satires of, 124, 127
King Arthur, 4, 6, 75–93, 96, 99, 106, 108, 110, 112, 121–122, 162
Love Triumphant, 110–112
MacFlecknoe, 141–142
The Medall, 12, 17–18, 43, 107–108
Ovid's Art of Love, 127
Religio Laici, 12
The Spanish Fryar, 26
Threnodia Augustalis, 180 n. 39
"To Mr. Congreve," 131–132
"To Mr. Grenville," 163

"To Sir Godfrey Kneller," 131–132
Tyrannick Love, 44
Virgil, The Works of, 1–2, 106,
    124, 126–127, 163; *Aeneis*, 35;
    Aeneis, Dedication of, 43, 109,
    117, 119, 120, 122, 123, 133,
    147–162, 164–165; *Aeneis,
    Postscript* of, 112, 123–124;
    Georgics, Dedication of, 108,
    113, 122; *Pastorals, Dedication*
    of, 108, 113
Dutch Design Anatomiz'd, The
    (1688), 174 n. 18, 185 n. 20
Duthie, Elizabeth, 186 n. 2

Ehrenpreis, Irvin, 172 n. 4, 177 n. 30
Elizabeth I, 24, 160
"English Triumphs at Sea, The"
    (1691), 182 n. 10
Ennius, 143
Erasmus, 141
Erskine-Hill, Howard, 132–133,
    181 n. 42, 184 n. 17, 189 n. 26
Etherege, Sir George, 9, 131
Eupolis, 143
Exclusion crisis, 15–18, 26–27, 30–
    31, 33, 77, 78, 80, 112

Fable, 22–24, 170 nn. 16, 19
Fairfax, Edward, 160
Falkland, Anthony Carey, viscount, 93
Feiling, Keith, 76
"Female Parricide, The," 174 n. 18
Fletcher, John, 131
France, 3, 6, 7, 76–77, 79, 96, 100,
    110, 119–120, 122, 136–138, 152,
    153–154, 156–157, 158, 164–165
Fujimura, Thomas, 2, 106, 112,
    167 nn. 2, 3, 188 n. 23, 189 n. 33

Gardiner, Anne Barbeau, 171 n. 27,
    186 n. 27, 187 n. 17
Garrison, James D., 64, 66,
    180 nn. 39, 41, 43, 188 n. 24
Geoffrey of Monmouth, 88
George, prince of Denmark, 46
Ginkel, Godard van Reede, baron of,
    and earl of Athlone, 90

Goldie, Mark, 180 n. 30
Grotius, Hugo, 180 n. 30
Guiborry, Achsah, 187 n. 8

Halifax, George Savile, marquis of,
    6, 48, 77–79, 108, 185 n. 17
Harth, Phillip, 167 n. 1, 168 n. 5,
    169 n. 13
Heinsius, Daniel, 147, 164
His Late Majesty's Letter (1689),
    174 n. 18
Hobbes, Thomas, 117
Hoffman, Arthur W., 105
Holiday, Barten, 121, 125
Holland, 5, 18, 90, 92, 119, 122,
    151, 152, 164
Homer, 122, 130, 140, 147, 148–149,
    153, 155, 156, 158, 161
Horace, 102, 113, 117, 119, 137,
    140, 142, 143, 144–147, 151, 152,
    157, 158, 162, 164
Hyde, Anne. *See* York
Hyde, Laurence. *See* Rochester

James II, 9, 10, 52, 70, 77, 81, 82,
    92, 96–97, 97–100, 101, 113, 123,
    132–133, 151; Dryden's
    presentation of, xi, 6–7, 9–34
    passim, 38–41, 55, 69–72, 87, 95–
    96, 134–136, 153–156
Jefferson, D. W., 171 n. 26
Jones, J. R., 177 n. 33
Jonson, Ben, 131
Julian, 141
Juvenal, 117, 119, 121, 137, 140,
    143, 144–147

Kenyon, J. P., 175 n. 24
Killigrew, Charles, 141
King, Bruce, 172 n. 4
Kinsley, John, 179 n. 37, 188 n. 23
Kliger, Samuel, 183 n. 13
Kneller, Sir Godfrey, 131–132

La Hogue (naval battle), 79
Lauderdale, John Maitland, duke of,
    52

Leicester, Philip Sidney, third earl of, 35–36, 56–57
L'Estrange, Sir Roger, 23
Letter to a Member of the Convention, A, 175 n. 25
Leveson Gower, Sir William, 57
Levine, Jay Arnold, 2, 109, 167 n. 2, 186 n. 2, 187 n. 8
Lloyd, William, 180 n. 30
Loftis, John, 171 n. 4
Lord's Speech Without Doors, A (1689), 168–169 n. 7, 172–173 n. 10, 179 n. 36
Louis XIV, 9, 13–14, 25, 74, 96–97, 119, 130, 132–133, 137–138, 140, 152, 164
Lucan, 120
Lucian, 141

Macaulay, Thomas Babington, 10–11, 175 n. 25
Maccubin, Robert P., 189 n. 30
MacDonald, Hugh, 169 n. 7, 171 n. 1
Maecenas, 102
Mainwaring, Arthur, 172 n. 5
Maitland, John. *See* Lauderdale
Management of the Present War Against France, The (1690), 182 n. 10
Martial, 122
Mary II, 80–81, 92, 93; Dryden's presentation of, 6, 47–48
Maydman, Henry, 183 n. 10
Merriman, James D., 183 n. 12
Merzbach, Margaret Kober, 177 n. 32
Milbourne, Luke, 163, 164–165
Milton, John, 38, 84, 87, 138, 147, 158, 160
Miner, Earl, 2, 10, 105–106, 117, 118, 132, 167 n. 1, 168 n. 6, 169 n. 8, 170 n. 19, 172 nn. 4, 6, 173 nn. 13, 16, 174–175 n. 22, 177 n. 28, 188 nn. 24, 26
Modest Enquiry into the Causes of the Present Disasters, A (1690), 182–183 n. 10
Molière, 5, 58, 59, 65, 71, 181 n. 44

Monmouth, James Scott, duke of, 18–20
Montague, Charles, 104
Montaigne, Michel, 118, 149
Moore, Frank Harper, 180 n. 41
Moore, John Robert, 52, 171 n. 4
Moore, Robert E., 183 n. 13
Mulgrave, John Sheffield, earl of, 121, 123, 133, 157, 158
Myers, William, 168 n. 2, 169 n. 9, 171 n. 4

Nantes, Edict of (1598), 9, 13, 25
Nathan, Edward P., 189 n. 31
Nero, 145, 146
New Test of the Church of England's Loyalty, A (1687), 168 n. 7
Noel, Thomas, 170 n. 16

Ogg, David, 185 n. 21
Old Cavalier Turned a New Courtier, An, 176 n. 25, 181 n. 1
On the Late Metamorphosis (1690), 64, 180 n. 40
Ormond, James Butler, second duke of, 48, 108, 122
Ovid, 120, 125, 130, 147, 160–161

Pandora's Box, 49, 174 n. 21
Patrick, Simon, 179 n. 36
Patterson, Annabel, 170 n. 16
Persius, 119, 143, 144–147
Petrarch, Francesco, 130
Petre, Edward, 26
Petronius, 102, 141–142
Phocion, 78
Pindar, 116
Plautus, 5, 58, 59, 65, 71
Plutarch, 94
Poem . . . in Opposition to the Hind and the Panther, A (1688), 169 n. 7
Poems on Affairs of State, 169 n. 12, 171 n. 23, 172 n. 8, 173 n. 11
Polybius, 100
Portland, Hans Willem. *See* Bentinck
Portugal, 38
Powell, George, 163–164

Price, Curtis, 81–82, 91, 92, 183–
    184 n. 14
Proffitt, Bessie, 188 n. 26
Purcell, Henry, 58

Radcliffe, Francis, lord, 121, 123
Raphael, 131, 156
Reede, Godard van. *See* Ginkel
*Reflections upon Our Late and
    Present Proceedings* (1689),
    173 n. 10, 176 n. 25
*Reflections upon the Occurences of
    the Last Year* (1689), 182 n. 10
*Remonstrance and Protestation . . .
    against Deposing . . . King James
    the Second, A* (1689), 173 n. 15,
    176 n. 25, 178 n. 33
Reverand, Cedric D., II, 188 n. 24,
    189 n. 27
Revolter, The (1687), 169 n. 7
Revolution of 1688, xi–xii, 75, 121;
    Dryden's presentation of, 5–6, 34–
    74 passim, 75, 96
Rochester, Laurence Hyde, earl of, 48,
    93, 101–102
Roper, Alan, 188 nn. 23, 26
Roscommon, Dillon Wentworth,
    fourth earl of, 158
Rothstein, Eric, 172 n. 4
Rymer, Thomas, 122, 131, 133

Sackville, Charles. *See* Dorset
Sallust, 38
Salus Populi Suprema Lex (1689),
    179 n. 36
Sammes, Aylett, 184 n. 14
Sandys, George, 125, 160
Savile, George. *See* Halifax
Scaliger, Julius, 122
Scott, James. *See* Monmouth
Scott, Sir Walter, 81, 183 n. 12
*Seasonable Reflections on a Late
    Pamphlet* (1689), 179 n. 36
Seaton, Ethel, 184 n. 14
Segrais, Jean Regnauld de, 119–120,
    122, 153–155
Seidel, Michael, 189 n. 31
Seneca, 141

Seymour, Sir Edward, 76
Shadwell, Thomas, 131, 164
Shakespeare, William, 84, 137
Sheers, Sir Henry, 76, 182 nn. 2, 10
Sheffield, John. *See* Mulgrave
Sherlock, William, 61
Sidney, Philip, third earl of Leicester.
    See Leicester
Sidney, Sir Philip, 37
Sloman, Judith, 124, 186 n. 27,
    188 nn. 23, 24, 25
Smith, Ruth, 189 n. 30
Socinians, 13
*Some Reflections on His Highness the
    Prince of Orange's Declaration*
    (1688), 172 n. 10, 174 n. 18, 177–
    178 n. 33, 184 n. 15
Sophocles, 41
Southerne, Thomas, 102, 131, 164
Spencer, Robert. *See* Sunderland
Spenser, Edmund, 5, 24, 37, 84, 138,
    139, 141, 147, 151, 158, 160,
    170 n. 19
Stanhope, Philip. *See* Chesterfield
Steward, Elizabeth, 105
Straka, Gerald M., 178 nn. 34, 36
Sunderland, Robert Spencer, second
    earl of, 52
"Suum Cuique," 175 n. 23
Swift, Jonathan, 163, 165–166

Tacitus, 146
"Tarquin and Tullia" (1689), 46, 50,
    174 nn. 18, 20, 175 n. 23
Tasso, Torquato, 84, 88, 120, 151,
    153, 155
Tate, Nahum, 164
Teignmouth, 79
Test Act (1672), 9, 16, 31, 155
Tillotson, John, 179 n. 36
Titian, 131
Tories, xi, 4, 6, 9, 75–77

Varro, 142
Villiers, George. *See* Buckingham
Virgil, 35, 113–114, 122, 125, 130,
    137, 139, 140, 147–162 passim,
    164

Waith, Eugene M., 183 n. 13
Wallace, John M., 41, 172 n. 7,
174 n. 19
Waller, Edmund, 147, 158, 160
Walsh, William, 101
Ward, Charles, 185 n. 24
Watson, George, 106, 188 n. 23,
189 nn. 31, 34
Wedgwood, C. V., 167 n. 2
Wentworth, Dillon. *See* Roscommon
West, Michael, 2, 167 n. 1
Whigs, 6, 9, 43, 52–53, 75–76, 80,
109, 163
William III, 70, 76, 77, 81; Dryden's
presentation of, 3, 6, 7, 18, 45–46,

48, 52, 54, 58, 60–66, 68–72, 74–
75, 82, 84, 86, 87, 89, 91–92, 94–
96, 99, 109–110, 111–112, 119,
121–123, 130, 132, 138, 146–147,
149–162 passim, 164; and
patronage, 81, 107, 147, 157–158
Winn, James A., 184 n. 14, 185 n. 25
Winterbottom, John A., 172 n. 4
Wycherley, William, 131

York, Anne, duchess of, 4, 9

Zwicker, Steven N., 109, 152, 155,
159, 170 nn. 14, 15, 20,
188 nn. 19, 22, 23, 189 nn. 31, 33

Designer: UC Press Staff
Compositor: Auto-Graphics, Inc.
Printer: Braun-Brumfield, Inc.
Binder: Braun-Brumfield, Inc.
Text: 10/12 Sabon
Display: Sabon